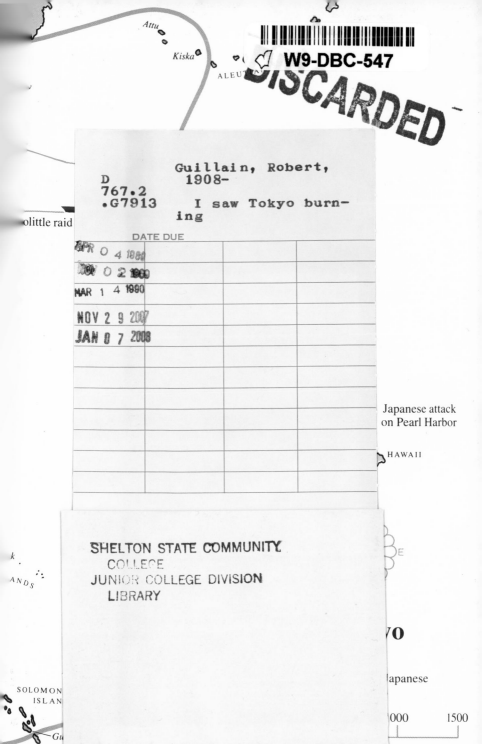

I SAW TOKYO BURNING

Other books by Robert Guillain

THE JAPANESE CHALLENGE
JAPAN I LOVE
WHEN CHINA WAKES
SIX HUNDRED MILLION CHINESE

I SAW
TOKYO
BURNING

An Eyewitness Narrative from
Pearl Harbor to Hiroshima

by ROBERT GUILLAIN

Translated by William Byron

DOUBLEDAY & COMPANY, INC.
Garden City, N.Y., 1981

Library of Congress Cataloging in Publication Data
Guillain, Robert, 1908-
    I saw Tokyo burning.

    Translation of La guerre au Japon.
    Includes index.
    1. World War, 1939-1945—Japan. 2. World War,
1939-1945—Personal narratives, French.
3. Guillain, Robert, 1908- 4. Japan History—
1912-1945. I. Title.
D767.2.G7913   940.53'51

ISBN: 0-385-15701-0
Library of Congress Catalog Card Number 79-8927
Copyright © 1981 by Doubleday & Co., Inc.
English edition published by arrangement with Editions Stock, Paris
Originally published in France as LA GUERRE AU JAPON by Editions Stock
Portions of this book previously appeared in *The Atlantic Monthly*
All Rights Reserved
Printed in the United States of America
First Edition in the United States of America

Preface

The Japan this book resurrects no longer exists. Today's Japan is profoundly different from that vanished Japan. I want to make this conviction clear at the start. In choosing now to describe the country in its militarist period, which I found detestable, I have no lurking desire to cast a shadow over today's industrial Japan, which in many ways I admire. On the contrary, I feel that by showing this industrial nation's roots, I am pointing up its merits. Knowing what Japan was like at war should not feed anti-Japanese sentiment; instead, it should show how satisfying it is that a whole people that had gone astray could rectify the course of its history.

Yet, after its defeat, there were many ways in which it might have added to the disorders of our time. Anything and everything was predicted for it, everything feared from it: Japan was going to begin, secretly and at once, to prepare its revenge on its American conquerors; it would inevitably revert to rearmament and militarism. Beaten, humiliated, ruined, it was going to slide toward communism. Or, if this was avoided, it would revert to fascism. Wasn't it still seeking vengeance by plotting with China against the West?

None of this happened. More than thirty years after Hiroshima, Japan remains allergic to atomic power and to militarism. It has behind it now over a quarter of a century of stable moderation. It is the liberal West's vanguard in Asia.

I have written elsewhere of the new Japan's postwar adventure in its race toward productivity. It seemed to me that I could complete my contribution as a journalist to the record of our time by also telling the story of Japan as it was, a Japan I was in a position to observe. Circumstances enabled me to watch the country from the inside, starting on the eve of World War II and going on from Pearl Harbor through Hiroshima and beyond.

The war began in Europe in September 1939. In Japan and the Pacific, it began with the surprise attack on Hawaii in December 1941, over two years later—two years during which Japan remained merely a spectator of the world tragedy's first act. Probably, though, it was the best placed of all spectators. In that interval, Tokyo was a fascinating observation post. All the tangled strands of great-power interplay converged there. Tokyo had a view—and this is an essential fact—over both camps, the Axis powers' and the democracies'. There you could follow the most brutal game—the one Hitler was playing—from the inside; beyond that you glimpsed the wiliest and most secretive: Stalin's. There was a better view from Tokyo than from Europe of the strategy being followed by the United States, heading for war but, like Japan, not yet actively involved. It was a total world view that Europe did not have because it was not limited to the West, but embraced Asia and the Pacific as well.

Despite this, how many correspondents did France—which will always have trouble understanding that Japan is not the end of the world—maintain there on the eve of the war? One, just one: the correspondent for the French news agency Havas, compared to ten Americans and five British correspondents. I was assigned to that job in 1938, after a spell in China. When the war blew up in Europe, I was kept on in Tokyo; the prime concern in Paris—and rightly so—was to maintain France's positions in the Far East. I was mobilized into the French embassy staff until the armistice in 1940. After that I stayed on; a Japan suspended between peace and war was supremely interesting to observe, and I thought I could always leave for the United States if necessary. Then, suddenly, Pearl Harbor, and some three hundred French nationals were trapped in Japan at war; we were forbidden to leave, and we could not have done so anyway, unlike the British and Americans, who were exchanged for Japanese nationals.

Were we ill-treated? Generally speaking, no. Japan looked on a defeated France as being out of action, and the French were treated as neutrals. Suspect neutrals, however, under police control, constantly spied on; arrests were made from time to time to keep the French colony in a state of salutary fear. But at least we were allowed provisional liberty.

Financially, we made out on the sizable French assets frozen in Tokyo. Professionally, I must stress, the situation was extraordinarily interesting, and I could still wire dispatches to the unoccupied zone of France. Japanese censorship was too obtuse to spot everything I slipped between the lines, information that was independent and useful. Beginning in 1943, however, when the Germans extended the occupation to southern France and the war began to go badly for Japan, this became too risky. Soon there was nothing I could do as a journalist but conscientiously look, listen and keep quiet. To possess documents or take notes was dangerous; the few I had I lost in the rain of fire-bombs on Tokyo or destroyed when the French were interned five months before the end of the war.

It was after the surrender in August 1945, when I resumed my correspondent's job in American-occupied Japan, that I was able to reconstitute and complete my files through interviews and investigation with the help of my Japanese sources. And it was on my return to France in 1946, after eight years of involuntary exile in the Far East, that I wrote the first version of this book. It sold out quickly, but it was not reissued in the torrent of publications that was then breaking over a French public which had only recently recovered its freedom to read. Besides, the French did not want to hear about the war in those days, and Asia was too far away to wrest their attention from nearer horizons and immediate problems.

Today, however, our shrinking world has telescoped us; Asia, Japan have become our neighbors, and they are posing urgent problems. We must fill in the gaps in our knowledge and understanding of them. Hence the idea of publishing this revised edition. In Japan, too, where the book is appearing in translation, people are trying to understand their past misfortunes, taking stock of their recent history. A flood of books has appeared in

Japan and the United States about the Pacific war and wartime history inside Japan. I have not attempted to use them to expand my own book; I would rather preserve it as a report written in the heat of events and based on personal observation. Nor have I made any fundamental changes in my analysis of the events or my portraits of the men of that period. Instead, I have tried to preserve the sense of immediacy in my report. At the risk of seeming somewhat prejudiced or unfair, I have preferred to see my story as that of a man who had just gone through the agonies of a war and who was enraged by its stupidity and its cruelty.

What has changed, then, in today's Japan from what it used to be? I am often asked the question and I am tempted to answer: why, everything! Let's simply say more cautiously that the changes have been vast. The Japanese are the same people, of course, but they have been profoundly marked by their earlier failure; now they are pursuing a wholly different aim, and they are absolutely determined not to repeat the past. To do something else, to do it well, very well indeed—this seems to be Japan's new project, even if the results and the means do not always square with its intentions. I am convinced that in postwar Japan, there is first of all a powerful current of good intentions.

In the depths of this people, in its masses, there is a basic fund of goodwill, an inclination to work for the community's welfare by endowing it with a great sum of effort, frugality and discipline. This willingness was terribly exploited and perverted during the war by Japan's military leaders, who to some extent were themselves victims of the extremists and fanatics among them. In defeat, the people understood how enormously they had been duped. Today's Japan is the result of a prodigious about-face, the beginnings of which are touched on in this book's final pages. To seek the world's forgiveness for what it did, to redeem itself, to establish its respectability in its own eyes, to catch up with the rest of the world and demonstrate that it belongs to the community of civilized, developed nations, that is, in a way, as "Western" as we are, up to doing anything the West can do and doing it better— these are the motivations of Japan's new forward surge. Add to this its memory of the suffering it endured during and after the war: for a while, the Japanese were literally dying of hunger and poverty. Their eagerness to work, to produce, is partly explained by their fear of falling back into want, of returning to their cruel past. These islands are poor; the people in them cannot live except by working very hard and being at peace with the entire world.

So the country's progress from a generals' Japan to an industrialists', from a destructive to a constructive nation, from militarism to pacifism represents a complete reversal. Few peoples are more pacifistic than the modern Japanese, more distrustful of military uniforms and the weapons of war. Another total about-face: the country's shift from nationalism to internationalism; Japan is now one of the world's most internationalist countries in its actions, its thinking. Different, too, is its decision, its determination to live within its islands and to have a better life there than it had before, even when its population reaches 120 million, as it soon shall. For half a century, with fewer than 75 million, Japan based its policy on a supposed overpopulation that, it believed, forced it, authorized it to explode over the countries around it. But it knows now that in today's world, conquest is no longer possible, any more than colonization or emigration are. Perhaps more than any other country, therefore, Japan needs a peaceful world. It can breathe only so long as the seas are free; it would suffocate if war were to cut off the oxygen of international trade.

A further change: freedom, that great postwar discovery by a people that had been subjugated for so long—political, cultural, religious liberty, freedom to think, speak, write, act, travel, love. Japanese use of all this is sometimes still anarchic, for they are only gradually learning the necessary limits of liberty. But in their daily lives, as in politics and business, they have developed an avid taste for freedom and they will not allow it to be snatched from them without fighting to save it.

Change: in their notion of personal conscience. To the people of old Japan, order derived first of all from external constraints, from collective pressure on the individual and the menace of an omnipresent police. The modern Japanese has discovered, or rediscovered, an inner voice of conscience that can guide him in choosing between good and evil. There is change, again, in his sense of reflection. The Japanese has learned to think for himself; he may be less given to it than the argumentative, rebellious French, but he is not the Japanese of yesterday, always ready to accept the ideas dictated to him by his leaders.

A major change: more and more people in Japan are allowing themselves to be intelligent. The old Japan was wary of awakening its people's intelligence. Among ordinary Japanese, it was better not to be intelligent, or not to become so—in any case, not to show one's intelligence. Westerners, aided by their arrogance, long believed that most Japanese were their intellectual inferiors. To believe this today would be a grievous mistake. The way is now open in Japan to maximum development of the general intelligence and the country's whole system is directed toward this. Within a few years, intelligence has begun to blossom even among the masses, in keeping with the rise in the whole people's educational level. Where popular education was once restricted to grade school, it has now expanded to the secondary-school and university levels. The Japanese are among the world's most educated people. Moreover, the volume of their information— that is, their knowledge of the world and their participation in their times—is superior to Europeans'.

Certainly, the Japanese form of intelligence is different from ours. It is not showy; it shines less brightly externally because it is suspicious of speeches and fine words. But it is richly intuitive. It is much less individualistic than ours, for it dislikes to work in isolation, but it is the common current that activates a group or emanates from it, and it is often the more remarkable for this collective animus. Japanese intelligence is linked to action; it seeks concrete results, aims for efficiency. These differences do not handicap it in the contemporary world's race toward progress; on the contrary, we are beginning to understand how competitive the practical, collective Japanese intelligence is with our own.

With these changes duly noted—and many others could be cited—the question remains: what has not changed after all? Aren't there still resemblances, transfers, a continuity between the country's abolished past and its reinvented present? However different its whole orientation may be now, hasn't today's Japan maintained certain structures and modes of behavior inherited from the past, if only to preserve the qualities and virtues—and there were some—of its militaristic past as well as those of what is sometimes called "eternal Japan"?

Three times in the brief span of a century, this people has amazed the world: at the end of the nineteenth century, by its perilous leap from the Middle Ages into modern times; in the 1930s, by its ephemeral military triumphs; in the 1950s, by its dazzling economic ascension. Here indeed is its continuity, and it stretches back into the past, beyond the beginnings of military Japan. And what we must really ask ourselves is what the springs are that have propelled this country through its many adventures and misadventures. What makes Japan tick?

There is more than one answer to this; in fact, a book could be written on it. I would offer a one-word explanation: dynamism. What are the sources of this dynamism, this vitality, this energy? I can suggest only a few clues. It is, to begin with, the product of a poor country which, as I have said, requires its people to work with unrelenting fervor. One aspect of this is their zeal for education, for acquiring knowledge and information, their interest in the world and in progress. Secondly, Japanese dynamism is a result of the country's population density, for this generates mass competitiveness that can attain a virulence unknown in the West. This is one of the roots of Japanese aggressiveness in business. The drive and what sometimes seems to us to be the shocking ruthlessness that Japanese traders and manufacturers show in their dealings abroad is really the way they do things at home. Finally, Japan's dynamism also stems from the feeling of solidarity and discipline that is one of this people's traits. More gifted than we for the collective society of the future, a Japanese needs to be part of a group. He loves his group, agrees with all the others who belong to it. Put three dozen French together, and they will soon be divided into rival parties debating the reasons they have found for their inability to work together. The Japanese, on the other hand, will begin by determining what unites them, and they will reach an understanding that permits a common effort, setting aside those things that could divide them.

Add to all this the fact that to the different social communities —family, firm, locality, the nation—the Japanese bring a spontaneous loyalty culminating in an instinctive patriotism, and you have the main keys to the dynamism animating their work and their ambition. They are fiercely ambitious, anxious to be first, in everything if they can. But, in my opinion, their ambition is a by-product of Japanese dynamism; it functions as reinforcement whenever they find that their thousands or millions of coordinated efforts, concentrated on a given sector, can achieve a breakthrough in domestic or world competition.

In its new forms, this dynamism remains explosive. First of all, Japan is exploding over itself, however pacifistic and "civilian" it may be. Capitalistic industrialization has been crueler there than almost anywhere else because of the country's natural environment and its cultural heritage. Japan's furious urbanization, the proliferation of factories and transportation systems, have been grimly devastating. But the country has also remained explosive toward the rest of the world under the peaceful guise of economic expansion. There is a major problem that still has not changed in Japan: the problem of recognizing its limits. Because they did not know when to stop, the leaders of militarist Japan were responsible for Pearl Harbor—and Hiroshima. Will the new Japan's managers have a nicer notion of when to curb their ambition in the interests of world economic peace? Will they repudiate their predecessors' temerity, probably born of too long a voluntary imprisonment in their islands during Japan's feudal era?

Their wisdom depends partly on ours. For the past century, the world has been faced with the problem of Japan's place as a partner in the community of developed countries. This is in part our problem: it is we who will have to arrange that place and we must understand that it cannot be a small one; Japan occupies and will continue to occupy a major place. Competition: that's the key word in connection with Japan. But we must remember—and we must remind the Japanese—that the word has two meanings. It means struggle and rivalry, but it also means convergence on a common objective, a sportsmanlike race run together, side by side. We—and they—must give the word "competition" this meaning. The world is approaching a new millennium. We must work together in the difficult and exalting task of building that new world.

Contents

1

Pearl Harbor Seen From Tokyo

Tokyo, December 8, 1941: In the biting early-morning air, a newsvendor dashes into the still-deserted Shimbashi intersection, yelling the announcement of war headlined in his papers.

"Sensô! Sensô!"

It is 7 A.M. Still no traffic in the square or the streets around it. The old man, seemingly furious that his sensational news is being ignored, gallops toward the electric-railway station. He waves his arms even more wildly, frantically ringing the bell the newsvendors' guild uses on great occasions to announce a special edition.

"Sensô! Sensô! War! War!"

A train passes over the viaduct, and the first passengers finally appear in the station portico. Alerted by the bell, they head straight for the vendor, pay their two cents and grab their papers. It is a very small sheet, more like a flier. It contains nothing but the astonishing announcement, in a few vertical lines of big Chinese characters: "At dawn today, the Imperial army and navy entered into a state of war with the forces of the United States and England in the waters of the western Pacific."

I watched people's reactions. They took a few steps, then suddenly stopped to read more carefully; the heads lowered, then recoiled. When they looked up their faces were again inscrutable, transformed into masks of seeming indifference. Not a word to the vendor, nor to each other. This was a Monday, and the war had stricken these people as they were returning peacefully to work after a fine, sunny Sunday. Not one of them dared voice his

feelings, open himself candidly to his neighbors or to his unknown countrymen pressing around the old man selling papers.
"*Sensô! Sensô!*"

I knew them well enough to understand their reaction. The astonishment and consternation they felt was visible under their
impassive expressions. They had instigated the war and yet they
did not want it. Out of bravado, and to imitate their leaders, they
had talked constantly about it, but they had not believed it would
happen. What? A new war? Another war? For it was now added,
superimposed, on the China war that had dragged on for three
and a half years. And this time, what an enemy: America! The
America that much of the press and the country's leadership had
still been courting less than six months before. The America
which the Japanese for a quarter of a century had thought of as
the champion of modern civilization, the ever-admired, ever-imi-
tated model.

"*Sensô!* War! War!"

Other vendors, ringing their bells, were invading the Ginza,
Tokyo's main thoroughfare, brandishing their special editions.
The weather was cold and radiant. A streetcar emptied and a
new wave of buyers swirled around the newsvendors. Farther
along, housewives were waiting in line (lines already, on this first
morning of the war). Slight women in white aprons and silk kimonos, they darted briefly away from the fishmonger's shop to
catch the vendor as he went by. Heads wagging, they silently
deciphered the single sheets, then returned to their places in the
line. At most, there were a few muffled exclamations, a scattering
of muttered comments.

Yet there had been enough talk of this war against the Anglo-
Saxons. For six months, nationalist propaganda, whipped up by
the German colony, exploited by the military clique, had violently assailed America and exalted Hitler's victories. The United
States, said the newspapers, by imposing economic sanctions on
Japan, depriving it of oil, scrap iron, loans, trade, was strangling
Japan. America must "reconsider its attitude" or Tokyo's patience would run out. Threats by General Hideki Tojo, successive waves of troop mobilization, civil-defense drills all clearly
pointed to war. But, deep down, the people had still believed that

a settlement would be reached. Tojo had sent Ambassador Saburo Kurusu as an eleventh-hour negotiator to Washington, and a compromise was near.

Then, suddenly, war! Japan was at war with terrifying America. The Japanese people's feelings had always been divided; they were torn between the official slogans exhorting them to intransigence and a secret intuition that told them this was madness. Their strongest feeling on that morning of December 8 was one of consternation. Collectively, the nation had let itself be carried away by war hysteria, but individually, each Japanese, always so different when he is on his own, isolated from the group, feared the war. He could already see himself giving up all his little comforts, uprooted by mobilization from the narrow compass of his daily life, and he knew perfectly well that on that day he would appear brave in public. Alone, or at home, he would be green with worry, would have sudden crying jags.

"*Sensô!* War! A Japanese-American war!"

Tokyo was afraid. The Japanese were frightened by what they had dared to do.

At Domei, the Japanese news agency, there was the excitement that always attends big events. News was already pouring in. "This morning, at a cabinet meeting convened at 7 A.M., Admiral Shigetaro Shimada, the Naval Minister, reported to his colleagues on the progress of the . . ."

I was reading over the shoulder of the Japanese newsman who was hastily scribbling an English translation of the latest communiqué. When he reached the key word at the end of the line, he mumbled to himself for a moment, hesitated, finally asked out loud: "Fight? Fighting?"

What? There was fighting already? Not just a declaration of war, but war in fact, fighting? Then Japan had not been content to break off relations; it had actually started shooting. Official confirmation came a moment later: the Japanese fleet was simultaneously attacking Manila and Hawaii.

Hawaii! So it was the Port Arthur tactic used against Russia in 1904 that was being repeated this time against America. Japan, hot-blooded and crazed with boldness, had struck first with the ferocity of an old Japanese warrior whose fury had been pent up too long. On February 7, 1904, without a declaration of war, Admiral Heihachiro Togo's fleet had attacked the Russian ships laid up in the harbor of Port Arthur, Manchuria, sinking two battleships and a cruiser. This was the first of the sneak attacks in twentieth-century history, the first attack by an Asian people against the whites and, incidentally, the first significant use of torpedoes in modern warfare. But had Japan again dared to strike without warning?

"Has there been an . . . American declaration of war against Japan?" I asked.

The Japanese newsman I questioned did not seem to understand the implication. "There is just a 'state of war,'" he replied curtly.

I rushed to the Foreign Ministry. Excitement was high in the wooden sheds that housed it (the other ministries had handsome stone or brick buildings, but while the War and Naval ministries were pampered, Foreign Affairs had always been a poor cousin). A press conference had hastily been called for 9 A.M. I looked in vain for my American and English colleagues; Bob Bellaire of the United Press, Max Hill of the Associated Press, Otto Tolischus of the New York *Times* and at least a score of other correspondents with whom I had worked every day for the past six months were all missing, probably arrested, imprisoned or under house arrest. A Japanese diplomat, wearing a cutaway coat as though he were at a cocktail party, distributed mimeographed sheets: a fifteen-page Japanese memorandum delivered to Washington to notify the United States that the diplomatic talks in progress were broken off; an aide-mémoire recapitulating the history—Japanese version—of Japanese-American negotiations; an Imperial proclamation announcing the war.

Some of the pompous sonority of the proclamation's original language survives translation: "We, by the grace of Heaven Emperor of Nippon, sitting on the throne of a line unbroken through ages eternal, commanding you, Our brave and loyal subjects, hereby declare war on the United States and the British Empire. . . ."

"Is this release designed for internal consumption," I asked the diplomat who was handing out the copies, "or is this really the declaration of war as it was delivered to Washington?" The question was probably too subtle for a Japanese spokesman. For years, the government had been careful to fill such posts with people whose wit was none too sprightly, and God knew there was no lack of these in the Tokyo bureaucracy. Spokesmen were traditionally mutes. So I received no precise answer.

"At what time was this declaration of war handed to Washington?" This time, the only answer I got was a scowl and a look of repressed fury. Other officials I questioned said they were not in a position to reply on this point; by the look of them, the importance of the question completely escaped them.

In fact, the declaration of war, as we would soon know, was conveyed to Washington nearly an hour after the first wave of Japanese planes attacked Pearl Harbor. As for the Imperial proclamation I was holding at 9 A.M., long after the time of the attack, the Japanese later admitted that it was not actually signed by the Emperor until 11:45 on that same Monday morning. It was also at 11:45 that the first radio announcement was made of the *declaration* of war. But listeners, to whom the first news of the *state* of war had been available since 6 A.M., who knew before 9 A.M. that the "battle" had begun on all Pacific fronts and—at 11:20—that the American fleet had come under surprise attack in Hawaiian waters, did not seem alarmed at the fact that for the five hours during which they had been hearing of a Japanese attack on America there had been no mention of a declaration of war from Tokyo or from Washington. And, in the weeks that followed, the Japanese government would shroud the facts in a prudent fog, carefully concealing from the people that the attack on Pearl Harbor had been made without warning. In the enthusiasm of victory, 75 million people would swallow official propaganda with the unreflecting credulousness typical of the Japanese at that time and would honestly suppose that Pearl Harbor had been a proper engagement in which Japan had exploited the element of surprise to win the "battle." Only those in the leadership class, perhaps, had some doubt about this; they were careful to keep it to themselves.

The Ginza at 1:30 in the afternoon: a radical change in the popular attitude. Of that morning's worried astonishment there was no trace. Japan had allowed itself only half a day of defeatism. Before the noon rice, people talked of a colossal victory. And Tokyo Radio's announcement that staggering damage had been inflicted on the American fleet was carefully timed for precisely the hour when offices were emptying out. First reports said at least two cruisers were sent to the bottom; further developments were expected. The American aircraft carriers, it was said, were also hit. (This was absolutely untrue: the attackers had fully expected to find them in the trap and were eager to destroy them; this is why the Japanese were already announcing the flattops' loss. As it happened, the two carriers they had thought to find at Pearl Harbor were not there that day.) At noon, a huge crowd flooded into the streets from shops, department stores, offices. Joyous relief and intense satisfaction shone in every face. Groups of clerks and clusters of young girls—servants and typists working in the district—strolled along the willow-lined boulevard; they were all alike, all of the same short, stocky race, but they maintained a careful separation, men on one side, women on the other. There were no shouts, no cheers, for one never applauded in this country; but across every face was spread a look of smug pride mixed with naïveté. "It was as easy as that," all those masks said. "That's how we are! One day at war, and Japan has already beaten America!"

There was no agitation, no hysteria of any kind. It was as though everything that had happened seemed to them to be almost natural. That morning's fright? It might have been a quickly covered loss of face, a spasm of petulance inadvertently let slip like a breach of the good manners that forbid any show of surprise. Now that the people's self-control had been recovered, it also squelched demonstrations of excessive joy. The outside world might at that moment have imagined Japan swept up by a powerful wave of violence and warlike chauvinism, its military leaders, the lords of war, bursting with cynical arrogance and demanding that the people applaud their aggression. There was really none of this. It was almost as if, with the war, everything had returned to normal. Hadn't Japan been at war for three and a half years, since the start of the China "incident"? Three years? Ten, really, since the Manchurian "incident" broke out in 1931. And this is why, on that afternoon of December 8, 1941, a kind of feeling of habit already weighed on the war, as though the victory itself were almost immediately going to seem routine.

In conversation, the tone was pretty much: "And we let ourselves be afraid. We didn't want to believe we could do it. We are at war. Well, everything is going very well; here we are, winning everywhere, and at the first crack. Really we did not have enough confidence in our leaders. We owe our humble apologies to the soldiers and sailors guiding us. We dared doubt them, they who know everything, whose plans were perfect and whose decisions were infallible. To think that we did not altogether believe them when they kept telling us that we are superior, heroic and invincible! They have proved our lack of faith was wrong and from now on we will return to blind confidence in them."

Kimonos massed before a radio store where a loudspeaker howled the latest news: "The Imperial fleet is attacking Hong Kong, citadel of British imperialism in China. . . . The army of the Rising Sun has made a first landing on the coast of the Malay Peninsula. . . . The Nipponese fleet has bombarded Davao, in the Philippines, Guam, Wake, Singapore." These names from the distant South Pacific—except for the last, Singapore—were scarcely better known to the office workers on the Ginza than they were to their counterparts on the boulevards of Paris or New Orleans. But the Japanese passersby were not very interested in finding them on a map.

Now the Imperial proclamation was broadcast, read by an army spokesman. The crowd listened, standing at attention, necks slightly bent, eyes staring at the ground in sign of respect. Before all these demonstrations of Imperial power, didn't propriety dictate a show of awe and trepidation? And who among those millions of loyal subjects would grasp the powerful and tragic irony with which history invested their sovereign's words?

"To assure stability in eastern Asia," said the speaker's raucous voice, "to contribute to world peace, this is the clairvoyant policy formulated by our High Illustrious Imperial Great-Ancestor and our High Imperial Grand-Ancestor his successor, a policy that we ourselves have constantly at heart. . . ." The persons thus solemnly designated were the legendary ancestors of the Son of Heaven: Ninigi-No-Mikoto, grandson of the Sun Goddess, and his great-grandson, identified in holy writ as Kamu-Yamato-Iwarehiko-No-Mikoto, more familiarly known to the populace as the Emperor Jimmu, supposed founder of the Empire. The official myth gravely affirmed that this happened 2,601 years ago, shortly after the founding of Rome. But the Roman Empire perished, whereas the Japanese Empire. . . .

"To cultivate friendship among nations and enjoy a common prosperity with all peoples, such have always been the guiding principles of Our empire in its foreign policy. . . ." The broadcast went on and this humble people, already hoaxed so long and destined to be bamboozled even more, listened to the Imperial statement in perfect obedience, in a spirit of patriotic credulity, of total and almost naïve submission.

> In truth, it is because of an inevitable situation, one far from Our wishes, that Our empire has been brought today to cross swords with America and Great Britain. . . . By their inordinate ambition to dominate eastern Asia, they forced us to take up arms. . . . Patiently have We waited, and long have We endured. . . . Our empire, for its existence and its own defense, had no other recourse but a call to arms. . . . The hallowed spirits of Our Imperial ancestors guarding us from above, We rely upon the loyalty and courage of Our subjects in Our confident expectation that the task bequeathed by Our forefathers will be carried forward and that the source of evil will be speedily eradicated and an enduring peace be immutably established in East Asia, preserving thereby the glory of Our empire.

What were the facts behind these pompous phrases that this throng did not know and would not know until after the defeat? How much responsibility does Emperor Hirohito bear? I had to wait until August 1945 to obtain the following information. The Foreign Minister, Shigenori Togo,* insisted to the cabinet that the attack be carried out within the legal rules. He was promised

* Not to be confused with the Prime Minister, General Hideki Tojo.

that Washington would be informed of the declaration of war one hour before hostilities were launched. In the last days before the attack, the government, at the armed forces' request, reduced that margin to a mere half-hour. The Emperor was kept informed, but vaguely, in a general way; he is above details of execution, or, at least, his subordinates affected to consider him so, informing him only of the broad lines of the attack plan worked out by the general staff. He was in any case reassured concerning the diplomatic procedure; he supposed that everything would be done legally. It was only after the attack that he learned the truth: the blow was delivered before the warning that should have been given thirty minutes earlier. No one in Tokyo, however, was to be punished. Everyone saved face before the Emperor by imputing the blame not to the cabinet, which delivered the rupture note on schedule the day before the Pearl Harbor raid, but to the Japanese embassy in Washington, which had failed to decode the document rapidly enough. So that when the declaration of war was delivered, late, to Secretary of State Cordell Hull by Ambassadors Kichisaburo Nomura and Kurusu at 2:20 P.M. instead of 1 P.M. (Washington time), the bombs had already spoken.

By their pride and their sheeplike passive obedience, the Japanese people were both dupes and accomplices of this trickery. From the first day, Pearl Harbor was a legend they credulously accepted. Hadn't the official version of events been the truth for them for years? And how, at this late date, could they have pierced the curtain of secrecy their leaders always drew between official truth and the real facts? The curtain was specially heavy over the final pre-attack maneuverings, particularly the last of the year's great Imperial conferences—we will speak later of those that preceded it—held in the palace in absolute secrecy on December 1; it was at this meeting that the supreme decision was taken to strike at Pearl Harbor and the date set for Monday, December 8, which was Sunday, December 7 in Hawaii.

At a telegraphed signal from Tokyo, the naval force readied for the attack had left its rendezvous in the Kurile Islands, in the extreme north of the Japanese archipelago, on November 26. The task force included Japan's six best aircraft carriers, four fast, modern battleships, late-model cruisers, fuel tankers. It raced at top speed toward a point 250 miles north of Hawaii, and it had orders to sink any ship it encountered—including Japanese vessels.

On December 3, Tokyo's ambassadors in Rome and Berlin informed Mussolini and Hitler of the failure of the Japanese-American negotiations. Without specifying how hostilities were to begin—Tokyo had no great confidence in the way secrets were kept in Berlin and Rome—they asked their allies to declare war on the United States as soon as the fighting started, which would be soon; Japan also asked that the three powers sign an agreement prohibiting any of them from seeking a separate peace.

At the December 1 Imperial conference, Admiral Isoroku Yamamoto, the fleet commander-in-chief, gave Foreign Minister Togo, at his request, an assurance that the attack could be put off if the government requested a last-minute delay. But this promise (and the illusion that it could be kept) was only one of the maneuvers that helped thrust more completely into the war those who had not given up a last hope of compromise; this probably included the Emperor himself. On December 2, the admiralty in Tokyo ordered the fleet to strike at dawn on the following Sunday, and on Saturday, December 6, the Japanese embassy in Washington received the text of the note breaking off relations with the United States. On the night of December 7, the carrier squadron was in American waters, within striking distance of Hawaii.

The attack schedule would be followed punctually, without a hitch, until the last minute. But it had not been adopted without disputes and some commotion. Three men had conceived this wildly daring stroke: Admiral Yamamoto, supreme fleet commander; Admiral Takijiro Onishi, chief of the general staff of the Eleventh Air Fleet, and Commander Minoru Genda of the naval air arm. Yamamoto, as we shall see, had long opposed the war; but when he finally bowed to the government's decisions, he hotly championed a "complete" strike against Hawaii. By this was meant not merely a bombing raid against the American fleet, but a landing on Hawaii followed by full-scale military occupation of the archipelago, advance bastion for defense of the American continent. It was a rash plan and it aroused fierce opposition; the army and General Tojo opposed it, and so did part of the naval command. Yamamoto was refused the troops he requested for the operation; he was told they were needed on other fronts. Much later, however, leading American military and naval authorities would agree that Yamamoto was right: had Japan placed Hawaii under military occupation, the consequences for the United States would have been infinitely more serious than the disaster at Pearl Harbor.

The plan adopted on December 8, then, was less ambitious. It simply called for an aerial attack against the bulk of the American fleet that had been concentrated for months at Pearl Harbor to intimidate Japan. The objective was to destroy the Pacific fleet's battleships at anchor, and especially the much-feared aircraft carriers. All through the first week in December and right up to the last minute, Japanese spies transmitted valuable information to Tokyo. The Japanese secret service knew that under still-prevailing peacetime regulations, the FBI kept no watch on apparently uncoded commercial telegrams sent through regular channels. The Japanese consul in Hawaii could transmit vital data disguised as innocent trading messages . . . via Western Union.

A Japanese submarine squadron in Yokosuka, the Japanese Norfolk near Tokyo, sailed four days before Ambassador Kurusu's arrival in Washington for the final stage of negotiations. Well before the attack date, the subs were in place, keeping watch on fleet movements around the Hawaiian islands. Moreover, two-man miniature submarines, displacing a maximum of 46 tons and built specially for this operation, were on station at the mouth of the enemy base. One of them managed to slip inside Pearl Harbor just before the attack, as a spy might sneak into the heart of a fortress. It seems to have entered at dawn that day, shortly after 4 A.M., in the wake of two minesweepers returning to port. The antisubmarine net across the harbor mouth was open at that hour and, through negligence, was left open. The two men aboard the tiny steel fish reconnoitered the fleet's three mooring areas without surfacing. Eight battleships were parked hull to hull behind the island that forms the "pearl" in the oyster-shaped bay—eight battleships sitting huddled and motionless like ducks in a pond. What a target for the Japanese bombardiers! At 6 A.M. the pocket sub's radioman, speaking softly on that slowly spreading Sunday morning, reported the boat's findings. This was Japan's first success, and it was an important one.

At 7:54 A.M. the first wave of bombing planes from the carriers north of Hawaii plunged down out of the sky over the airfields at the American base. An extra bit of luck cleared the sky over the attack zone while clouds covered the rest of the island. Then came the torpedo planes. With incredible daring, they loosed their torpedoes—equipped with fins for shallow-water attack and carrying unusually heavy payloads—at the battleships. Before 8 A.M., Admiral Chuichi Nagumo, the Japanese fleet ace commanding the attack squadron, cabled a message to Tokyo that simply repeated the one word *Tora! . . . Tora! . . . Tora!* —Tiger! . . . Tiger! . . . Tiger!—the code word for "Attack fully successful." The beast had killed; with a brusque roar it signaled its victory, howled its joy.

On the evening of that historic day, Nagumo still could not understand how the surprise could have been so complete. Hadn't the admiralty in Tokyo anticipated the loss of up to half the attack squadron? In fact, the Japanese had lost around 30 planes and fewer than half a dozen submarines, only one of which was of normal tonnage; the rest were pocket subs. Still less comprehensible today is how the Americans allowed themselves to be taken by surprise when, as was later established by a number of commissions investigating the Pearl Harbor disaster, we know that American intelligence analysts had broken the ultrasecret Japanese naval code well before December 1941. More than fifteen hours before the attack, the American high command, President Franklin D. Roosevelt and Secretary of State Hull, along with the rest of the President's closest advisers, knew that the two Japanese ambassadors had a declaration of war that they were going to deliver to Hull the next day, Sunday, in the early afternoon. There had been warning of the attack after all, not by the Japanese government but by the United States intelligence service. If there was any surprise to America's leaders, it concerned the site of the raid, not the fact that an attack was coming. The government and the high command were sure the Japanese would strike; the trouble was simply that they did not know where the blow would fall.

2

How the War
Came About

On the evening of December 9, the day after Pearl Harbor, telegrams reached Tokyo from Berlin announcing that Hitler had just halted his offensive in Russia and had given up the idea of taking Moscow that year. This was big news and should have aroused deep dismay in Japan because it killed hopes of a rapid German conquest of the Soviet Union. It should have left the Japanese rancorous and bitter: the news was a clear confession that the Reich had tricked its ally by dragging it into the mess just when Germany itself had to stop for breath. But this news was too embarrassing. It remained unnoticed by the general public, carefully minimized and buried in the newspapers among bulletins about the victory in Hawaii.

Yet it had mainly been Hitler's insistence and example that had pushed Tokyo into the war. It is easy to see today what madness it was for Japan to attack the United States in December 1941, but I can attest that even at the time, there was not a single foreigner living in Tokyo to whom that folly was not glaringly evident. Not one of the foreign observers whose painful privilege it was to watch the march of events closely failed to foresee from the very first day that the disproportion between the United States and Japan must sooner or later lead to an American victory. Even after the capture of Singapore, it was impossible to doubt that Japan would finally be beaten. Then how could the Japanese have been so blind? Because they were dazzled by the early German victories, fascinated by Hitler, bewitched by the promise of the coming partition of the world. They were so spellbound by the 1940 Blitzkrieg that they could not perceive in 1941 that Hitler had already made two fundamental errors: he had not dared to cross the English Channel, and he had been mad enough to attack Russia.

To the allure of the war in Europe for the Japanese was added the irresistible pressure of the Asian war that Japan itself had ignited. Ten years of imperialistic expansion, marked by the conquest of Manchuria in 1931, the step-by-step invasion of northern, central and southern China from 1937 to 1939, the first move against Singapore with the Tonkin invasion in 1940, and the occupation of Cochin China in 1941, led the Japanese war toward fusion with Hitler's war; it was entirely natural that the two should blend into a single world conflict.

This ineluctable train of events coincided with a calculated, premeditated design: Japan was bursting with a desire to prove itself as much a world power as the Western countries of which it had so long been the docile, patient pupil. This Asian people was determined to force its way on to the stage of history by chasing the white race out of Asia. This was an old ambition, nursed since Japan's first contact with the Western world. The war against America was the coronation of three generations of effort that had already crystallized in war three times: in China in 1895, against Tsarist Russia in 1904, and World War I, which Japan entered in 1915.

All this indicates that we must look beyond the logical causes of the Pacific war. Its true causes were basically emotional. Had reason been guiding Japan, it would have halted the country at the threshold of this impossible adventure. But Japan was guided by a chaos of passions and there are names for them: the old Japanese instinct for violence, eager for a share in the toppling of ancient empires; Japanese pride, which preferred a whole people's suicide to peace with the United States, if this meant relinquishing some of the country's Asian conquests; natural ambition, which chiefly saw in the collapse of the white empires the advent of a Japanese empire in Asia.

These passions were exacerbated in 1941 by a kind of race between Japanese expansion and the countermeasures it elicited from the other Pacific powers. Japan's rash plunge into the war cannot be fully understood without emphasizing the economic and political strangulation it brought on itself by its own actions. Sanctions replying to each new Japanese invasion wave—trade embargo, credit freeze, a ban on scrap-metal sales to Japan, an oil blockade, etc.—steadily reduced the choices left to the country until there was no longer any alternative but surrender or aggression.

I will not attempt here to give a detailed history of the year 1941 before Pearl Harbor; instead, I will simply sketch in the few highlights needed to illuminate the events that followed. From them, I hope, will emerge a factor that was indirectly one of the fundamental causes of the war, one that also contributed later to hastening Japan's defeat: I mean the extraordinary disorganization and incoherence of Japan's entire policy. The world now knows how much weakness lay under Japan's apparent power. But only those who lived in Tokyo in 1941 can gauge how much its supposedly "immutable" policy—that was the official phrase—was enfeebled by hidden disorder. There is just one word that can adequately characterize Japanese policy at that moment in its history: a shambles. The government was chaotic because authority was constantly disputed by at least two parties, the civilian and the military. Plans were contradictory because both war and peace were projected. Men were hypocritical, agreements were illusory, negotiations were contradictory and self-annulling.

The most surprising turns of this erratic policy pivoted on the tragicomedy of Japan's relations with Germany, in which the former's clumsiness combined with the latter's cynicism to make the tripartite Axis agreement a bizarre tangle of international intrigue.

The first act is set in 1938–39. During the conservative administrations of Prince Fumimaro Konoye and Baron Kiichiro Hiranuma, Germany pressed Japan to conclude a military alliance that would unite the two countries in a common assault against the Americans and the British. But Tokyo, which at that point was still anxious to conciliate the Anglo-Saxon countries, turned a deaf ear to the proposal. On the other hand, Japan was willing to ally itself with Germany against Soviet Russia, in keeping with the anti-Comintern pact of which Japan was a signatory. Berlin agreed; negotiations went ahead; Japanese policy toward Russia stiffened. The treaty was about to be signed when, in August 1939, Berlin announced that German Foreign Minister Joachim von Ribbentrop and the Soviet Commissar for Foreign Affairs, Vyacheslav Molotov, had signed a nonaggression treaty. In Tokyo, stupefaction and rage; the Japanese cabinet, which had never been consulted or even informed by the Germans, collapsed amid cries of treason. The sullen resentment born that day against Germany in a sector of public opinion and among Japan's military leaders was never to be completely dispelled.

The second act took place in September 1940; a year had passed, France had surrendered and the Nazi Blitzkrieg was triumphant. The Japanese reckoned that, after all, it was highly imprudent to distance themselves from the Reich just when Germany seemed all-powerful. They returned to the idea of a tripartite military alliance. But this brings us to a fascinating and paradoxical aspect of Axis history that deserves historians' attention. The determining factor in Tokyo's decision was precisely the German-Russian rapprochement that marked the beginning of the European war. Indeed, Prime Minister Prince Konoye, after long resistance, finally agreed to the tripartite agreement only on condition, formally accepted by the Reich, that it would become a four-power treaty to which Russia would also be a party. What practical value was there in a Berlin-Tokyo agreement if the two powers were separated by the vastness of the Soviet Union? If Russia accepted the arrangement, however, the most fruitful exchanges would henceforth be possible in every field between the Germanic West and the Japanese East, and the formidable European-Asian bloc thus constituted would be strong enough to hold the world in check.

Early in September 1940, in the course of discussions in Berlin between Ribbentrop and Japan's Ambassador Kurusu, aided by General Hiroshi Oshima (who would soon replace Kurusu as ambassador), the German Foreign Minister assured the Tokyo government's representatives that the proposed alliance would quickly become a four-power agreement; Russia, he said, had definitely fallen in line with German policy. When Tokyo cautiously asked for Ribbentrop's exact words, Kurusu confirmed that the German had specifically used the English expression *to fall in step.*

Ribbentrop even offered Tokyo a plan by which, after immediate signature of a tripartite treaty—Japan, Germany and Italy—its extension to Russia was projected under the following conditions:

1. Russia was to declare its adhesion to the triple alliance and agree to its objective, which was to limit the extension of the war and restore peace, or else to intimidate the United States, restraining it from entering the war against so powerful a coalition.

2. The principle of German predominance in Europe and Japanese hegemony in East Asia was to be proclaimed.

3. Japan, Germany and Italy would recognize a Russian sphere of influence in Iran and India, while North Africa would fall to Italy, Central Africa to Germany and the South Seas to Japan.

Didn't caution demand that Japan wait to agree until Russia consented to all the plans concerning it? The Emperor himself raised the objection: why the interim step of a three-power treaty if they were to wind up with a four-power agreement? Ribbentrop replied that events in Europe were moving fast; it would be highly imprudent for Japan to suffer the slightest delay in this period of lightning war. Britain was going to be invaded, the British Empire would soon be dismantled. It was urgent to sign at once. To help him wrest consent from the Japanese, Ribbentrop sent Dr. Heinrich Stahmer as a "special envoy extraordinary" to Tokyo. Stahmer brought all his eloquence and persuasiveness to bear to convince Prince Konoye of the fundamentally peaceful, friendly nature of German-Russian relations. He specially insisted on the remarkable fashion in which Russia was complying—"to the last drop of oil"—with the Berlin-Moscow trade agreement. He stressed that the Soviet Union's economic and industrial structure rested largely on the help of German technicians, particularly in heavy industry.

These assurances were accepted by the Japanese government, which was finally persuaded that dispute between Russia and Germany was now impossible. Besides, Foreign Minister Yosuke Matsuoka had been thoroughly convinced in advance of the rightness of Berlin's position. The resistance had come from Prince Konoye and that resistance now ended; he signed the tripartite military alliance treaty with the Reich and Italy on September 27, 1940. Extension of the instrument to Soviet Russia was not written into the pact, but constituted a tacit condition, as is confirmed by a number of notes exchanged on the subject by the governments in Tokyo and Berlin.

All this was to change in the first half of 1941, and this is the tragicomedy's third act. While Tokyo undertook a policy of rapprochement with Soviet Russia designed to fit in with the Russo-German understanding about a future quadripartite treaty, Berlin was quarreling with Moscow and the German Army, on Hitler's orders, was preparing to attack in the east. Dense secrecy masked these preparations, and Japan was unaware of the gravity of the crisis developing in the relations between Hitler and Stalin. It nevertheless received a warning at the end of March, during a visit by Matsuoka to Hitler and Ribbentrop. The German Foreign Minister told him that serious disagreements had arisen with Stalin. War was not impossible, he said, and much of the German Army was forced to face eastward. But if this were to happen, Stalin would be beaten within a few months. Was the warning too vaguely worded? Did the Japanese minister and his government refuse to believe it, or make the mistake of not trying to check it out? Whatever the reason, public opinion was completely surprised when, on June 22, Hitler unleashed what everyone supposed was a new Blitzkrieg against the Soviet Union; the effect on Japan, even on its government, was like that of a violent earthquake.

Again the Japanese cabinet cried treason. Again it had been caught off balance at a crucial moment, like a dull-witted spectator who cannot understand the play he is watching, who weeps when he should applaud and applauds when he should weep.

Matsuoka sent Berlin a formal note protesting actions diametrically at odds with the Reich's political commitments. Berlin replied with a harshly acrimonious note expressing Hitler's regrets that radical changes in the situation had forced him to reverse his policy; Germany also assured Japan that it would win the war against Russia in three months. And it admonished Tokyo not to worry: Germany really felt strong enough to handle the war without Japanese assistance.

Meanwhile, however—and the fourth act in this climax-studded drama opens here—Matsuoka, stopping in Moscow on his return from Berlin in April, had signed a neutrality treaty with Stalin. The structure originally planned for the four-power alliance had been a kind of bridge linking Tokyo with Berlin via Moscow; the German end had blown up while Japan was still building the bridge, and the Russo-Japanese treaty stood like an intact Asian pier of a ruined edifice. Circumstances would increasingly give this pact a decidedly anti-German thrust because it would allow Russia to throw all its forces against the Reich without worrying about Berlin's Japanese ally.

The upshot of this extraordinary imbroglio was clear, at least: less than ten months after the Axis agreement was signed, its two principal members turned their backs on each other. They were careful to mask this hasty divorce if only to avoid losing face altogether. And Prince Konoye, who had lent himself to this botch only out of weakness, now thought he could correct his mistake and gradually reverse Japanese policy; he would try to put the tripartite treaty on ice (his expression) and seek an agreement with the United States. But among the factors that led to his failure, there is one to keep firmly in mind: Washington did not know how serious the German-Japanese falling-out was and it profoundly mistrusted Japan's Prime Minister; the mistrust would only deepen because the pro-Germans in Japan and the country's military establishment were determined to patch up Tokyo's differences with Berlin at any cost and they would sabotage an attempted reconciliation with America by every possible means.

For Konoye, it was important to begin by officially detaching Japan from Germany in the war against Russia. This was decided at an Imperial conference in the palace on July 2. All the state's leaders, civilian and military, attended these grand councils, convened only on rare and grave occasions, at which the Emperor presided in person and decisions remained absolutely secret. At the July 2 conference, then, it was decided—and this was enormously important in the subsequent chain of events—that, for the moment, Japan would not go to war against Russia in support of its German ally.

Next, Konoye hurriedly took charge of the unofficial negotiations that had been going on in Washington since April. They were begun while Matsuoka was in Europe and were to some extent being carried on behind his back. A first storm blew up on the Foreign Minister's return from Moscow. He was furious to learn that such a step had been taken without his knowledge; at the same time, he thought he could continue to suit the triple alliance to his purpose: although its positive advantages were lost, it might still be used in a negative way, as a means to blackmail or intimidate Washington.

Matsuoka maneuvered in so many ways to sabotage the talks with the Americans that Konoye had to get rid of him; the Prime Minister submitted his government's resignation to the Emperor and then reconstituted his cabinet exactly as it had been, except that Admiral Teijiro Toyoda was appointed Foreign Minister.

A second storm soon broke, however. The July 2 conference had not merely decided to abandon Germany in its war with Russia; it had also authorized the Japanese Army to take a further step toward Singapore by moving south to Saigon the troops stationed in Tonkin since the fall of France in 1940. Thus, at the very time its policy was preparing the ground for an understanding with the United States, Japan, illogical as ever, was elsewhere taking steps that would touch off a violent explosion of anti-Japanese feeling in America. This is in fact what happened when the Saigon decision became known on July 26; Washington immediately took stern reprisals, paralyzing American-Japanese trade by freezing the credit it had granted Tokyo. Sales of oil to Japan were specifically banned.

This incredible contradiction in Japanese policy should not surprise us. It is explainable by the old quarrel separating the state's military and civilian branches, familiarly known as the uniforms and the cutaways. In every cabinet, the Army and Navy Ministers—always a general and an admiral on active service— were independent, under no obligation to obey the Prime Minister. A constitutional custom, originating with the poorly written and confusing Constitution of 1892, made the two ministers directly responsible to the Emperor, not to the Prime Minister, and thus in a position to appeal over the Prime Minister's head. And when a cabinet was chosen, they were appointed not by the Prime Minister, but by the army and navy, which imposed their candidates on the government. Formation of a ministry displeasing to the military, therefore, was impossible. Yet the armed forces did not openly take power; they preferred to pull strings from the outside. For the previous ten years at least, then, there could be said to have been not one Japanese government, but two. The cabinet could never, therefore, be held to a precise commitment; it followed a double policy, talking of peace and perpetrating acts of war. The Manchurian affair grew out of the system and so did the February 1936 military rebellion.* Feuding among the clans high in government turned Tokyo's policy into a series of internal accidents and external power plays. Its only logical result was Japanese militarism's territorial expansionism. The military preferred this lame system because it reaped its share of advantage from each successive crisis.

This is precisely what happened at the July 2 Imperial conference. The military leaders were chiefly concerned that Japan not remain immobile while everything around it was moving and changing. Deprived of a strike at Siberia, they were compensated by agreement from the Prime Minister and the Emperor for the troops' advance into Cochin China.

Nor did the high command flatly oppose the negotiations under way with Washington. Playing both sides of the board, it was perfectly willing to go far toward a compromise with the United States if, at the same time, it could end the war in China that was draining Japan's energies and restricting the country's freedom of action. Besides, General Tojo, the War Minister, like

* See page 101.

the army he represented in the government, thought the Saigon expedition, instead of damaging Japan's diplomatic position, would give the country added leverage in bargaining with the Americans.

But the army's policy was itself vitiated by deep internal schisms. Its leaders, relatively moderate because they were sick of the China adventure, were constantly outflanked by their subordinates and by their general staffs, whose party of young colonels insisted on a Hitler-style policy. The decision to invade southern Indochina was made primarily to satisfy the demands of the military extremists. Hence the astonishing confusion of Japanese policy in that summer of 1941: double betrayal within the tripartite agreement, with Germany duping Japan and being deceived by it in turn; Japan seeking compromise with Washington and making a show of force in Saigon; duality of a government torn between civilians and the military; the army itself split. To all this, as we shall see, was added discord between the army and navy and the alienation of the government and public opinion.

Faced with this disorder, Roosevelt adopted a simple, straightforward policy: offer Japan an agreement if it abandoned its armed conquests, retighten sanctions against it at each new Japanese advance. For the moment, the push toward Singapore in late July caused such a stir that Prince Konoye despaired of achieving anything through normal diplomatic negotiation. The only hope was to sidestep the muddle in Tokyo, avoid the clutter of conflicting programs and reach a decision away from the clan feuds. This is why, on August 7, Konoye suddenly proposed to Roosevelt that they settle the whole Pacific problem in a personal meeting.

At first, Roosevelt welcomed the idea; ten days later, he accepted it in principle and suggested that the meeting take place somewhere on the Alaskan coast. On August 27, Konoye sent him a personal message expressing his wish to work toward peace in a spirit of goodwill. Informed circles in Tokyo predicted that the Konoye-Roosevelt meeting would almost certainly succeed. The peace was as good as won and, for a few days, jubilation reigned. Then, on September 3, Roosevelt told Tokyo he had changed his mind; Tokyo and Washington, he said in substance, should begin with an understanding on the basic terms of a compromise reached through normal negotiations between chancelleries. Only when everything had been settled would the two heads of government meet to ratify the agreement.

Behind this about-face, apparently, was the advice of Secretary of State Hull. On reflection, the President and Hull decided that they had known the traditional attitude of Japanese governments too long and too well. They saw too great a risk that if Prince Konoye brought home a Japanese-American agreement from Alaska, he would be disavowed by his cabinet and disowned by public opinion. The Japanese Army would even resort to force if an agreement signed by Konoye imposed, as it had to, a retreat the military would doubtless consider unacceptable—for example, evacuation from China, the *sine qua non* of any compromise.

Were Roosevelt and Hull right? One thing is certain: if there was an unwitting Presidential policy error, it was here that it must be sought. In defense of their attitude of mistrust, Washington's leaders could point to ten years of Japanese history. Could they hope that the Japanese Prime Minister's word would be worth any more this time than it had been on a hundred previous occasions, when it was annulled by the actions of the Imperial army? Besides, Hull and Roosevelt could cite the words and actions of the Japanese themselves at that very juncture.

On August 14, a week after Konoye made his proposal, Baron Hiranuma, former chairman of the Emperor's secret council and a known supporter of compromise with the United States, narrowly escaped the bullets of an assassin belonging to one of the secret superpatriotic societies. In Toranomon, police arrested a gang of nationalists plotting to murder Konoye himself. At the very moment that the Prime Minister sent his message of goodwill to Roosevelt, the press in Tokyo was unanimously storming against the Atlantic Charter just signed by the American President and British Prime Minister Winston Churchill. Public opinion in Japan, six months behind events, was still being undermined by Axis propaganda. It was the prey of nationalist agitators, of pseudo-journalists drawing their pay from secret funds held by extremist groups, the army and, especially, by the

German embassy, which shrewdly orchestrated a violent campaign by part of the press against the British and the Americans. A deep gulf had existed for months between the public and the government. For Tokyo's policy, aside from the divisions and rivalries besetting it, was poisoned by still another factor: secrecy. The misfortunes of the Berlin alliance were kept secret. So were the issues behind the negotiations with the United States. Japanese opinion, ignorant to begin with and inexperienced in international affairs, knew nothing of the real facts of the situation—nothing at all, for example, about the comparative strengths of Japan and the United States or about Germany's chances of winning the war. Already powerless to redirect public sentiment before the proposed Konoye-Roosevelt meeting, how was the government to deal with the uproar that a final break with Berlin would provoke?

To all this, Prince Konoye and his supporters would reply that Roosevelt had been ill-informed of the real situation in Tokyo's ruling circles at the time. According to this thesis, the Prime Minister, instead of being isolated and exposed to repudiation on his return from Alaska, had arranged for backing from two sources that would have guaranteed his authority. First, he had the determined support of the Emperor, who profoundly wished to avoid war. In addition, he had behind him the army's three top officers: War Minister Tojo and Generals Kenji Doihara and Akita Muto. The latter two had agreed to accompany Konoye to Alaska; both were convinced nationalists, but, assert Konoye's defenders—whose arguments may be a little weak here—they were ready for any face-saving device if an agreement with Washington could rid them of the China war while giving Japan the access it coveted to raw materials in the South Pacific without having to fight for it. And so firm was the Emperor's support of the Prime Minister that the sovereign was determined to forbid any rebellion by army extremists; should such an uprising occur, he was prepared to shed his constitutional role as impartial arbiter and issue a formal order of obedience to anyone resisting Konoye's decisions. It would become clear later, at the time of Japan's surrender, what authority the Emperor's word carried. Roosevelt's mistake may have been to suppose that Konoye was virtually alone in attempting his crowning maneuver when in fact he had powerful backing. And, after all, the Alaska experiment was at least worth a try.

In any event, the negotiations were now thrown back into the chancellery machinery and, once more, all the disorder of Japan's governmental and diplomatic apparatus quickly made itself felt. While Konoye resumed negotiations with the American ambassador to Tokyo, Joseph Grew, the Japanese Foreign Minister worked to confuse matters by inaugurating more or less competing talks with the State Department in Washington aimed at tackling details one by one in the absence of agreement on basic principles. It was a clumsy move and it was obviously doomed to fail; its effect was simply to sharpen the Americans' suspicion.

Things were worsened by the fact that the rebuff to Konoye administered by Roosevelt threw the army's leaders in with the opposition. On September 6, the second great Imperial conference of 1941 began. Once more, its decisions reflected the deep contradictions in Japanese policy and the wrangling that was rife in the government. It told the Prime Minister to continue his negotiations, but it also authorized the military to make all necessary preparations for war. The diplomats were given a deadline—one more month in which to wrap up an agreement. If they failed, Japan's weapons would speak. The army man now pressing hardest for war was Marshal Gen Sugiyama, chief of the general staff.

Of course, the army had long been ready for hostilities, but this was the first time it had been officially authorized—indeed, urged to prepare. The September 6 decision involved a serious responsibility for Konoye; he accepted it—reluctantly, no doubt, but he did accept it—believing he could somehow get off the hook; at this decisive moment, he showed his weakness of character.

As for the Emperor, it is important to understand that under the Constitution he had no alternative to consent. The Constitution makes him a "sacred and inviolable" figure—in other words, not responsible, like the British sovereign. No decision of his is valid unless it is countersigned by a cabinet minister. He cannot intervene directly in politics except by deserting his normal role and assuming supralegal authority. He is certainly not the all-powerful god that legend makes him out to be. He would dare to take the helm actively only on a second decisive occasion —to deal with the question of surrender in 1945—and then in the light of his experience in 1941. For the time being, although he favored peace with the United States—the most reliable witnesses agree on this—he left the decision to his ministers, and Japan took another step down the slope toward war.

A characteristic incident at the September 6 conference proves how greatly confusion contributed to the making of Japanese policy. In Japanese, no distinction is made between the present and future tenses. The result was that the text of the resolution adopted that day by the state's highest assembly was ambiguous. The first part said in substance that negotiations with the United States were to be continued until the beginning of October. If no conclusion was reached by then, the document went on, "we decide on war at the end of October." But the Japanese words *"ketsui suru"* mean both "we are deciding" and "we shall decide." In the days that followed the conference, the army and civilian moderates squabbled over what the text meant—"we are deciding today to start the war at the end of October," or, as Prince Konoye maintained, "at the end of October we shall decide whether to go to war and we shall begin it on a date to be set at that time"?

In the event, the negotiations with Washington between September 6 and October 15 were no more successful than those that had preceded them. They remained blocked by a basic obstacle which, until the very end, would compromise any possibility of an understanding with the United States: the Japanese Army's rejection of the prime American condition: immediate evacuation of the troops of the Rising Sun from China. In mid-October, therefore, General Tojo, in the name of the army, informed Konoye that the deadline set at the Imperial conference had passed and that he had no choice but to withdraw. The Konoye cabinet resigned in a body and, on October 18, Tojo was named Prime Minister.

Over a month and a half were yet to elapse before the blow at

Pearl Harbor, but we will skip over the history of those last weeks; for all practical purposes, the Pacific war actually began in those mid-October days in 1941, when the head of the army assumed power.

3

Mass~Produced
Heroes

Who was the General Tojo who suddenly appeared on the world's stage in the dramatic dawn of Pearl Harbor? Shaved, eggshell skull, slit eyes encircled by horn-rimmed glasses—was this a new Hitler, the Hitler of the "yellow peril"? The world thought so briefly, in the wake of Japan's Blitzkrieg victories, and Japan made the mistake of thinking so, too.

Yet neither Tojo's personality nor his career were made of his model's stuff or built on that scale. His personality? There was nothing prophetic about Hideki Tojo, nothing heroic. He was merely an earnest soldier far readier to obey than to command—to obey the pressure of his clan. His career? He was luck's plaything; not, like Hitler, a man who made the world his toy. He did not create the Japanese Army, he was simply its product. Executor rather than inspiration of the group's will, he was nothing more than a kind of administrator delegated by the army, almost a strawman.

When Tojo emerged from the shadows at the age of fifty-six and moved from the War Ministry to the Prime Ministry in place of Prince Konoye, he was a man who had never risked anything, had never gambled; he had gotten ahead by studious self-application, by hitching himself tenaciously to his daily chores. His career as a general was swift, but without martial luster: a graduate of the war college in Tokyo shortly after the Russo-Japanese War (in which his father distinguished himself as a general), he had no brilliant feats of arms to his credit. His sole action of note was a rearguard victory over fleeing Chinese troops in the province of Jehol early in the Manchurian incident. But in the military bureaus in Hsinking, capital of the Japanese puppet state of Manchukuo, he found the climate that suited him then and afterward. In 1935 he commanded the military police (*Kempetai*), with the rank of colonel. When the China War began in 1937, he also functioned as chief of the Japanese Army general staff in Manchuria, the so-called Kwantung Army. It was the combination of these two posts that made him; Tojo would always be known as the former boss of the Kempetai. Behind the red-brick front of his headquarters building, what was to become the Japanese Army's Gestapo slowly took shape under his direction. Detailed files were assembled on majors, colonels, generals. Tojo was shrewd enough to stay clear of the clan feuds rampant in the army since 1930. He was interested in men, not ideas; when he had weeded out the army's right and left wings, only a single faction would remain: the Tojo clan.

Tojo liked to live in a group, to be surrounded by it, have friends and comrades. He knew how to listen, take notes, ask advice. Those he wanted to eliminate he handled carefully, patiently. Because he was an incisive speaker and clear thinker, he was considered a great brain by those dense, cloddish farmers' sons who themselves remained peasants. They nicknamed him "The Razor." Tojo a razor? A dull blade, wielded by other hands, who would commit murder on behalf of the gang. In 1938, having been named a general, he became vice-minister for war; in July 1940, when the superpatriotic friends of the Axis were exulting over Hitler's victories in Europe, he was made War Minister in the Konoye cabinet. He immediately purged the general staffs of his remaining enemies; in the name of the army he established control over war industries, pressed the Prime Minister to dissolve political parties, saw to the expurgation of every class of society. Liberals, trade-unionists, leftists, intellectuals and socialists, anyone who resisted Japanese militarism, disappeared into the prisons of the military and political police. In the stormy months preceding October 18, 1941, when he took power, Tojo still nourished some scruples, was still hesitant; only a few weeks before Pearl Harbor, he put up a show of favoring peace; vain gestures of appeasement—Kurusu's mission to Washington, for example—contradicted the cunningly engineered war machine that he himself had organized. But he was swept along by events and pushed by the clan. Just before he succeeded Prince Konoye, who was still desperately trying to keep Japan out of war, Tojo taunted the prince to his face. "Once in his life, sire," he told the prince, "a man should know when to throw himself from the terrace of the Kyomizu temple"—tantamount, for an American, to jumping from the top of the Washington Monument. On December 8, 1941, Tojo took another kind of jump, and behind him followed all Japan: 75 million sheep. For the first time in his life he gambled, betting on an Axis victory in Europe. But he was an uninspired gambler, really no more than a profiteer and mimic; like Japan itself, mimicking fascinating Germany, profiteering for over half a century from Western dissension.

Such was Tojo. He was the flashiest of the actors in the Japanese drama, yet he remains lackluster, gray, hazy. Some newsmen, especially Americans, like to depict the central figures of peace and war as colorful, brushing in characteristic gestures, intimate glimpses and striking comments. They have tried and will go on trying to do with Tojo what they have done, with more justification, with Hitler: seeing him in bold relief, with a character marked by destiny, a dramatic figure. His personality did not, however, lend itself to vivid imagery any more than those of the other leading actors in the Pacific war did. It is a poor observer of the Orient who would endow these men with grandeur for good or evil, with colors and shadows they did not have. And it is misleading to explain them by calling them inscrutable, impenetrable, mysterious.

No, Tojo and those behind and around him must be taken as they were, gray against a grayish background; let's not separate them artificially from the clan to which they belonged, from the crowds against which they are only dimly visible. Instead of inflating them with the genius of supermen or endowing them with the ideas that mark great fashioners of the future, we should see them as unsubstantial, without even the blackness of great criminals. There was a fatality, powerful and certain, behind the catastrophe they unleashed that always tended toward a single end, the war's disastrous denouement. But the men who severed the leash were merely weak, vacillating, shadowy—ordinary Japanese, products of a militaristic Japan that took a dim view of genius.

The main difference between these men and their Western counterparts lay in their low relief. Why this lack of distinctiveness? What might be called the "sense of man," the mark—Greek and Christian—of the Western world, is alien to Japanese civilization. Japan's society does not like individuals; it blunts them, effaces them. Japanese personalities therefore lack the strength of ours. "Know thyself" is a misconception in Japan, where men do not study themselves, where they scarcely know themselves; people *are* individuals, of course, but they avoid asserting the fact. Japan's masses do not require men in public life to indulge in the kind of publicity with which Western peoples like to surround the famous. Leaders are not subjects for anecdote: no human touches, no information about their private lives. Indeed, the State prevents the common man from knowing anything personal about his leaders; every effort is made, not to bring a public figure closer to the people, but to render him remote. And the less they know about him, the greater their obedience, their reverence and their fear.

Who is the Emperor of Japan? Western journalists tell us that he dines Western-style but lunches in the Japanese manner, that he gave up golf as too British a sport, that he studies plankton with oceanographers, that he is morally stern and has a happy home life. None of this provides a key to his personality. Making a living god of him is equally false. To the Japanese, he is simply a superior being; exceptional, but not a deity. The truth is probably that the Emperor is man without the right to be a man; first because he must live behind a wall the people may not penetrate and, more importantly, because he is somehow Japan itself, its living history, its aspirations and beliefs. He is a body of institutions; he is a throng, and his particular image is inseparable from the background against which it is projected: a multitude of 75 million people.

And who was Admiral Yamamoto, the hero of Pearl Harbor? Like Tojo, he was unknown to the public until, suddenly, he emerged to achieve glory. Commander-in-chief of the Rising Sun's fleet at 57, he had fought as a cadet in the Russo-Japanese War in 1904, losing two fingers in the naval battle of Tsushima. His career spanned general-staff posts, fleet commands and foreign missions (to Washington as naval attaché, to London as a delegate to disarmament conferences). With his shaven skull, his direct gaze and habitual pea jacket as austere as a clergyman's habit, bare of braid or decorations, he was indistinguishable from the naval officers around him. A systematic effort seems to have been made to invest him with a thoroughly abstract personality. He is known to have played cards. An occasional epigram is cited: at the London conference, to a delegate who tried to classify torpedoes as "defensive weapons," Yamamoto remarked, "Doesn't that depend on which end you are at, the departure or the arrival?" And when someone voiced surprise at his skill at bridge, he explained that "I have fifty thousand Chinese ideograms in my head; I can certainly add fifty-two cards to them." But all this does not add up to a personality; it tells nothing of the living man. He will always remain a haughty, distant figure because he is primarily defined by a function and a set of noteworthy actions at a particular moment in history.

What is true of the top men is even more so of their underlings. We can list the names of the leading generals behind Tojo: Kenryo Sato, the army's political brain; old Marshal Sugiyama, bland and foxy, with a prodigious memory; Koreshika Anami, whom we will find at the surrender; Akita Muto, head of the Bureau of Military Affairs, one of the three top army posts; Sadaichi Suzuki, chairman of the Planning Bureau, and a number of others. Their functions were well defined and their actions sometimes known, but as men they remain indistinct. And behind them, in the shadows, we glimpse an anonymous host of military clansmen, the young general officers and staff colonels whose names will never be famous, but whose work was nevertheless essential; for their leaders were never more than emanations of the group.

But then, why insist on trying to singularize these men whose very nature it was to escape the ordinary imagery of public life? It is nevertheless striking to note that these leaders of modern Japan were just as deficient in psychological relief, as elusive spiritually as they were physically. They seem immaterial because their actions were inconstant and illogical; their chief characteristic, probably, is that most of them seem to have lacked solid convictions.

Konoye's case is specially disturbing, almost tragic. This decent man was to be charged with war crimes because everything he attempted degenerated, liquefied, went haywire. He began the China affair by calling it an "incident" and allowed it to become a real war. He was the moderate, the advocate of a free society who opened the door to a kind of fascism in Japan; he was pro-British and he signed the Axis treaty; he was a pacifist who allowed the generals in his own cabinet to work toward war.

The Emperor? In the Imperial conferences in which the Empire's overall policy was set, he too allowed his ministers to prepare simultaneously, as we have seen, for peace and war. He asked that the war be launched according to the legal forms and he failed to see to it that this was done. And in his solemn December 8 declaration he admitted that war was "very far from his wishes."

The minor figures are no more ascertainable. Matsuoka, for example, was an internationalist, educated in the United States, who became a superpatriot and ally of the fascist dictatorships. Kurusu, signatory as Japan's ambassador in Berlin of the tripartite alliance, would later maintain that he signed against his will. He appeared as a messenger of peace to Washington on the very eve of Pearl Harbor, but his mission, whether he agreed or not, was mere camouflage for Japan's war preparations.

None of these men ever tried by a dramatic gesture to break away from his group or from national policy. None resigned or protested or refused the role assigned them. Whole groups acted the same way. The most striking case is that of the big financial trusts, the ones called the *zaibatsu*: Mitsui, Mitsubishi and others. Their history was internationalist and mercantile; until the last moment they stood aloof from the army and feared the war, knowing very well that peace was much more profitable. But they did nothing; they left action to others. Their leaders could have spoken up, could have acted—such men as Seihin Ikeda, the great financier, and Aichiro Fujiyama, president of the Japanese Chamber of Commerce and Industry. They were silent. They submitted.

Still more extraordinary, surely, was the case of the navy and its commander-in-chief, the indefinable Yamamoto. As Vice-Minister of the Navy in 1939, he secretly but vigorously opposed, as did his minister, Admiral Mitsumasa Yonai, the conclusion of the tripartite alliance demanded by the army. His very life was in danger; so heavy was the rain of threats against him from rightist extremists that he and his aides went permanently armed behind a hedge of bodyguards. A leaflet circulating throughout Japan called the man who was later to become a great hero a "traitor" and a "national bandit." When, a year later, Konoye signed the Axis treaty, Yamamoto was no longer in the ministry and so was no longer responsible, but couldn't he at least have spoken out, protested? Not a word.

Another year went by, ushering in the 1941 crisis in Japanese-American negotiations. The Naval Ministry and the navy's general staff strongly opposed the war; the army-navy quarrel flared anew. Having surveyed the navy's resources, the admiralty reported that the fleet would have trouble maintaining a two-year war. Yamamoto went it one better: in a letter to the government, he warned that he could not accept the responsibility of command for more than a year and a half; beyond that, he could see only disaster.

But all this opposition remained secret; it wavered, left all the responsibility to Konoye. The top fleet officers were afraid of stirring up public opinion, of sapping Japanese prestige by showing the rest of the world a picture of national disunity, and of displeasing their subordinates—for the navy had its own clan of fanatic young officers. So at last it bowed and went reluctantly to war. Then came the final paradox: Admiral Yamamoto, foe of the Axis, partisan of peace, agreed to lead an attack of which he disapproved and, rather than resign, he kept the supreme command of the Japanese fleet that had recently been given him.

Emperor and ministers, army and navy officers and civilians, leaders minor and major—what was it they all lacked? What was the missing element in these men? What they lacked, even more than the logic so foreign to their minds, was, first and foremost, moral courage. And this is one of the prime causes of misunderstanding about Japan: though it lacks moral courage, this country nevertheless has physical courage in the highest degree. Its ancient wars were marked by real heroism, just as the Pacific War would be. Militarist Japan was satisfied with this kind of courage; it knew no other and it exalted physical bravery at home while filling the world's ears with the din of its heroes' prowess.

A surprising contrast, this scarcity of moral courage and superabundance of physical heroism. The paradox is only apparent, however; it has a logical explanation, for the same causes produce similarly contradictory effects in Japanese society. It is the twin result of the law of the group to crush what resists it while exalting what serves it. Moral courage dwindled in the collective climate of a militaristic Japan that blocked individualism and self-affirmation. Physical courage, on the other hand, became something like a national industry because the group exploited the very lives of those who moved docilely with the herd. The nation-clan, fanatically self-conscious, feared ideas but cultivated its instincts, especially the old Nipponese instinct toward violence in which killing others, killing oneself or being killed were all blended in a single notion of heroism. Finally, it allowed morality, or, rather, amorality in its leaders while—and here military Japan recalls Nazi Germany—demanding morality and faith of the herd.

There have been endless postmortems about the attack on Pearl Harbor, but the domestic tragedy with which it was coupled may have gone unnoticed: a colossal hoax inside Japan that stamped the entire war; exploitation of the virtues of a whole people in support of its leaders' mistakes. There was a good deal of cynicism and nihilism in the feelings that launched Nazi Germany on its career of aggression, but the Japanese people went to war with considerable good faith, enlisting in the nation's service the physical courage which, in them, is a form of conviction.

And in a swindle that was their leaders' real crime, all this faith, elicited and maintained by the leadership, was used to deliver one of history's most terrible stabs in the back.

After Pearl Harbor, I was told a few revealing secrets about the atmosphere in which the blow was readied. Several hundred cadets and young naval officers, perhaps five hundred, perhaps more, were gathered in a training school. Almost all were unmarried, all were between the ages of twenty and twenty-five, and they knew they had been chosen from among the best in the fleet. They had hardly settled in before they began a training program like nothing then known in the West. First came physical training of almost savage violence: intensive gymnastics, fiery Japanese fencing, hiking, swimming, breakneck jumping, judo or jiujitsu, muscle building. Then came the cruises, aircraft-carrier maneuvers, training flights on which daredevilry was the rule for the young pilots in launching aerial torpedoes, dive-bombing, attacking target ships. Fatal accidents were not rare, but such an end was reputed as glorious as death in battle.

The rumor spread gradually through the ranks that all the men involved constituted an elite corps chosen for an exceptional operation, a higher, secret duty, the most glorious of all. Officers made only veiled allusions to it, fanaticizing their men with appeals to their heroic courage and evocations of old Japan's violent instincts.

Finally the admirals appeared. They were known to the whole fleet and they hinted at the likelihood of an extraordinary operation, a bold and sacred mission on which the nation's fate would hang. A promise was made to all those nerved-up young officers that their names would be linked with this historic adventure. They should know that their chances of returning alive were slim, but they had advance assurance of the deification in the Yasukuni Temple—the national pantheon—that rewards the shades of all warriors who die for the fatherland.

In the summer of 1941, all were given forty-eight-hour furloughs. These young people who had been living in conditions of monkish austerity, without leave, without distractions, without a drop of alcohol, spent two days with their parents without letting on that they would probably never see each other again. Reassembled near Tokyo, they were led in a body to the temple of the Emperor Meiji, the founder of modern Japan who was made a god . . . in the twentieth century! And there, bowing before the brown-wood altars under the tall, rosy-trunked pines, each man, in a silent prayer, offered up his life. Before November they were on their way to an unannounced destination.

In the first week of March 1942, exactly three months after Pearl Harbor, the whole Japanese press suddenly came out with a sensational story, a dramatic new development in the accounts of the initial strike. A long announcement by the naval ministry revealed the names of nine young naval officers and noncommissioned ranks who had taken part in the Hawaii attack aboard the pocket subs the Japanese referred to as the "special flotilla." The official announcement, read on the radio and front-paged by all the big newspapers, posted in public places and commented on for days by all the propaganda organs, told how the nine men, given up in advance for dead, had not only defied a thousand perils to enter Pearl Harbor, had not only joined Japanese planes in the attack on the morning of December 8, but had even returned to the attack alone that evening. One of the pocket subs was credited with sending the battleship *Arizona* to the bottom. They radioed a report of the results of their mission to the regular submarines waiting offshore. Then, silence. They never reappeared; either they were destroyed or they blew themselves up in obedience to the Japanese code of honor, which forbids a warrior to be taken alive.

The entire announcement was vague, the details hazy. No precise indication was given of how many submarines there were; the Tokyo communiqués, even at the beginning of the war, imitated classical Japanese painting—artistically foggy with lots of blank spaces. After the war, the Americans would deny the "special flotilla's" effectiveness; they would even report that a Japanese officer and his crewman were captured as they emerged from the craft they had run ashore at the harbor mouth; this was the sub that had reconnoitered the naval base at dawn on December 8.

Japanese propagandists ignored this; what mattered to them was not discussing technical or strategic secrets—these were jealously guarded—but raising a storm of publicity around the sacrifice of these nine heroes. Heroes? The word is too mild; they were called "hero-gods," an expression which a carefully orchestrated propaganda campaign would soon make a commonplace in referring to military who died in battle. Photographs of the nine officers were published in the newspapers, along with their grades at the naval academy, interviews with their parents, comments by their teachers and instructors. One Sunday, the Naval Minister, Admiral Shimada, visited the native village of Major Iwasa, one of the missing submariners (a pre-deification second lieutenant, he had been promoted posthumously to the rank of major). The press touchingly described the minister's visit to the dead man's folks; he was photographed on his hands and knees on a mat, bowing low to Iwasa's parents in solemn reverence. To reporters' questions, the hero's father, a gnarled peasant named Naokichi Iwasa, declared, "But it's to his mother that he owes it all!" The woman was astonished: had ever a Japanese husband—especially hers—been heard to praise his wife instead of introducing her to others, as he should have, as his "foolish wife"? "I can sew," she protested. "Except for that, I was no good for anything."

And here is a letter from Major Iwasa to the commander of his training camp, dated the day before his departure on the expedition from which he knew he would never return:

> I am speechless before the marvelous opportunity offered me, and I am resolved to give up my life there. I am humbly grateful to you for your kind and constant efforts to educate me, fool and dunce that I am. It has become necessary for the welfare of the race of Yamato* to take a decisive step and go on the offensive. To your humble servant has fallen the honor of striking the first blow; I know of no greater glory. And if I fail in my mission, know that the fault will lie entirely in my own inadequacy. . . .

Lieutenant Hiro, aged twenty-two, kept a diary, excerpts from which were published in the newspapers: "My parents think I'm

* The ancient name of Japan.

on vacation; that's what I told them when I left them. All of you, forgive my mistakes. I'm going to die for my country, for the nation. Maybe you will learn about it later, and you will probably say, 'Ah, the scamp, he made it after all!' "

Others left only laconic aphorisms or poems about death, such as it was fitting for a warrior to write before dying, set down in Chinese ideograms with a few bold brushstrokes. From Lieutenant Furano, these four syllables: *"Chin Yu Ka Dan"*—"Cold courage, harsh decision." From Hiro again, a precept: "Serve the State through seven reincarnations," meaning, "I will be reborn seven times, and seven times my life will end with my sacrifice in the fatherland's service."

Young Lieutenant Furano left a poem dedicated to his father:

> *The young cherry blossoms*
> *fall from the branches*
> *at the highest moment of their glory*
> *with no regret. . . .*
> *Myself, like a broken pearl*
> *I will scatter my bones*
> *in Pearl Harbor.*
> *The dawn is bright*
> *with the joy of our reunion*
> *at the Yasukuni temple!*

All this drumbeating on behalf of the "heroes of Pearl Harbor" was not done, we must bear in mind, for foreign consumption. It was aimed at the Japanese people, whom it profoundly affected. Their leaders lavishly sowed heroism and sacrifice to reap new harvests of heroes at every season. The public-relations budget for heroism paid off a hundredfold; it guaranteed a profit from the investment of violence in every Japanese citizen's education. It provided the human bombs and kamikaze fighters of the future, prepared people's minds for the campaign for national suicide that climaxed the Japanese war effort. This promotion campaign would make millions anxious to try their hands at that much-vaunted national art: dying honorably.

Responsibility for this breach of public trust, this exploitation of the people's courage, was not the leaders' alone. Japan's modern military society, heir in this respect to its ancestors, conspired by its very nature to make death easy by a kind of depreciation of life. In the West, classical and Christian wisdom established human life as a unique and primary value. A Westerner does not live his life fully unless he understands and realizes its inimitability; the very sense of his existence is its preciousness. If he gives his life, he gives something irreplaceable. More: our identities are not only precious, but they are also precise, clearly distinguishable from those around us, independent, even opposed to the group of which they are a part.

On all these points, how different Japanese psychology was! We have already noted, and will have occasion to do so again, how the mass there blurred the precise contours of identities, of individuality. This was not so much the result of military Japan's totalitarian regime as of Oriental civilization as a whole, the general tendency of which is to dissolve the individual in his surroundings.

Not satisfied with depriving individuals of their particularity, it subtly teaches these individuals that existence is not so valuable. What does sacrificing a life matter if it can be replaced by other interchangeable lives? What does it matter, as long as the group, which is everything, survives and if the idea for which the group has asked the individual to perish survives as well? Life is also replaceable because it is superabundant. Greater Japan, with its expanding population, wasted life ungrudgingly because the birthrate was high and every death was supplied by several lives. A young man married, or was married by his family, when he was barely twenty years old; he had time to father children before he disappeared, and at the age of heroic deeds, chiefly between twenty and thirty, he was already the head of a large family, as contrasted to white men, who usually become fathers after the heroic age.

A Japanese attaches less importance to the persons in his group and they are also less precious. As a group, his family constitutes an indispensable world, but individually its members are not all that necessary to him. Personal ties in Japan do not have the tightness, the sometimes tyrannical command they have for us. A Japanese family, while more coherent than ours, is not as devouring as a family can be in the West, where it is based on the love of specific individuals. Unlike a French or American trooper, a Japanese soldier did not feel that his absence was a material and emotional disaster for his loved ones, or an even greater one if he failed to come back. The great Japanese family looks after a lonely wife, is even more enveloping of a widow and her children. The State watches over them and takes care of them if necessary. The eldest son succeeds his father as head of the house, and everything goes on naturally without him.

Among all the groups that absorbed Japanese individuality, the most demanding, the most pervasive, was the nation. It kept the individual in a life that was poor, shrunken, obedient. In compensation, what proud satisfaction it gave him on a national level! How powerful he felt through Greater Japan! Japan taught him that he was nothing without the nation, everything through it. If the nation's fate was at stake in a war, therefore, his leaders proclaimed that it was better that each Japanese die than be vanquished, for living if the fatherland was dead meant living in a vacuum. It was this idea that inspired the campaign of national suicide, of which we will speak later, shortly before Japan surrendered. Was a battle lost? Better then that a Japanese soldier die rather than be taken prisoner, and the code of honor required a captive to commit suicide, for what good was survival if it meant living in an enemy group? How could a Japanese captive maintain his dignity there when the pith of that dignity was given him from outside, from the group?

Religion did its share in depreciating life. Death is made as fearful as possible to a Westerner. Even an unbeliever really believes in a fearful future—in nothingness; in losing life, he will lose everything he has and so, in the meanwhile, even his sorrows are dear to him. To a Japanese, death did not mean entry into an unknown and fearsome future, but, rather, a return to the past, to what was known. A Japanese about to die was not someone who went ahead as a vanguard to those still living, alone among terrifying shadows. He felt he was returning toward everything that was, that he was going to be reunited with the whole past and the dead he knew. He did not lead, he followed, taking the same road as his thousands of ancestors. Shintoism and Buddhism, tightly blended in his beliefs, put him in daily contact with the dead, who could be visited effortlessly since they lived with him, in the ancestral altar there, over the worktable or the family dining table. Popular Buddhism was still more reassuring, because a heroic death brought the certainty of promotion in the chain of reincarnations, the promise of a higher life in the ladder of beings and lives.

Again, the State seized profitably on this disposition to die. On Shintoism, an animistic and primitive religion, it built a sort of lay religion of the nation, endowed with a purely civilian and patriotic cult centered on the Emperor. This faith was crowned by the death of its faithful, conferring a guarantee of immortality on the heroes who sacrificed their lives to it. They became the god protectors of Japan, its new, modern deities, replacing the ancient tutelary spirits who dwelt in peaceful retreat among the rocks and woods. The war's hero-gods lived in Tokyo; their souls were "enshrined in the temple," the patriotic Yasukuni pantheon on the Kudan hill. Thousands of fellow Japanese visited them daily, asking their help and seeking to follow their example.

4

Tokyo at Play

On the afternoon of December 10, Tokyo Radio announced the torpedoing of the two most powerful British warships east of Suez. The ultramodern, 35,000-ton battleship *Prince of Wales*, accompanied by the 32,000-ton battle cruiser *Repulse*, en route to Singapore, had ventured into the Gulf of Siam without air cover, hoping to intercept Japanese naval convoys between Indochina and their landing points on the Malay Peninsula. Recognized and reported by a submarine, they were attacked at high noon by successive waves of incredibly daring Japanese Navy torpedo planes that sent both ships to the bottom in less than two hours. This, coming two days after Pearl Harbor, was a sensational defeat for the British fleet. Even more than the American disaster, it seemed to cast doubt on the basic value of all armored fleets, which were now at the mercy of aerial torpedoes. Evident in the enthusiasm reigning in Tokyo was an odd feeling of final relief. After all, the first day's victory was not to remain an isolated success; the last traces of the anxiety felt on December 8 now vanished. Japanese pride swelled with a double satisfaction: that of inflicting this affront on the British fleet, considered more redoubtable than the American Navy, and the more hidden satisfaction of carrying off this fresh strike against an enemy that, this time, could not plead surprise.

Soon the army's successes, coming on the heels of the navy's, would contribute to a kind of habit of victory in the first weeks of the war. Hong Kong, citadel of British imperialism in China, surrendered. The Philippines, a sort of second Japanese archipelago at the latitude of Indochina, was invaded. Siam was conquered. The Malayan peninsula, instead of being a barrier protecting the whites' Asian empire, proved to be an access corridor to their main military and naval bastion at Singapore. Only a month was needed for the Japanese public to pigeonhole the whites: confronted by Japanese troops, their soldiers were despicable and their leaders incompetent. The newspapers compared the lightning war in the Pacific with the Blitzkrieg in Europe and found that Japan had nothing to envy Hitler. For the first time since 1905, Asia's best soldiers met white soldiers on the battlefield and, as was to be expected, they won easily.

As though to further underline the automatic quality of Japanese victories, the announcement of each new success was regularly made to coincide with a holiday. In the Japan of bygone centuries, warriors usually refrained from fighting except on the days designated in the lunar calendar and by official astrologers as being of good omen. The samurais' motorized descendants, using a sort of reverse astrology, arranged to have their victories fall on the holidays in the modern calendar. They saw to it that the fall of Hong Kong occurred on December 25, as a "Christmas present" to the nation. The announcement that Manila's defenses had been pierced came on January 1, although it was not until January 3 that the propagandists could announce total occupation of the city. Japan's most hallowed national holiday, the *Kigensetsu,* or anniversary of the founding of the empire—equivalent to the American July 4 and France's July 14—falls on February 11. In anticipation of this fateful date, on maps that suddenly appeared everywhere—in the newspapers, on walls, billboards, signposts, shop windows, in the lobbies of the big dailies —all Japan excitedly followed the campaign in Malaya, the securing of a bridgehead on the island of Singapore, the advance toward the city itself. The military command speeded up its timetable, Japan's armies forced the pace and, on the evening of February 11, shortly before 11:00, Tokyo Radio solemnly announced the surrender of the British commander-in-chief which, it said, had taken place at 7:30 P.M.

The next holiday in the calendar was Army Day, celebrating

the Mukden victory over the Russians in 1905, and a new victory had to be ready for this mandatory rendezvous. News of the capitulation of the Dutch East Indies, which had actually happened five days earlier, was therefore held back in Tokyo until it could be announced on the holiday with much hoopla. So that even the Japanese calendar collaborated in the nation's victory. In peacetime, it had been a series of naïve, flower-decked festivals—the cherry-blossom festival, the doll festival, the firefly and autumn maple festivals; now it had come to resemble the program of national military festivals. On the appointed days, in every city, unprecedentedly large crowds massed at official ceremonies or spontaneously invaded the Shinto sanctuaries. Every roof, every door, absolutely without exception, was hung with the flag of the Rising Sun.

Tokyo suddenly secreted a crowd that swarmed like bees. The human tide flooded the approaches to the Meiji temple, poured into the sacred gardens with their dark, Elysian greenery, undulated across the half-moon bridge, rushed under the portico carved from giant cedars and broke in a million bows before the sanctuary. Elsewhere, tight phalanxes moved toward the palace in the center of Tokyo. A vast esplanade designed to keep the city away, to create an empty space around this sacred place and reduce the scale of everything else, slopes gently downhill to expire at the edge of the Imperial moats. A thick screen of pines with zigzagging branches, a white watchtower capped with a horned roof rising over a bridge giving onto an alley that disappears behind a heavy feudal gate—this is still one of Japan's sacred places. It was here that the Japanese, by the millions, converged to show their national devotion. Singly, in groups, in processions, by families, men in semimilitary khaki, women in multicolored kimonos and hundreds of children revolving around the grownups—from morning to night the flow of people coming to bow before the moats was unceasing.

A brief stop at the edge of the green ditch, a slight, silent bow, held for a brief instant, in the direction of Him who lives somewhere behind those ramparts and that somber curtain of trees—nothing more, and yet this was the holiest ritual in the whole Japanese cult of passive obedience. In those weeks of victory, this people's old inclination to reverence, its innate disposition to prostrate itself before its leaders became a kind of passion. Or rather, a national tic, because the ritual gestures were accomplished without frenzy or gaiety. There was just the rapid bob creasing the jacket or the kimono, then the marionette snapped straight with a slight hissing of saliva between the teeth, as though, in unfolding, it was filling itself anew with the air it had lost in bowing. This little operation took place every day, anywhere, at any time, on every occasion. In a trolley or train crossing Tokyo, whole carloads of passengers suddenly rose and, standing in their places, made their little bow, caught up in the national tic at every point in the city—around Shibuya, because it is within sight of the Meiji temple gates; in Yoyogi, because the train passes within 550 yards of the same sanctuary; in Kudan, where the Yasukuni pantheon stands, the resting place of dead soldiers' souls; around the Tokyo central station, because it's in a line with the palace; at the Interior Ministry, because the palace is even nearer. Bows at the beginning of every show in the theaters, when the whole audience bobbed in a single movement toward a point on the wall marking the direction of the palace; bows to a trainload of soldiers on leave, to a wounded veteran dressed in a white kimono, to the draftees escorted to the station by their families, to soldiers returning from the front with urns bearing the ashes of war dead. Bows before the temples of deified great men: Maresuke Nogi, the admiral, or General Tojo; before the sanctuary of Hachiman, god of war, or simply before any corner temple whose minor local god is supplied by the good people of the neighborhood with vegetables the priests can use; bows even before the idol of the god of harvests, dear to shopkeepers, or the altar of the fox, the genie of the fields revered by farmers, superstitious women and geishas.

Yet this same people simultaneously experienced its most intense spasm of collective pride, as though millions of individual feelings of humility were compensated in a sense of mass, in pride of race. The potent inferiority complex that had so long gnawed at Japan was now revenged in a contrary feeling that repaid it for all the too frequent blows to its pride, the rebuffs administered to its impatience to expand, to direct, to succeed. Japanese pride had felt itself ridiculed by the whites, not only when they were being arrogant, but when they were being what they are—too quick, too intellectual, too difficult to follow. Except on rare occasions, whites have never known how to talk to the Japanese; their attitude has been thought of as rude, jarring, vexatious. Contact between the two races in Japan brought out the whites' offensiveness and their feelings of superiority. In dealing with the unclassifiable, unpredictable Westerners, who were never to be counted on because their word was always tempered by some indiscernible quality of paradox or humor or bluff, the Japanese took refuge in their hidden strengths: silence, obstinacy, their sense of collective action and the patient power of their mass.

Now the Japanese citizen regained his self-confidence—more, he saw his victories as confirmation of his old notion that Japan was, after all, invincible. More than ever, Japan forgot that its invincibility was one of the legends taught it by its leaders. If ancient Japan had never been beaten, it was because, isolated behind its ocean, it had never been called on to fight. And, in fact, hadn't it been invaded and defeated in the very first days of its modern history? Under the guns of Commodore Matthew Perry's ships in 1854, it didn't fight, it capitulated.

Besides, the Japanese were giddy. They failed to look ahead to more difficult days. Why would they have thought of the future? Tomorrows were part of the general staffs' secret calculations and of their leaders' wisdom. To the people was left the right to live their humble daily lives and, now, to enjoy their triumphs with no afterthoughts.

Life was pleasant in Tokyo in 1942. Japan was at play. After the psychological shock of the war's first weeks, victory brought a hilarious relief. The nervousness and sometimes explosive tension of 1941 gave way to frivolous gaiety, a hunger for distraction and pleasure that was masked only when it was important to show the authorities a disciplined, martial face. Never mind the tightening restrictions. Inflation sired a new world of black markets and clandestine amusements and gave everyone the price of admission.

How different an image this country at war projected from the

one Japanese propagandists and even foreign authors had so long
spread in more peaceful days! How polished and distinguished
Japan was in the books! All was beauty, refinement, good taste
and good manners. Sad to say, this Japanesque aesthetic, while it
may in better times have flowered in the isolated upper classes,
was now swept away by a popular Japan about which the writers
had forgotten to tell us. What strange misunderstandings this
country has always engendered. It had been painted for us in
pastels, by such authors as Lafcadio Hearn or Pierre Loti, represented as small, simpering and delicate, whereas, in its mass, it
now was noisy, disorderly and, when it did let itself go, brimming
with life and an unbuttoned earthiness.

Evenings in Tokyo were an Oriental carnival. The nights
belonged exclusively to men; the women stayed home. Eating
well and drinking too much was the minimum program for the
thousands of men who gallivanted off at nightfall. In the narrow
streets, fittingly darkened by the blackout, almost all the
passersby entering or leaving the restaurants were either tight or
tipsy. They staggered, bawled patriotic songs in staccato
rhythms, dragged their wooden sandals and scuffed shoes dread-
fully as they zigzagged from bar to bar.

This surprising city does not, like other capitals, have three or
four districts specializing in night life, it has at least thirty. Some
hummed with people eating and drinking; in others, where whole
streets were given over to pedestrians, theaters and movie houses
were lined up door-to-door. The lights of countless bars and
cafés blinked in tiny buildings in other districts. In all of these
quarters, geishas rushed in their rickshaws to their teahouse as-
signations. Some sections were mainly geisha quarters, others
merely red-light districts. The aristocracy of pleasure spent its
nights in Tsukiji, between the port and the city, where the
houses of the most famous geishas and the costliest restaurants
stood hidden along the canals. High government officials liked
Akasaka, near the hill on which the Diet—the Parliament—stood.
The Sumida, that Oriental Thames, attracted the lovers of atmosphere who came to make love in the damp, blue setting of the
river flowing below them under a lacquered moon.

Scattered all through the city were half-hidden little pleasure quarters where the latest Japanese victories were celebrated nightly. There was Kagurasaka, perched on a hill: tiny inns with huge Japanese lanterns; geishayas (geisha houses), their labyrinth of alleys wrapped around an old temple; gigantic restaurants where the officers from the nearby War College went to carouse. There was Kanda, where students got drunk for three yen in the bars in the small dead-end streets behind the bookstores. Yotsuya, the geisha quarter, huddled in a circle in the trough of a dried-up old pond. Juban, where the foreigners' former servants had opened clandestine gambling rooms. And to Ueno, Shimbashi, Shinagawa, came the suburbanites who liked to do their reveling within sight of their railroad terminal.

Tokyo had its poles of attraction: Ginza, the district of chic central boulevards harboring some five hundred modern-style bars, the smoky, seductive haunts of the bar-girls who served the customers' drinks and sat with them, sat too close to them; Asakusa, cut-rate paradise for provincials and country people and refuge of an old spirit of rebellion hounded by the police. From the stages of the four-penny operas, storytellers would make veiled attacks on the government or comic samurais would whip accordions from under their kimonos to play a jazz tune.

Tokyo also had satellites in its outskirts where night life hid. Shibuya, in a tangle of white, pink and mauve streets planted with weeping willows like a set for a René Clair movie, concealed a hive of microscopic cafés where the bar-girls affected a sort of doe-eyed Madame Butterfly look. Shinjuku, behind its giant movie theaters, splayed out through the night a one-story city of countless beerhalls and disreputable restaurants; near the *Moulin-Rouge*, where the police still—not for long—tolerated mildly nude revues, houses recalling German red-light districts opened onto dismal streets. There were working-class restaurants on the muddy banks of Tokyo Bay in Omori, and open-air cafés in Ikebukuro for artists and people with no money.

And Yoshiwara should be mentioned—a red-light district famous throughout the Orient, as ancient as Tokyo, sung by Kipling. Still farther out, more inaccessible to the uninitiated, were the capital's cut-price hells—Tamanoi, Kameido, nightmarish hives of love for sale. Shadowy throngs made up entirely of lone men would jostle slowly along alleys dark as the inside of a movie theater, where two men could barely pass each other. Silently, they would file past the huddled rows of low, slightly recessed doorways, in each of which a square, violently lighted hole opened onto the black night like a television screen, illuminating the living face of a girl against a background of gold and blood-red silks. Young, often pretty, the girls would laugh, call out and, when a silhouette stopped at a girl's brightly painted smile, she would briefly open her door to her one-hour lover, then slam her peephole shut against the darkness.

But of all pleasures, the most sought after in that period of tightening shortages were those of drinking and eating. Hundreds of restaurants prospered in Ginza and Nihombashi, in the center of Tokyo. They served all the seafood delicacies—the golden fish and lobster fritters called *tempura,* shellfish and sea urchins, the pearly maws of raw John Dory that one dipped in soya vinegar perfumed with wild thyme, *fugu,* or moonfish, a gourmet's delight and a terror to the uninitiated because its bile contained a fast-working poison that only cooks who specialized in it knew how to eliminate. In attractive rooms paneled in natural-colored wood, one sat down among men on rustic benches around heavy tables carved in a block from half a tree-trunk. Or, upstairs, one squatted in small Japanese rooms where the straw mats, the whitewashed walls, paper screens and sliding doors all reflected a golden light. Golden too was the sake, the rice wine drunk in treacherously small cups; revelers were soon as red as the crab shells dumped into their porcelain bowls; the protocol and the hierarchical order reigning at the beginning of the meal was disrupted by noisy *kampei,* toasts at which everyone at the table was expected to drain his cup and refill it to start over again at once.

This was the time for good war stories and the latest inside information on victories past and future. The talk was of how the heroic Japanese pilots attacking the *Prince of Wales* sent eighteen torpedoes into its hull despite hellish antiaircraft fire. And, by the way, what were the famous aces of the Luftwaffe and Mussolini's fliers doing in Europe? Had they ever sunk so many of their enemies? And there were the latest reports about the battle for Singapore. Nearly 100,000 British troops surrendered there; the week's newsreels showed immense crowds of disarmed soldiers, many of them Indians. The story went that on the day before the Japanese landed on the island, British officers drove in to drink their daily whisky at the bar of Raffle's Hotel and explain why the Japs would never cross the water.

And Pearl Harbor! People never wearied of talk about December 8. All Japan repeated the juicy story told by Commander Hideo Hiraide, the admiralty spokesman, of the torpedo planes who took off to attack at 6 A.M. because Japanese intelligence knew perfectly well that Hawaii's air-defense listening posts were shut down at precisely 7 A.M. on Sunday mornings. Nor, as Hiraide said, "was it by chance that we struck on a Sunday: for ten years we'd been studying how the American Navy spends its weekends." Another man at the table embroidered on this: "Do you know what the days of the week are in the Japanese Navy? Monday, Monday, Tuesday, Wednesday, Thursday, Friday and Friday. There is no Saturday and no Sunday."

Stories circulated of fantastic battles in the Malayan jungle, of the astounding exploit by Japanese Olympic swimmers who dived naked into the straits between Hong Kong and the mainland and disarmed enemy mines to open a channel to Japanese assault troops. The wretched General Douglas MacArthur—the man the American press before the war called "our $50,000 general" (his fabulous annual salary)—was covered with ridicule; he dishonored himself, the Japanese newspapers affirmed, by leaving the Philippines for Australia; shouldn't he have had himself killed there, as any general of the Rising Sun would have done?

So went the pleasures of Tokyo and elsewhere. The Japanese joyously abandoned themselves to them in the euphoria of their early victories, especially because their consciences were clear. Ten years of tendentious reporting and official secrecy had convinced them that Japan never went to war except in self-defense —in Manchuria, to protect Asia from the Red peril; in China, to check the wicked Chiang Kai-shek; at Pearl Harbor, to save the Empire, strangled by Anglo-Saxon imperialism. Did they really believe all this? But what might be called "nominalism" was one of their basic character traits, that is, their tendency to let themselves be taken in by the nominal value of people and things without concern for their real value. To them, what was official was true. Catchwords were accepted without question. All leaders, from the Emperor to the local ward-heeler, were automatically respected. Just as the King of England can do no evil, the Japanese State could never err; an attitude that seemed very like the Germans', but that was really different on many points because it stemmed from Oriental, and specifically Japanese, habits.

Japan was part of a ritualized civilization that organized exterior signs of inner feelings for aesthetic, not moral, reasons and codified body movements to signify emotions. Finally, only the show became important, repressing what was happening in the heart. The Empire's subjects had only to make their gestures of obedience, devotion and loyalty to be good subjects; the State was not concerned about whether their consciences agreed. Nor were its subjects; they were satisfied with the collective beliefs demonstrated by official ritual, affirming their ready-made faith through their ceremonial gestures.

Japan was also a civilization of symbols, in which an idea's value resided in the word or the written character that contained it. Japanese education, intimately linked to the deciphering of Chinese hieroglyphics, was hypnotized by ideograms. A Japanese saw only the written character; he did not penetrate to the abstract notion behind it. Victim of a deceptive verbiage, different from ours because it is not verbal but visual, a Japanese saw a series of strong and splendid ideas in what was no more than a line of difficult and artfully chosen characters. Moreover, his language, grammatically imprecise, illogical and complicated in syntax, was a poor tool for abstract thought. All this made of the military-era Japanese the most inclined of the world's peoples to be deceived and to deceive themselves with words.

Their leaders, an elite group living above the crowd, masters of the national rituals and authors of the official slogans, systematically cultivated the people's inclination toward obedience. Reserving higher education for the governing class, they saw to it that the nation received typically primary schooling. They taught everyone to read, but only a few were taught to think. Everyone was to know just enough to read and to believe what was written. The populace was taught a complete system of national legends that refurbished the country's old beliefs—the divine origin of the Japanese people, the holiness of the Son of Heaven—to serve their leaders' political aims. Unlike Nazism, a political system that became a religion, the Japanese transformed the old Shintoist religion into a political system.

The country's leaders, skeptical because they were superior, were very careful not to believe the legends they taught. In this they truly sinned against intelligence and, in so doing, prepared the way for an unprecedented punishment to themselves and the people they tricked so badly. Japan might not have suffered so intensely in defeat had it not lacked a signal quality: a sense of— and desire for—truth.

The dearth of moral courage we discussed in connection with their leaders was repeated in the multitude. Nothing better shows this than the support of the Pacific war in its happy beginnings by a whole segment of the population that had in fact resisted militarism in 1936–41—that is, as long as the military had not completely proved itself. But once the army was victorious, those who had favored peace now lightheartedly agreed to war: the progressive middle class, intellectuals, businessmen trained in the school of international trade. This was coat-turning on a national scale. Indeed, the sartorial switch was literal as well as figurative: in the first months of the war, thousands of men adopted the civilian uniform favored by the government, a military-style, olive-drab garment of synthetic fiber with a cap to match that was almost exactly like the army's fatigue cap. It was precisely those people whose former opinions had left them feeling insecure who were the first to put on this unbecoming disguise because it testified to their zeal, functioned as a kind of patent of patriotism and enabled them to slip inconspicuously back into the crowd. There they were, cut from the general pattern and therefore loyal and obedient subjects! The trick was to act like a chameleon. Those who excelled: Japanese back from London or New York or California, diplomats, bankers, exporters, businessmen who had once been proud of speaking English with an Oxford accent or dressing like an American; the minority of Nisei (American children of Japanese parents) who rallied to Japan; artists who had followed the artistic fashions in New York or Montparnasse for too long.

The conformist wave swept over artistic and literary circles. Every pen served the state, everyone who spoke English made Japanese propaganda broadcasts. Every brush enthusiastically painted frenzied pictures illustrating the victories of Great Japan. The best painters vied for the honor of fixing the war's historic scenes on canvas—the capitulation of Singapore, dictated by General Tomoyuki Yamashita to the British commander, Sir Robert Percival; the capture of Manila by General Masaharu Homma; the sinking of the *Prince of Wales* and the *Repulse,* and, of course, the whole series of naval and air battles, all rendered in a naïvely theatrical style. Fujita, a fine painter who had to seek pardon for the long years he lived away from Japan and for his excessive love of Parisian freedoms, fell ostentatiously into step. There would be no more cries of *"Vive la frange"*;* when he cut off his famous bangs, it was announced in all the papers. With his head shaved like a colonel's, wearing the civilian uniform, he became the army's official painter, touring the fronts in a military plane, flooding the magazines with his sketches of tanks, planes, equipment, barracks life. He had himself photographed reading *Signal,* the illustrated Nazi propaganda weekly. Soon there was no show of painting that he did not honor with a huge slice of bravura work on a giant canvas— jungle combat, terrifying tank actions, infernal battles in the Aleutians, a heroic charge in the Solomon Islands—all signed by Fujita in Japanese characters in place of the Latin alphabet he had always used.

It might even be said that the war itself shared in the nominalism we've been talking about because it was the first of the artificial notions to be believed in without reference to its basic realities. The war? Japan had been waging it and talking about it

* Translator's note: The French pun is untranslatable. For the standard patriotic cry *"Vive la France"*—"Long live France"—the bang-wearing Fujita, in his Montparnasse days, cried *"Vive la frange"*—"Long live bangs."

for ten years without ever seeing it. It was something that happened far away, that was always successful and that one never had at home. Official propaganda did nothing to make it more concrete and to bring it home to the people. Instead, it portrayed the war in facile imagery with a victory obligatory at each phase and, at each, a new hero: Yamamoto for Hawaii, Yamashita before Singapore, Homma in the Philippines.

The communiqués were couched in ready-made formulas and pompous ideograms. The fleet was called, with Homeric splendor, the "invincible navy"; fliers were "Japan's wild eagles"; the dead, of course, were "hero-gods." A plane shot down was counted as "self-destroyed," for a Japanese aviator was also supposed to be invincible; if he went down, it was presumably because he had deliberately dived into enemy troops or an enemy ship. Believing that giving new names to things changed the world, Japan rechristened conquered places. Singapore became Shonan, meaning "Light of the South," and Java became . . . Djawa. The Japanese people called themselves "the rear front" or, more sonorously, "the Hundred Million"; Japan had only 75 million people then, but 100 million sounds better. The Japanese Empire called itself the "coexistence and co-prosperity sphere." General Tojo gave the war itself an official Japanese name: *Dai Toa Sensô,* meaning literally, "The Great Asia War," but official English translations preferred the more resounding "Greater Asian War."

The Hundred Million, meanwhile, continued living the easy life of little Japan while the war, instead of growing more pressing, receded farther and farther toward the inaccessible rim of that Greater Asia.

5

Under Doolittle's Bombs

April 1942: the wave of enthusiasm raised by three months of uninterrupted victories rapidly subsided. An astonishing people! One supposed the war had cured them of the mercurial moods they showed in the months before Pearl Harbor, of the brusque spasms of hysteria suddenly followed by a kind of sadness on the part of the whole nation. Not at all; for those who could take Tokyo's temperature, here was the drop, when overtaut nerves relaxed. The letdown.

After Singapore, as though by magic, the war lost its interest. People continued to enjoy themselves, it is true, but the pursuit of pleasure merely became one of the forms of national indifference. Government propagandists made a great fuss over the latest victories, the great naval successes in the Dutch East Indies, the fall of Java, the occupation of Rangoon, the Burmese capital. But such triumphs had come to seem so automatic that they no longer excited the public. The Information Bureau headed by Ei'i Amau, a colorless fellow whose violently nationalistic outbursts had earned him an unmerited renown, tried to shake the public's apathy with such devices as newsreel films of the war. For a while, every victory was quickly shown on film rushed home from the front in military planes (this did not last long because the Japanese Air Force would shortly have other things to do). The rush of those hordes of diminutive Japanese across the Eldorados of the southern seas came to life on the screen; here were these men parading among bare-breasted Balinese, swarming around tall oil rigs in Borneo and over the ruins of Angkor Wat, yapping their *banzai* at the top of a Burmese mountain. Movie-theater audiences' eyes popped, but there was never any applause. Why continue to be surprised at these incessant victories when people had been told time and again that the Japanese soldier is invincible? And besides, the war was so far away.

One morning in the first week of March, all the sirens in Tokyo suddenly began to wail lugubriously. The first alert of the war! Yet people were unmoved. Probably a test, they said. The afternoon papers carried long official declarations reproaching the public for its excessive unconcern. American planes, some thirty of them, had attacked the island of Minami-Torishima (the new Japanese name for Marcus Island), less than a thousand miles southeast of Tokyo. The raid had failed, the papers said, and it showed the disarray of a United States in the throes of defeat; this was a war of nerves, not real war. Yet, continued the propagandists with a thoroughly Japanese lack of logic, it was vital that the populace be alert. That very evening, the police imposed an absolute blackout on the city.

One bit of news, however, in that April when, for the first time, the cherry blossoms were ignored, stirred a reaction that showed what people were really uneasy about. It was announced that General Yoshitsugu Tatekawa, the ambassador to the Soviet Union who had signed the Japanese-Soviet neutrality pact in the spring before Pearl Harbor, had been recalled to Tokyo; he was replaced by Naotake Sato, one of Japan's best career diplomats. This was enough to send alarmist reports coursing around Tokyo. Japan, it was rumored, was going to war with Russia; the spring offensive noisily announced by Berlin to cover up Germany's failure before Moscow was soon to be launched and the German embassy had demanded—successfully—that Tojo strike in Siberia while Hitler struck in the Ukraine. Russian planes might be over Tokyo any day!

Judging from these rumors, which sounded like deformed echoes of real discussions at top Axis echelons, it was clear that no one was sure of anything in the north. On the other hand, the press, probably aware of this renewed anxiety, hastened to reassure the public by proving that an American raid on Tokyo was impossible. Its reasoning was simple and categorical: any raid would have to come from China, but Japan had slammed shut the back door to China by occupying Burma; it was therefore impossible for the United States to supply fuel, equipment and personnel to air bases in China. Tokyo could sleep peacefully; there was no danger of a raid.

On April 18, at 12:30 P.M., I was at home when, from not very far away, I heard a ragged, powerful series of explosions. Bombs? Suddenly, there was the sound of feeble antiaircraft fire. Still, if it were a raid, we'd have heard the sirens.

Four minutes later, the staccato moans of the sirens filled the air with a dismal call that soared into the blue, sunlit sky over Tokyo. A raid at high noon! Our first raid! So *they've* come! I rushed outside. I lived in the center of the city and it took me only minutes to reach Toranomon, a large intersection near the principal ministries. This was the time of day when clerks and typists in their blue smocks ate, usually at their desks, the box lunches they brought—four rice balls, two or three sardines and a bit of preserved seaweed. Instead of sending everyone to shelter, the sound of the bombs and the warning brought people to their windows or out into the streets and then to the square. Noses in the air, they waited. Suddenly, there was the sound of a plane. At the windows, fingers pointed toward the Ginza. It was at that instant that, looking in that direction, I spotted a dark airplane traveling very fast, practically at rooftop level. Far behind it exploded a line of small, thin, ridiculous-looking clouds, the air defense's shells. A much smaller plane, well behind the bomber and all alone, came into sight: a Japanese fighter. A second series of explosions was heard—more bombs.

And that was all there was to Colonel James Doolittle's famous air raid.

Now, before the ministries, the typists—laughing, childlike girls, who at twenty still looked like fourteen-year-olds—chattered breathlessly, as Tokyo's sparrows do after an earthquake. I toured the Ginza: everyone was out of doors; they had watched the raid from the middle of the street to get a better view. Besides, where would they have gone for shelter? There was not yet a hole or a tunnel anywhere in the capital in which to hide from a bombing. The people were not visibly worried, but at least they showed a lively excitement.

The alert was not lifted until that afternoon, but no official word came on exactly what had happened. Without news, people became alarmed and by 4 P.M. the rumor was all over the city: "Notice that we still don't know the nationality of the planes this noon; and since all the authorities asserted, as recently as yesterday, that Tokyo was safe from American raids, the planes must have come from elsewhere; they must have been, they were, *Russian* planes!" The rumor circulated, faces lengthened, people grew frightened. Domei finally produced a communiqué that made no mention of the attackers' nationality. And, spearing itself on its own clumsiness, the semi-official agency added: "His Majesty the Emperor and the members of the Imperial family are safe and sound and the palace is intact." Thousands of Japanese, especially those outside the capital, hearing the broadcast of the communiqué, imagined that half of Tokyo was in ashes, since the government felt obliged to specify that the sovereign, at least, had escaped unharmed.

It was not until the middle of the next day that a communiqué finally explained what had happened. Two American aircraft carriers had appeared far to the east of Japan at dawn on the previous day. A few hours later, some planes—the number was not given—appeared over Tokyo and several other big cities farther south: Kawasaki, Yokosuka, Nagoya, Yokkaichi and Kobe. Kyushu, the big southern island, and its northern counterpoise, Hokkaido, had also been placed on alert. So it had been the Americans! The newspapers said nothing about the damage done in the raids, reporting simply that it was slight. On the other hand, with the furor that marked great occasions, they proclaimed that American propaganda was going to make a fuss over the raid and that everything was all lies and invention in the clamor the Americans were, uh, *going* to make.

The affair suddenly flared up again three or four days later. Perfectly orchestrating their violence, press, radio and the official propaganda machine launched an extraordinary campaign of ra-

cial hatred of a virulence not to be equaled at any other time during the war. The American fliers—with Colonel Doolittle personally leading his "boys" in what the title of a famous film would
later proclaim as their *Thirty Seconds Over Tokyo*—were accused
of machine-gunning innocent civilians, massacring children,
bombing schools and hospitals. Articles and appeals, unprecedentedly violent in tone, accused America of a deliberate crime
against the civilian population, represented the Yanks as savages
brimming with hate and insisted that the guilty, if caught, must
pay for their evil deeds with their lives. Finally the army announced that the aviators responsible would be punished. A decree (it may have been an Imperial ordinance—my recollection is
vague) was hastily framed for proclamation throughout Japan,
throughout the world. Any enemy flier falling into Japanese
hands, the newspapers announced, would be sentenced to death
if he was found guilty of indiscriminate bombing of innocent civilians. The decree's exact text was not published. Were we to
conclude that American airmen had already been captured?

The answer came the following day in newspaper stories and
pictures. The *Nippon Times,* which continued to appear in English for foreign readers, specially distinguished itself for its odi-
ous stories which it accompanied by a photo spread across the
front page. It showed an American Army Air Force officer, tall,
blond, bursting with youth and superbly equipped, being brutally
manhandled by two Japanese gendarmes who gripped him by
both arms—two very small men turning grimaces of rage to the
camera. A second photo on page two showed the same officer
standing on some steps and surrounded by seven of his crewmen.
By the size of the building behind them, I surmised that the picture had been taken in China. The livid, pitifully haggard face of
one of the men mutely cried out that he had been beaten and tortured. Another's also portrayed the punishment he had suffered,
but it showed a pride stronger than all the cruelty of his captors.
To each face one could attach a word that summed up its tragedy: anguish, serenity, dejection, exhaustion, courage, resignation, hatred for its persecutors. And, in the middle, was the
young officer around whom the rest clustered, a magnificent representative of that American breed whose extraordinary force of

personality truly shone in that unhappy group. "These are my boys," it seemed to say. "They are unlucky and God have mercy on them, but I am their leader and I will lead them unflinchingly to that death we have been promised."

The photos became even more tragic when one read the stories that accompanied them; in sibylline language they indicated that the eight men were to be shot.* A wave of indignation swept the small foreign colony in Tokyo. The Swiss reported that the most furious were the Nazis and the people at the German embassy, who received the shock of their lives when they read in all the Japanese newspapers of this horrendous insult by the "yellows" to representatives—even if they were enemies—of the Aryan race. German correspondents were primed with questions by the embassy at the Japanese press conference called to report on the capture. How many American fliers were arrested? Were they to be executed? And how did the authorities explain the retroactive application of a decree enacted after the raid? But the Information Bureau's spokesman, Mr. Izono, was as lovable as a prison gate. His evasive replies, printed in the next day's papers, brought out only one concrete point that must have made the German reporters' blood boil. The honorable Izono-san had given them a word of advice—excellent advice, he insinuated—on how to stop the irritating enemy raids on Hitler's capital: the Nazis had only to imitate the Japanese and shoot British aviators who parachuted into Berlin during the bombings.

The clear impression received from official statements on the Doolittle raid was that it was a stunt with no real military value. All available information seemed to indicate that the damage to Tokyo was slight, even slighter than it had been in the other cities which had only one or two "visitors" each. How much damage could be done by sixteen planes—the figure was not revealed until later in the war—spread over the whole length of Japan?

---

* An American investigation after the war established that all eight Doolittle men caught by the Japanese were sentenced to death in Shanghai, but only three were actually shot; the sentences on the rest were commuted to life imprisonment by the grace of the Emperor. One of them died in prison. All were tortured under interrogation.

The government nevertheless exploited the raid to its own advantage. In the United States, it certainly stimulated the war effort and boosted morale as the first sign of recovery after Pearl Harbor. But, at the same time, it clearly provided a useful experience for the Japanese authorities and an unexpected way of alerting the Japanese public, of rousing it from its indifference. The air-raid warning services had been surprised; the sirens had sounded *after* the first planes made their runs; pursuit planes were absurdly late getting off the ground; firefighting was inefficient, and the populace had watched the raid as though it were a circus act instead of looking for shelter. The lesson took effect on all these points and, in the long run, the raid did the Japanese more good than harm. Air defenses were reinforced; in Tokyo, rooftops in the business and ministerial districts sprouted spotters and heavy machine guns. Parks were dug up for anti-aircraft batteries. Barrage balloons soon encircled the capital and new bases were built for fighter squadrons. Air-raid drills were frequent and for a full day, sometimes two, every month, normal activity was suspended in an entire quarter, occasionally in the whole city, by firefighting drills in which hundreds of thousands of men and women took part.

These amateur firefighters' equipment was sadly inadequate; what was worse, absolutely no bomb shelters were provided for the mass of the population. There were no public shelters in the city; the subway system was too shallow to provide proper protection. Nor were any private shelters built, except for hurriedly dug holes in a few gardens. People did not dare to take precautions for fear of losing face. All the neighborhood associations had been able to come up with so far were instructions to their members on how to make an excellent shelter in one of the closets all Japanese homes are full of. Cushions, mattresses, a chest of drawers in front made a kind of grotto lined with silk and down—in those houses of wood and straw and paper; this done, people could feel truly safe when the incendiary bombs began falling!

It was as though the government were thoroughly indifferent to the losses a serious raid might cause, wanting merely to use the threat to regain control over the people; it was not a question of assuring public safety but of reinforcing discipline. The continuing campaign against "American atrocities" was also a part of this plan for what the newspapers called "spiritual mobilization." Curiously, it misfired; one felt no deep hatred of the United States in the Japanese people.

The propagandists succeeded only too well, however, in implanting a skittish aversion to all the whites who remained in Japan, not excepting the Germans and Italians. "Spyitis," as we, its victims, called it, was a disease of militaristic Japan, its national vice. Systematically encouraged by the authorities, beginning with the police, it took on a double aspect: not only was every white person living in Japan considered an active or potential spy, but every Japanese was expected to keep permanent watch on foreigners and report their every act to the police. A foreigner, then, was a wicked *spaï*—a Japanized version of the English word was used—and the Japanese were good citizens if they did their duty and spied on foreigners.

In July, an Anti-Espionage Week was staged, prefaced by a long official campaign promoting xenophobia that followed the "atrocities campaign" excited by the Doolittle raid. Japan was covered with melodramatic posters exhorting the people to beware of foreign spies. Schoolchildren were taught to hate the *gaijins* (foreigners), who were pursued in the streets by urchins yelling *"Spaï! Spaï!"* Anti-spy drills were organized in the big cities, and even in Tokyo, in which actors disguised as foreigners were arrested by real policemen in the streets, in stores, in factories amid terrified and excited crowds who did not know if the scene was real or simulated. The newspapers went all out over the campaign. For example, they bannered supposedly sensational revelations depicting the British Information Ministry's whole prewar Far Eastern organization, which had always operated in the open, as a vast spy network enmeshing Japan and its Empire. Betraying, as usual, the inconsistency of their accusations as well as the Japanese public's credulity, Japanese authorities charged that the "ring"'s all-powerful master spy, whom they designated by the mysterious initials V. H. (for Vere H. Redman, director of the British Information Ministry's Far East service) frequented the Tokyo Club, where foreigners were regularly admitted, and . . . that he ordered English translations of local Tokyo Radio broadcasts.

An army spokesman, Major Yahagi, reported in the major daily *Asahi* that a recently unmasked foreign spy had converted his piano into a shortwave radio transmitter. "Consequently," the major warned, "any foreigner playing a piece of music that is not to be found in a book of music is dangerous." *Asahi* added a commentary to this: "Therefore, let's all have a smattering of musical culture." A typical editorial in the prominent daily *Mainichi* admonished: "Some may think that the campaign against espionage is useless given the Hundred Million's unshakable patriotism. But this facile attitude is particularly dangerous. The spaï is everywhere. Like an omnipotent phantom, he is in the street, he is in the trolley car, he listens to the people's naïve and innocent conversations." General Nakamura, commander of the military police, told reporters: "The essential idea is to keep an eye on anyone acting in an unusual way." All this was admirable proof that not much had changed in method or spirit since medieval times, when the *shogun* (military dictator) Iyeyasu authorized his samurais to cut off the head of anyone "incorrect," specifying that "an incorrect man is a man whose conduct is unusual."

When I arrived in Nagasaki from Shanghai for the first time in 1938 aboard a Japanese ship, leaflets were distributed to the foreigners aboard before landing. On them was a map of the Japanese coast with fortified zones circled with dotted red lines, and a list of the Draconian penalties—including death—applicable to anyone caught taking photographs, sketching, making notes or observing inside the restricted zones. A brief note added: "The same penalties can also be applied outside the dotted line." Guilty or not, a foreigner was automatically suspect to the police. Everything he did, habitual or not, was recorded, watched, interpreted and reported to the authorities because, as we have noted, all good Japanese were expected to spy on the wicked white spy. How could a white man escape this omnipresent conspiracy when he stood out so sharply among the Asians, when anyone he accosted automatically became suspect, contaminated? Japanese who consorted with whites were questioned, intimidated, often jailed for a day or two simply to make them spy-conscious. The police were particularly merciless toward Japanese women who kept company with foreigners; spyitis here was paired with racial jealousy.

Gaijins' servants were forever being questioned by the police, who expected them to report on an employer's comings and goings, to take note of the visits he paid or received, listen to his telephone conversations (which in any case were tapped and often recorded by the police), learn his opinions, admit a police officer to the house and hide him, if necessary, in a place where he could see or hear the employer, or allow him to search the place in the tenant's absence. Despite my servant's faithfulness, papers disappeared from my home; photos of Japanese beaches I had taken before the war vanished although other pictures with them were left in place. On the only closet I locked, an unknown hand changed the lock for another, almost identical, to which there was obviously a duplicate key. Police visited my neighbors and even posted themselves in their homes to observe me and listen to my conversations from a nearby window. Saying that in a Japanese house the walls had eyes and ears does not tell the whole story; in fact, in Japan, eyes and ears had no walls: paper partitions and wide-open doors and windows allowed anyone outside to see and hear what was going on indoors.

So I formed the habit of always acting as though I were being watched by a spy behind the door or overheard by a microphone under the table. I never discussed politics in public and only indirectly even in private. I learned to spell out proper names instead of pronouncing them, because it was names that alerted eavesdroppers or helped them understand what I was saying; never to take notes or keep a diary; to mistrust the telephone; to destroy papers, jottings, press clippings.

I had years in which to cultivate all this caution. Surveillance of foreigners—reinforced by a whole system of police permits, residence permits, travel permits—tightened from year to year beginning well before the war. The violence of the 1939–40 antispy campaigns repeatedly subjected the foreign colony to a reign of terror. This was fiercest during the summer of 1940 and coin-

cided with the blockade of the international concessions in Tien-
tsin and the crisis in Anglo-Japanese relations; it was then that
some fifteen prominent Britons were arrested by the military
police and my friend and colleague Jimmy Cox, the Reuters correspondent, was murdered—it was called "suicide"—in atrocious
circumstances. We grew used to seeing the campaign renewed
every six months or so, when the special police and the Kempetai
decided it was time to stimulate public suspicion and so keep it
alive. The dreadful national security laws pushed through the
Parliament by the army between 1937 and 1940 gave prosecu-
tors, judges and police murderous weapons; they teemed with
ambiguous passages, each of them a trap. There was, for example, the notion, deliberately left vague, of "state secrets"; the language of the law could be stretched to make this mean anything
at all. Anyone in possession of a state secret or, worse, com-
municating it to someone else or selling it was subject to penalties ranging up to death. Practically speaking, any foreign busi-
nessman, banker, journalist, priest, by the very nature of his
work, was in possession of confidential information and thus
subject to arrest and imprisonment at the whim of the police.

Because the police were perfectly aware that their powers
were exorbitant, they did not insist on immediate arrest and
imprisonment. They much preferred to make their weight felt everywhere, on everyone, and to fatten their files on foreigners by
unrelenting surveillance so that, when they did decide to strike,
they had only to open the file—always ready and up to date—and
choose whatever charges they pleased. There was not even any
point to launching a formal investigation or troubling the courts.
The penal code was truly a disgrace in military Japan, a sinister
counterfeit of Western penal codes that was designed merely to
mask the methods of a still-medieval Oriental police establishment. It provided for virtually indefinite preventive detention;
persons arrested on security charges were not assigned by the
courts to official prisons, but remained in the hands of the police
in local jails.

A half-dozen Frenchmen arrested on espionage charges at the
time of Pearl Harbor suffered over two years of ill-treatment in
gendarmerie prisons. Their ordeal was the ransom that liberated

the rest of the French colony in Japan, some three hundred people, half of them Catholic missionaries, monks and nuns. Here again, police policy was to emphasize the conditional character of the mock freedom granted to foreigners; the arrest of only a few French citizens placed the rest under permanent threat. They were given to understand that, sooner or later, proof could be provided that they were enemies of Japan and deserved mass arrest and confinement in a concentration camp. And throughout the war, as the first victims were released—usually half-dead of hunger—sporadic new arrests were made among the French, the principal reason obviously being to maintain police pressure on the whole group.

A few weeks before Pearl Harbor, on the day General Tojo took power, my friend and assistant Branco de Vukelich was arrested at home by the military police. A Yugoslav national, he had been the second man in the Havas bureau in Tokyo since 1935. The special police made it plain to me that my interference would not be welcome, not even in the form of a written or verbal statement on behalf of a man who had worked with me for years and who was now accused of having been a spy instead of a journalist. I was personally subjected to increased surveillance and was confidentially warned that I was also to be arrested. But, gradually, the vise was relaxed; I was probably saved from the lightning by the fact that it had already struck so close to me when it hit my unfortunate friend.

On May 16, 1942, a month after the Doolittle raid, the news of Vukelich's arrest, kept secret until then, was suddenly announced in the newspapers. Half a dozen other Japanese and foreigners, including master spy Richard Sorge, had been rounded up the same day. The case set off a tremendous propaganda din. It was now disclosed that all those arrested were members of an international spy ring working for the Soviet Union. Sorge, correspondent for the *Frankfurter Zeitung* and a well-known figure in Japan since 1932, was the ringleader, a particularly dangerous man because he was the close friend and confidant of General Eugen Ott, the German ambassador to Japan. Through Ott, Hitler's plans were an open book to Sorge, and the information he collected was funneled back to Moscow. He was also in close contact with some of Prince Konoye's closest advisers and, to top things off, with aides of Wang Ching-wei, the pro-Japanese head of the puppet Republic of China in Nanking. Sorge was sentenced to death and hanged in 1944, after a trial lasting nearly two years. Vukelich was sentenced to life at hard labor for violation of the laws on protection of military secrets and national security. I was to learn on August 15, 1945, the day Japan surrendered, that he had died the previous January in the prison at Abashiri, a kind of Japanese Siberia in the extreme north of Hokkaido. True enough, he had been a spy for Stalin. But at the time, Hitler, his enemy, had also been mine, and I chose to remember him as a friend whose solid morale, joyful optimism and strength of character had made him an exceptional human being.

6

Naval Victories
"Made in Japan"

Since its debut in the community of nations, military Japan had shown a morbid interest in what the world thought of it. Significantly, a mirror was one of the symbols of the national religion; international esteem was a mirror Japan could not do without. It was to win this esteem that it had spent so long posing, masking its violence and its weaknesses under an often artful layer of cosmetic propaganda purporting to show the outside world "the true face of Japan" and "Japan's real intentions." The world's opinion was constantly probed and scrutinized by hundreds of diplomats, observers and spies, among whose principal tasks was to mirror for Japan the flattering image it tried to create abroad.

None of this was changed by the war. On the contrary, early in the summer of 1942, following Tojo's lightning war, Japan passionately contemplated the redoubtable image it had at last succeeded in projecting on the world. Whenever Churchill or some other foreign statesman spoke of Japan's surprising power, whenever an enemy newspaper conceded it a victory, major or minor, the comment, speech or article was given maximum coverage by Tokyo's news services. The government hoped thus to galvanize the nation's energies by showing it how strong and feared it was. But the world, which had so long underestimated Japan, was now overestimating it, and the country was fooled by the frightening image its mirror reflected. The West saw it as a formidable power. From Hawaii to Suez and Madagascar, the

Pacific and the Indian Ocean seemed to be Japanese seas. The American Navy had disappeared after Pearl Harbor, and there was no British fleet in the Far East. Where would Japan strike next? General Tojo, in his speeches to the Diet, liked to keep the world guessing, alternately threatening to expand its colossal "co-prosperity sphere" toward India and to annex Australia.

On the afternoon of May 9, 1942, Tokyo Radio announced with great fanfare that a major naval engagement had taken place in the previous two days in the Coral Sea, in the South Pacific northeast of Australia. That evening, in a sensational communiqué, Commander Hiraide, the Japanese admiralty spokesman, announced a great victory. An American battleship and two aircraft carriers had been sunk, he said, another carrier damaged and two cruisers put out of action, not to mention damage to lesser units. Another dispatch on the following day further magnified the "American disaster," adding a few minor losses to the preceding list, but admitting that Japan had also lost a flattop.

Had the high command in Tokyo finally opted for a strike at Australia? Nothing was said about this to the Japanese public. The propaganda service did its best to convince the public that this was a real victory, but it also seemed determined never to give a coherent interpretation of events or precise explanations of ongoing operations. In war even more than in peacetime, the deep secrecy with which the Imperial government surrounded its policy counteracted its propaganda efforts with seeming mockery.

Nature itself was party to this mania for mystery. The ocean enveloped Japan in a world of silence. Battles were fought far away, beyond the horizon, across the seas and for days, even weeks, the Japanese government could conceal the real outcome of a battle, merely announcing noisily that its arms had triumphed. What really had happened in the Coral Sea? In fact, the high command had decided to move against Australia and the attack had failed. The key to the defense of northern Australia was Port Moresby, on the southern coast of New Guinea. The Japanese had occupied the northern coast since March, but their attacks through the jungle and their intensive bombing of

Port Moresby had not overcome the Australians' heroic resistance. So the Japanese Navy had opted for a landing on the south coast near the Australian strongpoint. The task force had been spotted as it was getting under way, however, and fiercely battered at its base in Tulagi by American planes, then beginning to demonstrate their growing power. The fleet was set on again in the Coral Sea by a powerful American squadron as it prepared to round the eastern tip of New Guinea.

This first great Pacific naval battle was also the first battle between aircraft carriers in the history of naval warfare. Never before had two fleets fought out of range of their heaviest artillery. Surface ships did not once use their guns; all the work was done by planes from the floating airbases. It was a costly meeting for the Americans, who lost the carrier *Lexington*, but the Japanese fleet was turned back from Port Moresby. For Tokyo, it was a defeat, one that was to have grave repercussions. Japan's threat to Australia evaporated; its march toward the south had been stopped.

Yet what was the use of conquering a chaplet of Pacific islands without Australia? Certainly it was an enormous undertaking to try to occupy the whites' last fortress in the South Pacific. But how much more fearful the danger was for Japan when the United States, with the help of the Australians, made the island continent their base for recovery of the north.

June 10, 1942, the hour when 75 million Japanese were squatted on mats before their lunches of fish and rice. Fanfares sounded over Tokyo Radio. One month after the "Japanese victory" in the Coral Sea, the admiralty announced a new triumph, off Midway Island. So the fight that had been waged up to then in the South Seas had moved into the central Pacific! Midway, a small island held by the Americans, is, as its name indicates, midway between the American and Asian coasts. Its mid-ocean position gave it prime importance as a naval relay station and air base. It was the key to the West's defense of the Hawaiian Islands 1,100 miles to the east, and it enabled the United States to advance its observation and attack planes over a vast circle that reached the 180th meridian on the west—that is, into what Tokyo had considered even before the war as Japan's half of the Pacific.

The Imperial general staff's communiqué announced that the Japanese fleet, boldly sailing within range of Midway, had surprised the island's defenders; its bombing planes had seriously damaged its fortifications and had sent two American aircraft carriers to the bottom. Moreover, operations had spread into the northern Pacific: at about the same time, the Japanese fleet had bombarded Dutch Harbor, the main naval base in Alaska, and Imperial troops had landed in the Aleutian Islands.

Once more the Japanese public trustingly swallowed the news of this "great Japanese victory" spiced by the propaganda machine with more than usually inflamed comments. Yet there was at least one disturbing fact about the communiqué: its lateness. Through a slip by the Domei news agency, word leaked out that the announcement of the battle had been held up for several days. It was a common practice, as we have noted, for the Japanese information agencies to put good news on ice for service as an example on a national holiday. They might have been expected to release it on June 8, for the eighth of every month was a ceremonial day—"East Asia Day"—in commemoration of Pearl Harbor. But the eighth went by without an announcement.

That announcement finally came on June 10; at least part of it referred to an action that had occurred a week previously, the bombardment of Dutch Harbor on June 3. And the Tokyo communiqué carefully combined three obviously different operations: the same Japanese squadron could not have struck at Alaska on the third, landed in the Aleutians on the fourth and attacked at Midway the same day. Nor did it indicate which of these actions was to blame for the losses it admitted: a carrier and a cruiser heavily damaged. Most suspicious of all was that, while acclaiming the victory, or simultaneous victories, of the invincible Nipponese fleet, newspapermen, radio commentators and spokesmen of all kinds resumed their long-winded vituperation of lying American propaganda which, it was admitted, had been shouting victory for the past five days—and shouting it louder and louder.

And rightly so! The Japanese people did not learn until after the war that the Battle of Midway had marked a decisive turning in the course of the naval war in the Pacific. Fleet commander Admiral Yamamoto had not planned a brief raid on Midway to reduce its defenses; he had intended a landing on the island. Capture of that vital base would have reversed the situation in the central Pacific in Japan's favor. To some extent, taking Midway would have corrected Japan's initial error on December 8, 1941, the first day of the war, when, despite Yamamoto's warnings, the general staff had failed to occupy Honolulu. The Dutch Harbor and Aleutians operations were planned by Yamamoto as diversions.

What the admiral did not know was that his adversary, Admiral Chester Nimitz, had a sensational secret weapon: American intelligence cryptographers had cracked the ultrasecret Japanese naval code. And this feat was to be seconded by another, no less remarkable: despite a few close calls, the United States naval command so skillfully concealed its possession of the code that Tokyo did not discover that it had been cracked until after the surrender.

Japanese messages intercepted in mid-May, then, apprised Nimitz that an attack on Midway was imminent. By the time the Japanese invasion convoy appeared west of the island on the morning of June 3, hastily reinforced American air defenses were ready. That afternoon, U.S. Flying Fortresses attacked Japanese cruisers and transports. The bombing continued until nightfall. On the same day, a Japanese flotilla reached its rendezvous with the invasion force before Midway. It included two battleships and four of Japan's best aircraft carriers, all veterans of the strike at Hawaii, under the command of Vice-Admiral Nagumo, who had led the raid on Pearl Harbor.

The massive assault it launched on the morning of June 4 against Midway's land fortifications aborted. Not only did the fleet come under attack by the powerful American air defense, but it fell into a still more dangerous trap. During the night of June 3–4, an American battle group including 3 aircraft carriers and several cruisers had arrived from Hawaii. It suddenly appeared on the Japanese squadron's flank northeast of Midway; its planes made a surprise attack on the fourth and, on June 5, they completely routed Nagumo. Under the pounding of American dive bombers and torpedo planes, 3 Japanese aircraft carriers went up in flames; the fourth, damaged by the bombing, was finished off by a submarine. A heavy cruiser was sunk, and 6 other surface vessels damaged. More than 300 Japanese planes were destroyed and 3,500 Japanese seamen and fliers killed. Aside from the damage to land fortifications, American losses were limited to one flattop, a destroyer and 150 planes. On Yamamoto's orders, the fleet of the Rising Sun fled northward toward a bad-weather zone to cover its scramble for Tokyo.

Six months after Pearl Harbor, the Japanese Navy had suffered a resounding defeat—resounding, at least, in the rest of the world. In Japan itself, the echoes were assiduously smothered. For the first time, the Japanese had tried to grab an enemy base east of the 180th meridian, on the American "side" of the Pacific; they failed, and they never tried it again. Just as the Battle of the Coral Sea had halted the Japanese Navy's advance in the South Pacific, Midway set up a mid-ocean barrier the Imperial forces were never to breach.

Yet this was the battle the Imperial general staff trotted out to the public as a splendid Japanese victory. And this time it was not only the people who were fooled; the truth about Midway was hidden from the Son of Heaven himself. Information I received later indicated that the false reports used to trick the Japanese public were also given to the Emperor. Only by comparing contradictory reports and extracting belated confessions from his officials did the sovereign learn, weeks later, the real consequences of the Midway engagement. Did his aides know the truth and conceal it from him? Or was the lie framed at the scene of the battle? In other words, did the Japanese general staff, its plans overthrown by the American counterattack, send false reports to Tokyo? Probably both are partly true; the government in Tokyo must have been duped, but it connived in the hoax and deceived others in turn.

According to my information, General Tojo himself was misinformed at first. He had the American communiqués, however, and he grew concerned over the extraordinary discrepancies between Hawaii's version of the facts and the news given out in

Tokyo. He summoned Admiral Seiichi Itoh, his chief of naval operations, and demanded the truth. Itoh, with the stormy fury of an offended Japanese—or one pretending to be offended—retorted curtly, "Has Your Excellency, then, lost faith in the admiralty's communiqués?" Tojo, thus accused of defeatism, said nothing, and Itoh's report stood. From other sources, the general learned that the Americans had indeed been telling the truth about Midway, but he made no effort to publicize this. He permitted diffusion of the lies that misled his Emperor and the public.

Tokyo Radio was nevertheless shrewd enough to play down the Battle of Midway, emphasizing instead the diversionary operation in the Aleutians that had been carried out without a fight. Commentators insisted on the real advantages of occupying the small islands of Kiska and Attu: the northern route the Americans might have used for an air-sea attack against Japan was now blocked, they said; Japanese aerial observation was extended to Alaska and was now in a position to survey the big Dutch Harbor base; maritime traffic and fishing in the Bering Sea were hampered. Radio reports described how angry the American press and public were at the islands' loss. And it added comments and information, all fictitious, about the threat posed to the United States by those few Japanese battalions lost in the Alaskan mists. Fog in the Aleutians did serve one purpose, however: it helpfully hid the defeat suffered at Midway.

7

"Withdrawal Deployment" at Guadalcanal

August 1942: the radiant Japanese summer plunged Tokyo into a kind of dazzled laziness, a happy indifference to the war, to all wars, the one in Europe and the war in "Greater Asia." It was as though the government and its propaganda machine had vainly shouted itself breathless trying to make this uncertain, ambiguous people show its violent, somber side, to keep its fears and hatreds awake and participating in the required alignments, orders, in the collective hysteria. But no: the intense heat had briefly brought out the other side, the other Japan that was so anxious not to die. All its intact, long-stifled reserve of kindness, sensuality, love of life surged forth in an access of uncontrollable languor. For the last time, the living was easy. Factories and offices released a throng of vacationers. Mobilization may have conjured away whole armies of young men, but there were obviously still thousands more in this overpopulated country. Still, there was an oversupply of girls, and the summer blossomed in bouquets of kimonos. On the beaches, naked crowds sprawled on the cindery, porous sand where the long, peaceful Pacific swell expired in a foamy, brilliantly white fringe. What was there to suggest that somewhere over the horizon this blue expanse was being dirtied with the oil and blood of great battles? *Sensô*—war: the word dissolved in the heat.

Yet a name—cropping up from who knew where?—was on everyone's lips: Guadalcanal. This was just another name among many. The Imperial high command seemed to take pleasure in

confusing all the names on all the fronts across the immense
Pacific, so far from tiny Japan. There was a daily bombardment
of communiqués: occupation of Kweiki, in China's Kiangsi province, and Sanshui, in Kwantung province; Chittagong (in what is
now Bangladesh) and Townsville (Australia) were bombed; Japanese submarines attacked Diégo-Suarez and Sydney (another of
the pocket subs' heroic epics) and "sowed panic" on the coast of
Oregon. How were all these dispatches—these stews of China,
Burma, Australia, India, Alaska, the South Seas—to be kept
straight in Japanese heads?

Two major battles were ballyhooed: a first naval battle in the
Solomon Islands on August 7, and a second engagement there on
August 24. Two great victories, naturally, for the banner of the
Rising Sun. Sensational reports on the first were filed by Japanese reporters describing in their now-familiar style the confusion
of a night fight and the Japanese destroyers' incredible audacity
in torpedoing everything that floated by them in the darkness.
The enemy was in full flight, a disarray that apparently did not
prevent it from waging a second battle two weeks later; the accounts of this one were even more obscure even though, this
time, the fighting had taken place in broad daylight.

Press and radio worked to arouse the public, but without
explaining just why the Solomon Islands, including Guadalcanal,
should suddenly be so important. To do that they would have
had to make clear that the locale of battle had shifted and that
this archipelago of jungles and malaria-infested swamps was now
the very hinge of the sea fronts, at the junction of the horizontal
line marking the southern limit of the Japanese advance toward
Australia and the vertical meridian on the eastern boundary of
that part of the Pacific controlled by the Japanese fleet. They
would have had to admit, furthermore, that the Americans had
begun their counterattack to save threatened New Hebrides and
New Caledonia and forestall a new Japanese advance that, by
occupying its forward bases, could cut the American supply line
to Australia. As always, however, Tokyo issued nothing but one-
way communiqués, announcing only victories. It was only by
carefully studying detailed maps, unavailable to the public, that

the retreat was traceable. Once more, the heady vicissitudes of a decisive battle escaped the Japanese public's notice.

The fight for Guadalcanal began on the beaches: Japanese troops installed on the island on June 16 were attacked by United States Marines hastily landed there on August 7. In the first sea battle of the Solomons (the battle for Savo Island, in official U.S. terminology), the American fleet on hand to cover the landing lost a heavy cruiser in the fierce night-fighting and two aircraft carriers soon afterward. The Marines were stranded on Guadalcanal without cover and without reinforcements. But the Japanese command, despite the noise its propagandists made about the battle for Savo, was unaware of the extent of its success. Fearing a trap, it threw away its chance to annihilate its enemy.

Then the battle over reinforcements developed, with both sides sending in troops to support their forces on shore. In the second battle of the Solomons (called the Battle of the Eastern Solomons in the United States), the Japanese admiral, who had inflicted heavy losses on the American fleet, again broke off the fighting prematurely because he too had lost one carrier and suffered damage to another.

Attention was now focused on the action ashore. The Japanese public was at last becoming aware of how ferocious the fighting had been in late August and September in that pestilential island's jungles. Press and radio borrowed the terrifying accounts broadcast in the United States on the fierce Japanese resistance. But nothing precise was revealed about the failure of the Imperial offensive, still less about the Americans' successful counteroffensive, which had won permanent land and air superiority.

The American Navy still had to regain control of the sea around the archipelago. During an engagement that lasted from November 11 to November 14, Japanese destroyers launched a murderous night attack off Guadalcanal that in fifteen minutes sank ten U.S. vessels. Tokyo announced a great victory, counting eight enemy cruisers sunk and nine other warships, including two battleships, damaged. On the other hand, Tokyo admitted losing only one of two Japanese battleships actually sunk and carefully said nothing at all about the loss of its troop transports. The American transports—the battle's real stake—were untouched and were able to land their men and materiel. Henceforth, the Japanese infantry, outclassed despite its stubborn resistance, retreated steadily westward during December 1942 and January 1943.

With the autumn, uneasiness had finally replaced Tokyo's blithe summertime indifference. Japan's information services, its propagandists and its spokesmen, were still trying to depict Guadalcanal not as a failure but as a relative triumph, vaunting the Imperial troops' heroism and endurance against their assailants' purely material superiority. They slipped over into caricature in describing the panic of American relief forces who, they said, refused to land on the accursed island; they mocked the Yankee soldiers who were allegedly unable to fight without chocolate and cigarettes against Japanese warriors feeding on roots and tree bark.

On February 9, 1943, the Information Bureau released a disturbing document, a summary of operations at Guadalcanal since the battle began. It listed every last American patrol boat and freighter sunk or damaged. This was a way of conceding that the engagement was over and of preparing the public for the truth. It was in fact on that February 9 that the Japanese command evacuated the debris of its infantry from Guadalcanal by sea.

Several days of deliberate silence went by. Then came the unprecedented announcement of the defeat. It was only a few lines long; one might almost have said it was only one word long, and that word stopped the Hundred Million short; it fascinated them. It was a Japanese word that had never been heard and above all never read. The Imperial general staff must have thought hard to come up with this strange, original, wily word. Since Japanese script lends itself to the infinite coinage of composite words by combining various characters, the word—the famous word—was minted of an alloy of two ideograms, one meaning "deployment" and the other "retreat." "Deployment" normally suggests a body of men fanning out as it advances, but the second character, "retreat," immediately made clear that in this case they were advancing backwards.

The "backward deployment" at Guadalcanal (the *Nippon Times,* translating the Domei dispatch, called it *withdrawal-deployment* in English) alarmed the Japanese. Remarkably, what shocked them was not so much the defeat, in an operation whose exact importance they had never really grasped, as the withdrawal—the fact that the last of the defenders left the island instead of remaining there and being killed to the last man. Army and navy spokesmen, sensitive to the slightest twitches of public opinion, were at pains to explain in the days that followed that troops have the right to "deploy to the rear" if their mission is to shield a real line of resistance organized behind the front, ready to surprise the enemy at the right time.

To correct the public's unfortunate attitude, the newspapers also ran stories of heroism to prove that troops had been sacrificed after all, as was fitting. In long showers of tiny hieroglyphs, the papers retraced, for example, the glorious end of the Inagaki unit. Grouped around their leader, Major Inagaki, the handful of soldiers was surrounded by the enemy, who had fenced them in with barbed wire and fortified positions in the marshy jungle. They were under constant shelling. There was nothing but grass to eat. After dark, patrols crawled to the enemy lines and killed sentries to steal their miraculous K-rations. "These are really living gods, these soldiers of mine," Inagaki exclaimed, at least according to the daily *Yomiuri*'s story. But their position was untenable. A council of war was held and decided unanimously on mass suicide that would take the form of a last-ditch attack at dawn on January 22. At midnight on January 21, all the men gathered and sang the *Kimi Ga Yo,* a sad and solemn hymn to the Emperor, then shouted three *banzais* to his eternal well-being. Everyone bowed toward the Imperial palace. And, in the darkness, while American loudspeakers set up over the lines continually repeated their invitation in Japanese to surrender, the two hundred men, including the walking sick and wounded—the others were killed by their comrades—rushed to their deaths in a final assault.

Twelve men were assigned by the major to try to sneak past the Americans, the newspaper said, to carry the suicide squad's final news through the jungle to the Japanese command. Here the newspaper's recital reached new heights of ferocity. First there was the melodramatic farewell scene in which the major gave his last message to Sergeant Kainuma, who led the twelve men. "Life is in death," Inagaki said.

Only four of the twelve made it through the enemy lines. They split up into two groups and, with soldier Niwa, Kainuma began his exploits. An ace with a combat knife, he killed a first American sentry alone in the jungle; farther along, a second: his knife flew toward the enemy like a javelin and nailed him at twenty paces. Niwa was shot; Kainuma carried him on his back through thorny jungle and across crocodile-infested rivers. But Niwa, seeing that he was tiring his friend, committed suicide while the other was briefly out of sight, slashing his wrists and dying with a banzai on his lips. Kainuma buried his friend and, brandishing his blade over the grave, swore vengeance. "There was murder in his eyes and every drop of his blood boiled," *Yomiuri* informed us. Off he went, killing man after man with his terrible knife and, each time, saying, "And did you see that one, friend Niwa?" Stumbling on a machine-gun nest, he killed the four-man team in a flash. Coming to a road, he stole a car, was chased, melted back into the jungle. By the eleventh day of his adventure, he had stabbed sixteen victims to death. He rested briefly with another band of Japanese soldiers cut off in the forest and living on roots, then once more plunged through the enemy lines.

"He came across a tent where eight Americans were sleeping heavily. He stabbed the one on the extreme right in the stomach. The man emitted a bizarre groan, but none of the others heard him. After reflecting on how to kill the second noiselessly, he struck, experimentally, through the mouth. The victim died without a sound. Then he stabbed the others the same way and, collecting their kits, returned to the Japanese position. Having killed twenty-four enemies, Kainuma felt a measure of relief."

This was the kind of prose the Japanese press served up daily to those on what it called the "rear front." Such recitals moved the public only moderately, since its leaders insisted that the fate of a few Pacific islands had no real influence on the overall progress of operations.

By an absurd paradox that clearly revealed the atmosphere

prevailing in Tokyo, it was the loss of another island, the relatively unimportant Attu in the Aleutians, that truly alarmed the Japanese for the first time. And instead of reassuring the country, the government, having decided that public opinion was too torpid and dangerously optimistic, inopportunely exploited this unexpected wave of fear by baldly announcing the loss. The upshot was that people in Tokyo began to imagine that an invasion route had suddenly been opened to the enemy from a direction hitherto thought secure: the north.

On May 11, under cover of the region's usual bad weather, the Americans had landed a full division on Attu. For more than two weeks, all Japan hung on the rare official communiqués reporting the Japanese garrison's heroic resistance. Outnumbered ten to one, they dammed the invading tide throughout the whole first week; finally forced to fall back, they fought for every foot of ground, inflicting heavy losses on the Americans. The Imperial general staff revealed the name of the man commanding the small force of defenders: Colonel Yasuo Yamasaki. Then, in late May, silence descended over Attu. Everyone in Japan knew it was all over. And in a broadcast on May 30, preceded by a dirge, an army spokesman solemnly announced the defenders' "last charge." The event received enormous play. Again, because there were no Japanese newsmen in a position to communicate with Tokyo, battle reports broadcast in the United States were used.

On the night of May 29, Colonel Yamasaki had launched the approximately 150 survivors under his command in a frantic suicide-charge against the weakest point in the American line. Before the charge, over 400 sick and wounded had committed suicide or were killed by their comrades. Having pierced a front loosely defended by an enemy who thought the battle was already over, the Japanese found no one before them and, at dawn, they moved five miles ahead, reaching the American artillery emplacements Yamasaki had fixed as their objective. They were able to turn the guns against the beaches where the enemy's stores and bivouacs were concentrated. The Americans finally pulled together a defense force of engineers, quartermaster units and cooks that just managed to pin down the marauding Japanese. Several more days were nevertheless needed to mop up the small, isolated groups that fought to the death like enraged tigers; some clasped grenades to their heads or hearts and blew themselves up rather than be taken prisoner.

The island of Kiska was still held by the Japanese—nearly seven thousand of them, far more than there had been on Attu. The Japanese command decided against sacrificing them uselessly and again resorted to a "withdrawal-deployment." On July 29, it evacuated its forces under cover of heavy fog. On August 15, the Americans, unaware of the withdrawal, sent no fewer than five battleships to shell the island before throwing in assault troops—who found the place abandoned.

An event unique in history marked the end of Kiska's defense. For the Japanese public, at any rate, there was proof of it in the account the newspapers relayed when they were finally allowed to announce the loss of Japan's last foothold in the Aleutians. Army spokesman Major Yahagi gave the event official credibility by reporting it in a special broadcast. Troop-laden Japanese destroyers left Kiska in dense fog. A few hours later, the fog suddenly lifted enough to enable the men clustered on the decks to see a shoreline dimly, as though through a veil, some distance away. It was Attu. All eyes were turned to this theater of heroic struggle when, suddenly, hundreds of Rising Sun flags were clearly seen waving in the mist. What was happening? Were there still Japanese alive on the island? No, said the official version gravely published in every Japanese newspaper and broadcast by Major Yahagi, "these were the souls of the hero-gods who died in defense of Attu, who had come down to the shore to salute and encourage our soldiers as they passed and who waved the standard of the red sun in the fog with a shout, faintly heard, of banzai for Japan!"

Shortly before the end of May, a piece of news as sensational as it was unexpected convinced the "rear front" that the situation was serious. A brief communiqué from the Imperial general staff, issued at about the time the reports were coming out concerning Attu, announced that Admiral Yamamoto had been "killed in

action at the front, in a plane, at the end of April." Astonishment
and consternation in Tokyo! The commander-in-chief of the Japanese fleet killed in a plane like some common pilot? All Japan
wondered about this strange death, but the high command kept
mum—so mum that rumors began to circulate. The great admiral, it was said, had simply committed hara-kiri. The whispered
"tip" was always followed by a loud guffaw to show that no one
was going to be taken in by that kind of nonsense. More detailed
information revealed, however, that in 1941 Yamamoto had
insistently opposed war with the United States. The admiral, it
was added—and this much of the story was true—had declared in
an argument with Tojo at the beginning of the war that the Japanese Navy would suffer its first defeats within a year. People saw
a strange coincidence between the admiral's mysterious death
and the time limit he had placed on his victories.

It was interesting later on to compare the scraps of information I picked up at the time with what really happened. The Japanese command, I was told, blamed Yamamoto's "bad luck" on
the excellence of America's aerial observation. The admiral was
on a round of inspection somewhere in the southern archipelagos, and enemy reconnaissance planes spotted the unusual activity caused by his passage. Suspecting the presence of big game,
U.S. fighter planes patrolled the area and, by what Tokyo
thought of as a stroke of luck, shot down the fleet commander's
plane. Thinking that the Americans were unaware of what they
had done, the Japanese command kept the business secret for
over a month. But a new commander had to be appointed; there
was a danger, too, that the navy general staff, which knew about
Yamamoto's death, would leak the news. The decision to make
the announcement finally came in late May.

As it happened, the American high command knew perfectly
well—this would be learned after the war—that Yamamoto had
been killed. He was attacked and shot down knowingly, not by a
"stroke of luck." This represented another victory by U.S. intelligence agents and cryptographers. An ultrasecret message announcing a tour of inspection by Yamamoto of bases in the
South Pacific was intercepted and decoded by the Americans; the
message gave the admiral's precise itinerary and the type of plane

he would be using. On April 18, at 9:43 A.M., exactly two minutes before Yamamoto's plane was scheduled to fly over the coast of Bougainville (in the Solomons) en route to Kahili, Japan's main air base in the area, sixteen American fighter planes were waiting for him. They had come from Guadalcanal and were at the outer limit of their combat range; if the admiral were late, they could not wait around for him and still conserve enough fuel for the return trip; they would simply have to miss him and head for home. But Yamamoto was exactly on time for his rendezvous with death—as usual, he was even a minute early. Suddenly, flames flared from an engine and one wing of his Mitsubishi bomber under attack by the leader of the American squadron. Yamamoto's craft crashed into the jungle in a jet of flame. Another Mitsubishi carrying his staff officers plunged into the sea and the Americans, having lost only one of their planes, were gone by the time the six fighters in the admiral's escort recovered from their surprise.

8

The "Co-prosperity Sphere"

At the beginning of 1942, General Tojo announced the creation
of a new cabinet ministry—the *Dai Toa Sho,* or Greater Asia
Ministry. Along with the *Gaimusho,* the Foreign Ministry, the
new department was to coordinate the administration of all territory conquered by the Japanese in the South Pacific. Plans for it
were grandiose and seemingly liberal. The flag of the Rising Sun
floated over an empire stretching from Siberia to the Indian border, and this vast expanse was now to be rid of the old ways of
Western colonialism. Japan would establish neither colonies nor
protectorates, but a free association of nations grouped around it
like a family around its father. Except for a few strategic spots
such as Singapore, where the military governments set up on arrival by the Japanese army would be maintained, all the associated peoples would have the right to independence. Burma,
Thailand, Malaya, the Philippines, the Dutch East Indies and Indochina (which Tokyo already treated as a state independent of
France even though it was still technically administered by the
French), all these newly conquered regions would be grafted to
the empire—an empire scarcely senior to the planned association
—that Japan had carved from the face of continental Asia:
Korea, Manchukuo, Outer Mongolia and the eastern half of
China.

With its love of pompous phrases, the government revived a
term it had invented two or three years earlier and called the new
association the "Coexistence and Co-prosperity Sphere." And in

the midst of the *Dai Toa Sensô*—the Great Asia war, aimed at destroying the old order—the *Dai Toa Sho,* the Greater Asia Ministry, busied itself at once in building the New Order in Asia.

By the end of 1942, however, it was obvious that Japan, preoccupied by its military problems, was merely improvising when it came to this much-touted "constructive project." It had neither the time, the daring nor the methodical mind necessary to prepare, as Germany had, squads of conquering administrators and gauleiters to re-educate and "liberate" occupied countries. Nor did it have the political instructors or the linguists it presumably needed for its program of schooling people for independence. This alone was already enough to show what the program was worth in practice. The entire south was firmly in the hands of the troops who had conquered it. That was the real program. Even supposing the political plans were sincere, they were purely theoretical; for the moment, they could represent no more than Japan's intentions.

Only consider the haste and disorder with which the government recruited the men it sent into the south, most of them totally untrained for the work they were to do. At first they were Japanese who had been routed out of Europe and the United States by the European war and who prudently returned home before Pearl Harbor or were repatriated later in an exchange of nationals: diplomats, businessmen, representatives of the big combines such as Mitsui and Mitsubishi, bankers, shipping-line agents, exporters, journalists. All these people would continue as Japan's political cadres abroad, but now they were to operate in regions they knew nothing about; branch managers in London, San Francisco or Buenos Aires were, without any preparation, to become administrators and civilian advisers in Kota Baru, Balikpapan or Mindanao. Their staffs? Anyone the authorities could find who once hawked gimcrack Japanese goods from Singapore to Rangoon, traders who worked the Borneo-Timor-Australia circuit and anyone who, under any sort of cover—journalism, business, fishing, travel agencies, for example—had acted as a penetration or espionage agent in the south. The latter were perhaps a little more knowledgeable than the others of the areas assigned them, but their education just barely equipped these liberators of Asia to understand and carry out the orders of the all-powerful generals now sitting in the swivel chairs of the white men who had fled or been captured.

Any Japanese who spoke any of the languages of the co-prosperity sphere—English first of all, then French for Indochina, Spanish for the Philippines, Dutch for Java—was guaranteed a good job. Hundreds of students waiting to be drafted into the armed forces applied for sinecures in those countries, only too happy to swap their military service for a spell in the dreamlands of the South Seas. Ancestral instincts were stirring in the depths of Japanese minds. These tropical countries called to their blood and they discovered what Japanese pseudoscience, custodian of the national myths, had always hidden from them: that there is an Oceanic strain in every Japanese. All Japan waxed enthusiastic about what it called the march toward the south. The word *minami*—the south—was forever cropping up in newspapers, in conversation; it was a theme in plays and a refrain of popular songs. It suggested not only the happy islands and sunny cities of the tropics, but the more specific advantages of a part of the globe where the whites had left behind them a kind of comfort and abundance of goods and food unknown to the Japanese. Indeed, for a little while, these flowed into Tokyo: rice, sugar, tobacco, whisky, well-tailored suits from Singapore, elegant shorts from Hong Kong and Saigon that shamed their wretched Japanese rivals. The supreme distinction was to ride in an automobile stolen in Shanghai, Manila or Singapore; this was a privilege reserved for the luminaries of the hour, for with shipping already scarce, only they had a long enough reach to enlist the military's cooperation in importing the 1941-model Buicks and Fords that looked so chic parked outside the teahouses.

All this fine enthusiasm, part of the 1942 euphoria, was short-lived. Indeed, had this people ever been known to hold for more than a season to its fads? Besides, minami—the south—quickly gained an unsavory reputation among those in the know. You were torpedoed on the way there. If you did arrive safely, you were at the army's orders; the war was still going on, construction was just a word and the rain of enemy bombs continued. Recruitment ran dry at the beginning of 1943 and the government had to mobilize a fourth of its metropolitan civil servants. The paper-shuffling, overcrowded Japanese administration was summoned to deliver hordes of bureaucrats who, like prisoners and other unfortunates, were uprooted from their routine lives and dispatched in terror to the unknown south. Only the craftiest succeeded in ending their journey in Tokyo itself by wangling a job in the new Greater Asia Ministry.

This was chiefly a hustlers' operation, a hunting ground for people with contacts. It was born of the clan quarrels that continued to sputter in the government despite the war. The army and the so-called progressive elements in the administration—the army's vassals—were anxious to humble and decapitate the Foreign Ministry, which for years they had accused of being too liberal and internationalist. The Foreign Ministry lost nearly half its personnel to the new Greater Asia Ministry; its powers were enfeebled by withdrawal of its authority over Asian affairs, leaving it with nothing on its plate but diplomatic relations with the Axis and a few neutrals, including the Soviet Union.

Clan disputes at the local level, which had always plagued the Japanese administration in the occupied countries, raged more fiercely than ever. Instead of stifling the eternal rivalries among the army, navy and diplomatic delegates by making them all responsible to a Greater Asia official, the system merely brought a new brawler into the free-for-all.

Moreover, the upstart ministry sparked bitter personal quarrels. The minister's portfolio should have gone to General Teiichi Suzuki, who had conceived the new department. But Tojo feared this would make Suzuki too powerful; he preferred to appoint Kazuo Aoki, a suitably docile Finance Ministry bureaucrat. At the same time, Foreign Minister Togo, already at odds with his Prime Minister over general policy, resigned in protest over the amputation of Asian affairs from his ministry. He was replaced by a minor figure, Masayuki Tani, Tokyo's ambassador in Nanking, the army's lackey in occupied China.

Disorderly bureaus, lack of preparation, personnel shortage, all these were merely secondary to the profound failing that had marred the Japanese empire in Asia since its inception: its lack of ideas. This was a decisive moment in Japanese history. This hermit people, so long isolated from the world, had become a leader. The mirror-nation, that for years had reflected the outside world, for the first time proposed to illuminate a part of the globe with its own light. Yet in this historically important role, in what it called its mission abroad, Japan showed itself to be poor in ideas and weak in expressing those it did have.

It had always preferred concrete action to reflection. Anyone familiar with Japanese policy from the inside always found it to be an unparalleled muddle of ideas; a perpetual row divided those who favored expansion to the north from those who looked toward the south; there was eternal rivalry between the principles of continental and oceanic policies; the conflict was never resolved between officials' moderation and their leaders' extremism; there was a confusion of theses, one for each clan, and a surfeit of slogans from everyone, the army, civilians, the navy, the diplomats.

Yet how sharp the contrast between the muddle of ideas and Japan's sureness in action! Was anything more logical, more rectilinear, did anything seem better prepared and planned than Japan's expansion in the previous half-century and especially in the previous fifteen years? It was a steady advance, undeviating, unhesitant, that seemed to know exactly where it was heading, what its main objectives and flanking maneuvers were. Japan's welter of contradictory ideas seemed to distill a unified strength. The explanation is that the logic of military Japan was instinctive, not reasoned. It was a mob instinct, moving as a mass, indifferent to its inner disorder, compact and sure in its advance, guided by unreasoned knowledge and collective impulses that were far stronger than the commands of its supposed leaders.

But now the moment had come when the problem was less one of action than of sowing ideas. The new order demanded more intelligence than instinct. A civilization cannot be imposed on a fourth of the planet by force alone; it must reach people's hearts and minds—we saw this clearly enough with Nazi Germany. But Japan, to which we cannot refuse credit for having harbored surprising dreams and for amazing the world in action, once again

gave only a miserable account of itself. The Japan put forward
by the Japanese was always prodigiously inferior to what it really
was. It was forever slipping into its mistake of taking prefabricated formulas for ideas. It served up to foreign peoples the slogans by which it deceived itself, the catchwords it adopted in
keeping with the nominalism we have already discussed. It
persisted in its inclination toward pompous display that concealed deep-lying truths.

The weariest of these clichés, these shams, was the "co-
prosperity sphere." Born, apparently, in the fertile brain of Matsuoka, it served in peacetime to cover aims presented as pacific,
mercantile and internationalist. When the time came for large-
scale military operations, the notion delineated the battlefield for
Greater Japan's warlike and nationalistic expansionism. Now it
masked improvised plans for a kind of Asian League of Nations
under Japanese tutelage. For Japan's formulas were as chame-
leonlike as its people.

Anyway, who knew where the sphere ended? Here, vague
words concealed the flexibility of Japan's intentions and its insatiable appetites. Australia would share in the "co-prosperity" if it
could be absorbed; India wouldn't do it any harm either, and
why not Siberia, if the chance ever arose? The formula was specially deceptive in its prescription of relations between Japan and
the lands of the South Pacific. Japan was poor and those lands
were rich. Associating them meant enriching Japan and stripping
the others of their substance. Prosperity flourished before the
Japanese armies arrived and vanished as soon as they settled in.
Everywhere Japan brought its co-prosperity, good-bye prosperity.

Another favorite bromide, this one squeezed from the ancient
writs of the national religion, was that of *Hakko Ichiu*, which
means "Put the eight recesses of the universe under a single
roof." A fine idea if it meant a desire for universal brotherhood.
But this too was a chameleon idea; after hearing it used on a
hundred different occasions, one understood how many meanings
it had. Japan wanted to group a family of nations around it, but
this was to be a Japanese-style family. Ancient Japanese tradition
made the family a hierarchy in which the oldest son is the supe-

rior of his younger brothers and the father is the unquestioned master of his household. Any Japanese association, of persons or peoples, had to be feudal, not egalitarian. Japan is a country in which each individual is always inferior to some of his fellow citizens and superior to the others. Putting all the Asian nations under one roof naturally meant treating them as inferiors. Hakko Ichiu's elasticity of meaning also gave nationalistic extremists a buzzword for worldwide expansion. Asia wasn't enough for them; it did not include all eight of the world's recesses. They were already looking beyond the Greater Asia war to other struggles to come, the one, for example, they would surely have to wage someday against Hitler's New Order in Europe.

Japan conquer the world? But its chief weakness as a civilizing nation was precisely that it had no world sense, a major failing that counterweighed and nullified its military strength. This people that thought it had a world mission, that longed to compare itself with history's great empire-builders, merely offered other nations images of its narrow particularism, displaying the manners of a special and unassimilable civilization. What isolated it most of all and rendered its message unintelligible, assuming that there was a message, was primarily its language. On an already extremely complex spoken language it had long ago plastered a wildly difficult Chinese script expressing a wholly different language from its own. This Sino-Japanese braintwister imposed years of study on Japanese children. But Japan also had two syllabic alphabets with a total of ninety-nine characters. This, it reckoned, was enough to make its impossible language the common tongue of its entire co-prosperity sphere in place of English; instruction in it was made obligatory.

The new masters of the South Pacific said they would respect foreign beliefs and make no changes in local customs. This may have been true of local superstitions and unimportant customs, but life was nevertheless expected to rapidly take on a Japanese tint. As in Japan, the police infiltrated everywhere and soon constituted the occupying administration's basic tool. Subject peoples were forced to form *tonarigumis*—neighborhood associations —that introduced two typically Japanese constraints: spying by neighbor on neighbor, and the organization of rationing.

Since the south was expected to become as industrious as Japan itself, its days of dancing and singing and, especially, of jazz were over. To work, everybody! Even siestas were banned. Education conformed to the Japanese pattern, with emphasis on violence through the teaching of martial sports and military exercises. No deeply entrenched system of beliefs was tolerated unless it fit into and submitted to the Japanese order. Persecution of the Roman Catholic religion began throughout the co-prosperity sphere, and especially in the Philippines, when it defended its independence and affirmed its attachment to a universal system led from Rome, not Tokyo. And, everywhere, the conquerors raised Shintoist temples to celebrate their own cult.

For centuries, Japan had shut itself into a cranky isolationism, teaching its subjects that anyone dealing with a foreigner was trafficking with the enemy and hence punishable by death. What prepared such a nation for the great tasks of international life? Its past had bequeathed it a profound misunderstanding of and incompetence for international relations. This showed in the attitude of individual Japanese toward foreigners: their reactions were suspiciously hostile or naïvely admiring; to them, a white man was either a god or a demon. A parallel incoherence on a national level made Japan's relations with the West veer constantly between idolatry and xenophobia.

Once, behind the "Chinese wall" of its oceans, Japan had developed a civilization with its own values. Ancient Japan would not have been so sturdy, so well balanced politically and socially had it not rested on solid political and moral foundations. But in the late nineteenth and early twentieth centuries it had again—for the second or even third time in its history—opened itself to a tide of foreign cultures. The country that boasted that it had never been invaded, that for two thousand years and more had protected the sacred soil of Japan from conquest from abroad, was then invaded by foreign ideas.

Pity the Japanese at the beginning of the twentieth century. Rushed headlong from the Middle Ages into the American century, they were awash in a sea of old Chinese words and modern expressions imported from the West. They were stuffed with foreign food, new foreign ideas, borrowed terminology, force-fed with translations of other cultures while still enmeshed in their own anachronisms and their ancient superstitions. With their heads ready to burst, they were hustled into the maelstrom of modern life, ill with all the world's fevers, easy prey to all the outside world's fads and fashions.

What, in the final analysis, did military Japan bring the world? It sensed obscurely that all its vices were closely mixed with virtues it had once half-succeeded in winnowing out, that in its ancient civilization it had lived by authentic truths. But it never managed to think through its values, or to rethink them. Had it tried to do so, had it not spoiled its chances by its schoolboy zeal to do everything faster and better than its teachers, it would, like every nation, have had a kind of mission in the world. It could, for example, have applied its frugality and its sense of collective effort to the development of a democratic spirit. It could, like the British, have shown that monarchy does not necessarily preclude democracy and that hierarchical structures need not be barriers to liberty. It could, in fact, have been the salt of Asia, for it intuitively sensed that its highest contribution to the community of nations might have been a salutary resistance to the West's scientific materialism. But in its disorderly thinking and its hysterical rush to act, it confused God and Caesar and ranked the saber above ideas.

The more accentuated these weaknesses became, however, the busier the directors of the New Order in Asia were. Never had the Greater Asia program seemed more brilliant than when Japan's first defeats announced the coming catastrophe. In 1942, increasing numbers of the Imperial government's ambassadors extraordinary were sent to visit the associated nations. Prince Takamatsu, Emperor Hirohito's brother, visited Pu-yi, the puppet emperor of Manchukuo. Old Baron Hiranuma and former Foreign Minister Hachiro Arita carried Tojo's compliments to Wang Ching-wei, the Chinese Quisling. In Bangkok, ex-Premier Koki Hirota, a member of the Black Dragon Society, conferred with Phibun Songgram, the tyrant of Siam. Wang Ching-wei went to Tokyo in December 1942, saw the Emperor, pocketed a loan of 100 million yen and declared war on Britain and the United States. This enabled the propagandists to announce "a reinforcement of 200 million men for the Axis" and produced a promise to the Chinese strawman that the international concessions in China would be restored to him.

Then Burma's U Ba Maw arrived in Tokyo. His tall frame was swathed in pink silk and topped with a mauve turban and he was visibly infatuated with himself. Bending toward his diminutive Japanese allies in their formal cutaways, he delivered endless speeches in impeccably Oxonian English. Tokyo worried about him, though; he was not to be relied on. Hadn't he been an avowed Anglophile until 1940, the Prime Minister in a British-assembled cabinet and Burma's representative at a Dominion conference? He had turned his coat while German bombers were pounding London in the autumn of 1940, believing, a little hastily, that Britain was finished. Since then, he had been irresolute and difficult, but there was no one better to deal with. During his March visit, Tojo promised him that Burmese independence would be announced in August, along with a Japanese-Burmese alliance.

The next on the list of Asian visitors was interesting in another way. Subhas Chandra Bose, president of the League for Indian Independence, was an enemy Britain took seriously. A former chairman of the Indian Congress Party, an astute London-trained politician, he ranked with the best of the new India's leaders, Jawaharlal Nehru and Mohammed Ali Jinnah. He was convinced that India should abandon the tactics of nonviolence preached by Gandhi and learn that freedom is bought with blood. Imprisoned by the British in 1939, he escaped and turned up in Berlin, where he briefly supported Hitler, until Germany's defeat before Suez convinced him that the road to India did not begin in Berlin. A specialist in sensational escapes, he dumped Hitler and reappeared in Tokyo after a mysterious voyage, probably in a Japanese submarine. Now he was betting on the Japanese. In Singapore he formed his league and organized the first Indian Army of Independence. Elegant, dynamic, extremely persuasive, speaking perfect English, he hoped to draw Japan into a campaign to conquer India. But all he accomplished in Tokyo was recognition of his provisional government and, of course, an alliance, insisted on by the Japanese, which brought him nothing but a few weapons for his soldiers. His "march on New Delhi" was to carry his army no more than a few dozen miles into India; it finally collapsed before Imphal in 1944.

Now it was Tojo's turn to play the globetrotter. He had already visited Nanking in March 1942 and Hsinking, the capital of Manchukuo, in April. The hoopla surrounding his travels was redoubled when he flew off on a Pacific tour. In Bangkok and Rangoon in July, he met Phibun Songgram and saw U Ba Maw again. From Thailand he went to Shonan (Singapore to the rest of the world). Marshal Count Hisaichi Terauchi, commander-in-chief in the South Pacific, reportedly gave him a surly reception and drew a grim picture of the situation there. Moving on to Sumatra, Borneo and Java, Tojo stopped in Rabaul, a forward oceanic strongpoint on the northeastern coast of New Guinea, where he came under intensive Allied bombing; he had time, deep in his shelter, to reflect on Terauchi's pessimistic predictions.

While the New Order in Asia seemed to be forging ahead, Hitler's New Order was experiencing its first major setbacks in North Africa, Sicily and Italy. The Japanese people, however, were still fooled by the government's "co-prosperity" propaganda because it flattered their love of sonorous words and official reality, masking the truth behind utopian visions. The more the facts pointed to the programs' failure, the more extravagant the propaganda became.

Tojo, in fact, had decided to change plans and shorten the Asian liberation schedule. Where would Japan be a year from then, in 1944? And in 1945? It had to act before what now loomed as the inevitable catastrophe occurred. The program for construction of the New Order had been devised in terms of a final victory; it now had to be revised to provide for probable defeat. This was one of the secret reasons for the Prime Minister's tour. At an extraordinary session of the Diet before his departure, he issued an unexpected proclamation: "We will bestow the honor of independence on the Philippines this very year." Of all the conquered peoples, the Filipinos, in whom spoke their ancient Spanish blood, were the most rebellious. Until now, Tojo had carefully refrained from setting a date for their promised independence. The Philippines, he had said, must first show the sincerity of their collaboration with Japan as an Oriental nation; only then would they be granted independence. Now it was being promised immediately and unconditionally.

In the Dutch East Indies and especially in Java, such promises had been dispensed with because, unlike the Filipinos, these people were the most docile in the co-prosperity sphere. This policy was also revised, and Tojo promised that he would soon establish a kind of native council that would be "consulted" by the occupation army. Finally there was Indochina, the best governed of the southern regions. The cheapest solution had hitherto seemed to be to allow the French under Admiral Jean Decoux to remain in control. This too was to change: with an eye to coming policy shifts, the independence movements that until now had received only lukewarm encouragement were to be vigorously supported. The Vietminh's day was coming; the conflagration in Vietnam was being kindled.

Japan's plan was clear. It no longer sought to build. If it was true that the Greater Asia war was already lost, the problem was to look beyond the defeat, to inflame the hatred in native hearts before the white men returned and to sow independence like a mine field in the terrain Japan would cede to the enemy. Never mind that the local peoples in the Pacific were learning to detest the Japanese Army, whose grip mercilessly tightened as the war news worsened. Catchword though it was, Asian revolt against the whites was one Japanese idea that was enthusiastically welcomed, that grew and prospered throughout the co-prosperity sphere and enabled Japan to keep local leaders in hand until the end.

In Tokyo, the stage was set in October 1943 for Filipino "independence"—made in Japan, of course. The actors in this farce were received in great pomp in the capital. In the leading role was José Laurel, a Filipino lawyer and politician who had courted Japan for years and had once received a *hogakuhakushi* degree—something like a doctorate in law—from the Imperial University in Tokyo. Two bit-players came with him: Jorge

Vargas, former secretary to President Manuel Quezon and once a determined supporter of the United States, who was now to be the Philippines' first ambassador to Tokyo, and Benigno Aquino, an ex-senator who had become head of the Kalibapi, the Filipino Fascist party. Laurel, with his messy haircut, his shifty eyes behind horn-rimmed glasses, his olive skin and striped pants, had a sly air about him. Not long before, he had narrowly escaped the bullets of a Filipino resistance fighter in Manila, which may have accounted for his anxious, almost hounded look, and he was permanently surrounded by police bodyguards.

The three men were solemnly received at the palace. Their claque had been mobilized: at the appointed time, schoolchildren lined their route and, at their teachers' commands, merrily waved both Japanese flags and little paper Philippines flags, red, white and blue with a sun and three stars in the middle. On October 14, with the visitors back in Manila, Tokyo noisily announced the declaration of independence, Laurel's nomination as the Philippine Republic's first president, and proclamation of a constitution for the republic that was a monument of totalitarian law. A few days later, Laurel declared war on the Philippines' former master, the United States.

Then, on November 5, Tojo set off the fanciest of the co-prosperity sphere's fireworks: the Assembly of East Asian Nations. Delegates flew in from all the associated countries and convened ceremoniously in a Parliament conference room in the presence of Greater Japan's leading dignitaries. Wang Ching-wei was there from China, and so were Chang Ching-hui, the hunchbacked, opium-addicted Prime Minister of Manchukuo; Siamese Prince Wan Waithayakon; Laurel for the Philippines; Ba Maw, in a general's uniform, for Burma, and Bose, who had been given "observer" status as a general of Free India. Tojo, his voice shrill, developed at length the idea of Asia for the Asiatics and promised his friends that the enemy's "desperate offensive," which was secretly worrying everyone in the room, would be repulsed. Hollow speeches were heard from Wang, Wan and Chang and then from Laurel, who scrupulously avoided mentioning that his capital was already being heavily bombed and that his country was under martial law. Nor was there any hint in

Ba Maw's address that his capital had been reduced to ashes. Bose, as an observer, allowed himself a little plain talk: "All these dreams," he said, referring to the New Order in Asia, "depend entirely on whether we can win this war!"

Tokyo made short work of the Assembly: there was one day of speeches followed by adoption of a "Joint Declaration of the Countries of East Asia" before batteries of cameras and radio microphones. No promise was made to hold similar meetings periodically, as the annoying Ba Maw had urged; no constitution was drawn up for the Eastern League of Nations, and the Declaration, a solemnly empty document drafted and proposed by Tojo, was unanimously approved without debate. Within a year, Wang Ching-wei would die in a Tokyo hospital of spinal injuries inflicted in 1940 by a partisan of Chiang Kai-shek; within two years Chang would be a prisoner of the Russians, Laurel a war criminal imprisoned by the Americans, Ba Maw a fugitive in the Burmese jungle. Bose would die in a mysterious plane crash on the day of Japan's surrender. But weren't these puppet heads of state, as they carried off their forced enthusiasm, also carrying a spark that would burn after they were dead—one which would light a fire on the ruins of the Japanese Empire to set all Asia aflame?

9

Tojo, the New Shogun

In the middle of Tokyo, at the foot of Sanno Hill, on which the Diet stands, hides a kind of small Japanese village called "the Three-Years district." No one remembers the origin of the name. It was there, at the end of a long, tidy alley, that I lived in a little Japanese house I had furnished in European style. Obscure, complicated, tiny—my "geisha house," I called it. This peaceful neighborhood, shaded by large gardens, was the scene of one of modern Japan's grimmest episodes: the military uprising of February 26, 1936. Rebellious regiments had dug in on Sanno Hill and occupied the approaches to the Diet and the Prime Minister's residence.

Like many rebellions in history, the 2-26 uprising, as the Japanese call it, was an immediate failure but a long-term success. The rebels, who wanted to topple the few liberals and big capitalists from power and set up a socialist-leaning military dictatorship, were overpowered, disarmed and punished. But Sanno Hill, the heart of Tokyo's political life, was now more thoroughly occupied than it ever had been by the rebel regiments. Only one man occupied it, but the man was General Tojo, the head of the army, and he lived in the Prime Minister's residence. This was a red-brick palace, a baroque mixture of European and Japanese styles that local architects, unaware of the expression's irony, called a "semi-style" that was widely used in Japan. From there, the uniformed Prime Minister had only about a hundred yards to cover to reach the Diet, a massive, white building that was also occupied by the army's people—some five hundred members of Parliament who were at the army's command.

This could be an awkward neighborhood to live in. At the head of my street, at least one police sentry and sometimes two or three observed my comings and goings, never failing to note them down, day or night. I frequently saw my irritating but illustrious neighbor during his brief automobile trips to and from his residence. For some time now he had preferred an open car, an impeccable black machine. Usually escorted only by an army chauffeur and two other figures in uniform, the general confidently exposed his highly energetic profile to public view. One or two motorcycles—no more—followed him, saddles and sidecars filled with goggle-wearing police. All this seemed exactly patterned on the sorties I had seen Hitler make in Berlin and Nuremberg. Tojo obviously wanted to show that he was like his German partner, the people's beloved leader who feared nothing and had nothing to fear. He had developed a taste for appearing in public. The ceremonies in 1943 in honor of all the Asian Quislings filing through Tokyo gave him excellent opportunities to circulate between two rows of banzai, parading his jovial face and his frightful khaki uniform, which he seemed to have chosen deliberately in the worst possible baby-shit color, hideously set off by a red collar and cap.

Every morning, the general went walking or riding. Hadn't he been seen at the central fish market the other day, as early as the Tsukiji fishmongers? Simply, good-naturedly, he had questioned the people in the market about their merchandise, their prices and the black market. A few days later, the vegetable market was honored—or terrorized—by his impromptu visit. The places crawled with plainclothes police, a fact ignored in the stories by the reporters who also just happened to be on hand to give the Prime Minister's early-morning excursions their due publicity.

This beloved leader, this Far Eastern Harun al Rashid, would frequently don an elegant British riding habit and, mounted on his favorite horse and followed by a lone aide-de-camp, trot to the Meiji temple before seven o'clock in the morning. If he spied a line of women in front of a grocery store he would stop and toss questions down from the saddle. He never got any but monosyllabic replies from the housewife or domestic he questioned, while the other women's faces puffed with laughter, a sign that they were frightened silly. Again, however, the newspapers published, at length, the martial declarations of Yoyogi mothers who were fully satisfied with their lot. Another time, Tojo the benevolent tyrant stopped a group of schoolchildren, all of them appropriately dressed in shoddy artificial khaki and armed with wooden rifles.

"What times does the drill begin?" the general asked one of the kids.

Frozen at attention, as custom dictated in his militarized grade school, the youngster barked out his answer like a good Japanese soldier: "Eight A.M.!"

"And what time did you leave school?" Tojo asked, peering down at him.

"Seven-thirty!"

"What time did you take the train to go to school?"

"Six-fifteen!" answered the boy who, like many Japanese pupils, spent an hour every morning on a train getting to class.

"And when did you leave home?"

"A quarter to six!"

"And what time was it when you had your morning rice?"

"At five-fifteen!"

"And at what time did you get up?"

"At five A.M.!"

"And your mother—what time does she get up every morning, then?"

"At four o'clock, sir!"

At which, according to the newspapers that gave this little story the prominence it deserved, Tojo declared: "Your mother is a true Nipponese mother! It is mothers like her who are winning the war!"

Still, the strange Japanese people, so easily fooled when it came to big issues they were too shortsighted to understand, were not so readily taken in by the small daily events that came within their scope. Tojo's poor imitation of his Axis partners fell flat; it rang false because it was not the custom. Perhaps, too, an instinct remained in Japanese hearts that somehow guided their true respect to where it really belonged—to the Emperor—and secretly denied Tojo the reverence with which they were normally so prodigal.

Quite a number of stories circulated about Tojo that never appeared in the newspapers. Everyone knew that scandalous fortunes were being built by those around him. In his shadow, a whole clique of bureaucrats and army men, active and retired, were mining gold out of military supplies. One of the most visible was Nobusuke Kishi, the Minister for Trade and Industry. Only forty-five years old, slender, elegant and energetic, he had begun to amass his wealth as a functionary in Manchukuo, where he befriended Tojo. From the outbreak of hostilities, he had kept war production in high gear, had brought the big industrialists under state control and placed army comptrollers in their companies. But for months there had been veiled talk of a "Kishi affair" that was now threatening to explode. Kishi's bribes were said to be so fat and his cut on major war contracts so big that the feared *kempei*—the military police—had reportedly decided to arrest him. Kishi counterattacked by accusing other functionaries of graft, notably General Akita Muto, head of the Military Affairs Bureau at the War Ministry and reputedly one of Tojo's two closest lieutenants. It was rumored that Tojo himself, knowing he would also be spattered if the blister burst, restrained the kempei's zeal and the case was dropped.

The man considered the industrial emperor of Manchukuo, Yoshisuke Ayukawa, dealt out millions of yen to this group of speculators and soldiers. Tojo had been subsidized at the start of his career by the Ayukawa group, which had a monopoly on heavy industry in Manchukuo; this was before he gained access to the funds of the *zaibatsu*, Japan's "hundred families" which, in fact, came down to five families who constituted the country's financial plutocracy. Tojo is said to have received millions from the Mitsubishi trust. And, above all, he and the army men around him were known to be dipping freely into the enormous military budget that remained absolutely secret, immune from any governmental or parliamentary control.

As in the greatest periods in Japanese history, all these people were living high. In the nineteenth century, the revolutionaries who restored the Emperor's power over the shoguns and who were hunted by the shogun's police, hid out in the teahouses; it was there, in nights soaked in sake and blooming with nubile girls, that the Saionjis and Itohs and other familiars of the Emperor Meiji founded modern Japan. Now it was the members of the government who caroused in the geisha houses. With rice growing scarce in Japanese households, leading public officials lived it up in the restaurants and teahouses with the most celebrated of the geishas, whose fee for an evening—as opposed to their prices for the night, which were higher—could reach a then exorbitant hundred yen an hour. In the sin-sodden alleys of Tsukiji and Akasaka, even during blackouts when no ray of light filtered through the sliding shutters or glowed behind the paper windows, piercing sounds of women's laughter rang in the darkness along with the coarse voices of drunken men, the nervous plucking of the *samisens*, the shrilling of songs and rhythmic clapping. Luxurious ministerial automobiles, their headlights covered with black hoods like carnival masks, rolled out of the shadows of the amusement districts carrying clusters of kimono-clad girls toward mysterious rendezvous. Other women waited in the night, sometimes until dawn, for the rich client who, as they said in the teahouses, "stayed over."

Tojo, it was whispered, set the example, maintaining a stable of beautiful mistresses. Not that any sympathy was wasted for all that on the general's honorable wife, Mme. Tojo; her ambition was said to be unbridled and her greediness for money insatiable. The people muttered that she had spent a fortune on a posh residence for her family on the banks of the Tama River. In the same neighborhood, the homes of a number of families were requisitioned by the army for use as nightspots for staff officers. The women's bitter laughter used to be aimed at Mme. Chiang Kai-shek, whose name in Japanese was *So Bi Lei;* now the sarcasm was directed at Mme. Tojo, who was derisively, if secretly, tagged *To Bi Lei.*

In the spring of 1943, Tokyo walls were suddenly covered with hundreds of colored posters showing the general's broad face smiling under a khaki cap. Heavy bombers soared through a sky-blue background along with a brief message urging young men to enlist in the air force. The portrait was clearly designed, however, as a puff for Tojo himself. It was an unusual gambit and it nettled a public already disposed against him; such personal publicity was alien to Japanese political customs; it stank of Hitlerism, which the public secretly detested. And it was all the worse for promoting Tojo as top dog when, it was felt, he should always have thought of himself as a subordinate, the lieutenant, the servant. There was only one chief, the people murmured, and that was the Emperor. But the Son of Heaven was more invisible and more silent than ever; he was hidden by Tojo's shadow.

This was certainly the general's most telling mistake, the one that was to center the whole country's hatred on him when the major defeats began to accumulate. Slowly, Tojo was changing from Prime Minister to shogun—military tyrant, like the shoguns of the old Tokugawa dynasty of shameful memory. Under his government, Japan seemed to be backsliding, falling into its old vices of an obsolete police and military state in which, as in Japan's Middle Ages, power was held by the head of a warrior clique while the Son of Heaven withdrew, remaining invisible, useless and secretly mocked. The Japanese people, despite their submissiveness, remained surprisingly aware of the significance of the nineteenth-century revolution that had briefly brought them near to freedom. They smelled imposture in the posters glorifying Tojo; they were scandalized by the portrait of this upstart general and they grumbled about the "Tojo shogunate."

Tojo was shown up even more clearly in another incident, this time in the closed world of politics. It happened during the winter session of Parliament. So enveloping were the mantles of censorship and secrecy covering the affair that the public had no clue as to what was going on. The newspapers did mention a dispute in Parliament over "Article 7" of the wartime criminal code, but they merely reported that the law had finally been unanimously approved; no hint was given of what the article in question said. From private sources and through leaks, I was able to piece together what had happened: nothing less than the muz-

zling of the last handful of liberal deputies—a dozen at the most—
who had survived the 1942 legislative elections. To silence them
and to fortify himself against any possible future opposition,
Tojo had asked the House of Representatives to vote an exceptional measure of which Article 7, an extraordinary example of
Japanese wartime "law," provided: "Anyone who, with the intention of creating disorder in national policy or of disturbing
public order and peace in wartime, shall propagandize on behalf
of matters susceptible of causing a notable breach of the public
peace, shall be subject to a maximum penalty of seven years'
imprisonment."

Even the deputies who owed their election to Tojo balked at
this. It meant giving their master too potent a weapon, one he
could turn against them. Influenced by the small group of representatives who had been elected without government endorsement—that is, despite and against Tojo—some of the government's stooges rebelled. A violent debate kept the dreaded
article's fate in suspense for several days. But the army had ways
to cut short this scandalous attempt to render a semblance of dignity to this rump of a parliament. The group of irreconcilables,
led by Dr. Ashida, an ex-diplomat and former director of the
Japan Times, was publicly derided from the tribune by speakers
in Tojo's stable. In a final session at which insults were hurled—
the last time this would happen during the war—the opposition,
accused of antipatriotism, was denied the right to vote. Tension
reached the breaking point. The independents stood up, massed
around Ashida, in sign of protest while the other deputies voted.
Fists clenched, eyes filled with tears of rage, these courageous
men watched impotently while a rigged ballot closed the debate.
Article 7 was unanimously adopted, the newspapers would report, without, as we have noted, revealing its contents. Ashida
and his friends disappeared from the House, prudently preferring
to retire to the country, where they were kept under constant
police surveillance.

I got wind of the angry discussions that followed the vote.
The Empire was finished, the independents agreed. Tojo and his
gang were now the undisputed masters of everything and everybody, beginning with the Emperor. The country was headed for

disaster. And this would be a good and profitable thing, because in a ruined and punished Japan, it would at least be possible to rebuild. In this new Japan, the Imperial regime would of course have to be abolished, since it had made the sovereign the tool of clans which legitimized their abuse of power by covering themselves with his name. And if the people refused to give up their sovereign, then he could be frankly demoted to the minor role of high priest of the obsolete national religion and exiled to Kyoto while the new men tried to reconstruct democracy in Tokyo.

The government's economic policy further helped to sap the short-lived popularity enjoyed in the first months of the war by the Pearl Harbor cabinet and its leader. In the spring of 1943, the regime, armed with powers it had forced through the Parliament, sharply tightened its hold on industry and labor. Company presidents and plant managers were inducted into the army, working henceforth under military discipline, and industry as a whole was run according to a German-style *Führerprinzip* which made the head of a firm personally responsible for its production. Workers were drafted into the National Service Association, a Japanese equivalent of the Vichy French Labor Front. Japanese girls and women, Chinese and Korean coolies and Allied prisoners of war constituted a new pool of cheap labor for industry.

Limitations on working hours were formally abolished. What this meant was obvious in a military Japan where the labor slavery that Europe had virtually abandoned in the late nineteenth century had found refuge in the twentieth. In June the screw was given another, more drastic, turn. Through surprisingly brutal decrees and, even more effectively, through secret instructions to the police, the Japanese people's living standard was systematically lowered. Their rice ration was cut. The Japanese, even more sensitive to poor-quality rice than Europeans were to poor-quality bread, now were given very inferior rice mixed with wheat, then potatoes and, soon, with beans. Neighborhood associations charged with supervising distribution of victuals doled out ridiculously small rations that barely fed a family for four days a week. People rushed to the countryside around Tokyo and

other big cities in search of provisions, but police in the trains
and railroad stations stopped them and confiscated their food,
usually to their own profit. Besides, long-distance train tickets
were rationed and any kind of travel became difficult to arrange.

In the stores, clothing and yard goods suddenly disappeared;
the government was releasing no more stocks. Just when prewar
clothing was wearing out completely, ration-card points for new
clothing were first devalued, then cancelled. Trade Minister Kishi
announced in July that no new cloth would be put on sale before
1945; clothing ration cards were not renewed, and regulations
encouraging the purchase of silk fabrics were rescinded. A great
many other staples vanished in the second half of 1943: soap,
shoes, pharmaceuticals, household articles, dishes, rice bowls, all
kinds of ceramic and porcelain ware, metal objects and many
more items.

To provide a diversion, the government made a great to-do at
the beginning of 1944 about closing luxury establishments, especially those in the amusement districts. Farewell to the geishas'
painted laughter; there would be no more flower-spattered, gold-
embroidered kimonos at the nightly rendezvous in the ritualized
world of clandestine sex. Would Japan ever see all this bawdy,
laughing Japanesquery again?

Meanwhile, ten thousand geishas were out of work. In the alleys of the nightclub districts, discreet doors of unpainted wood
were bolted on more than three thousand teahouses. Tragicomic
mini-dramas erupted like strings of firecrackers and the people
heard each little explosion. At first there was a rush in the profession toward marriage. The prettiest and most pampered girls
were quickly grabbed off to be transformed into honorable wives
or recognized concubines hidden away in the city or its immediate suburbs. Others became inept secretaries and typists in the
ministries and business offices; a geisha out of her element is like
a bird fallen from its nest. Or they went back to the country
towns where they were born. Many even let themselves be
drafted into the labor service where hands trained to pour sake
and arrange flowers learned to sew white-silk parachutes and
fashion aluminum parts.

Soon, however, there was a black market in geishas; it was

murmured that Tojo and other high government officials were celebrating their revels as before, joyously and seductively accompanied. Besides, in closing the geisha houses, the government had gone too far; the move had caused the instant closing of hundreds of restaurants providing an almost indispensable supplement to family food rations. Official propagandists explained that the restaurants had been diverting great quantities of foodstuffs to the black market and that now they were to be brought back into official distribution channels. Nothing like this happened; the black market thrived as never before.

To add to the gloom, the same decrees closed most of the theaters. European-style dance halls had been banned well before the war, in 1940. There remained only the countless bars in the Ginza and other quarters where girls of often slender virtue served watered-down drinks at exorbitant prices. Tokyo suddenly found itself without amusements, except for the bad war films shown in overcrowded movie houses. People began to understand that the situation was more serious than the authorities dared to admit; once more, popular resentment focused on Tojo.

Japan was worried about the progress of the war in Europe. Just as Japanese forces were retreating in Guadalcanal, the Reichswehr fell into the pit at Stalingrad. With the Tokyo government anxious to remain on good terms with the Soviet Union in view of Russia's vital importance to Japan, the battle of Stalingrad was given full play in Japanese newspapers. For once, the reports were truthful, abundant and sustained; the Red Army was frequently praised, to the detriment of Hitler's troops. From the autumn of 1942 to February 1943, the war in the West, so often belittled by Japanese propagandists conveniently forgetful of what was happening on the other side of the world, was again given its rightful dimension. From time to time, that struggle was so titanic that Japan seemed to suspend its own war to watch, breathless, as the spectacle in Europe unfolded. This happened in June 1940, at the fall of Paris; in September 1940, during the Battle of Britain; in 1942, with the Allied landings in North Africa. Through the long months of the battle of Stalingrad, Japanese fascination was heightened by their deep-seated belief that

Hitler really was not going to beat the Russians. Japan had never received anything but talk from the Reich and, to tell the truth, it was still betting on both sides of the board. The news early in February 1943 of the Nazi armies' surrender at Stalingrad had profound repercussions in Japan. A German victory in Europe now seemed definitely unlikely; the Japanese realized that henceforth they had only themselves to rely on.

The continuing deterioration of the military situation altered General Tojo's personality. He knew better than anyone else what the real facts were; he felt that victory had already slipped from his grasp and, along with it, his ephemeral popularity. Even to the army he was no longer the respected commander the military clan had unanimously raised to power in the autumn of 1941. He became increasingly bitter, scorned advice, stopped listening to his subordinates' opinions, no longer surrounded himself with intimates who kept him informed. His enemies came into the open, and he made new ones by shunting aside anyone who dared challenge him.

Retired General Kanji Ishihara, one of the country's most respected military men, was maintaining a disquieting reserve. Tojo knew Ishihara detested him. Nevertheless, Japan needed men of his worth and the general was a noted expert on Russian and Chinese affairs. Mutual friends arranged a meeting at the Prime Minister's residence. Ishihara immediately volunteered to return to his country's service. Tojo's satisfaction was shattered, however, when he added: "There is one condition: that you turn the post of Prime Minister over as soon as possible to someone more competent." Tojo never forgave the affront. Ishihara was confined to his home somewhere in Akita province, in northern Japan, and kept under surveillance by a network of spies and police with instructions to isolate him and see to it that he made no political contacts.

Even more feared by Tojo were the generals who distinguished themselves in the victorious early battles of the war. Yamashita, immensely popular after his conquest of Singapore, was the most dangerous of them all. The story goes that he went to Tokyo early in 1942 to try to persuade Tojo of the need to offer the United States a negotiated peace. In any event, the "Tiger of

Malaya" was disgraced in a way that set tongues wagging in the army: he was stripped of his command in Singapore and sent to the Manchurian front, facing the Russians, in a subordinate position under General Yoshijiro Umezu, the Japanese army commander in Manchukuo. Publication of the news was banned by the censors.

Marshal Terauchi, another of Tojo's possible rivals, was sent to the South Pacific as commander-in-chief of land forces there. General Seishiro Itagaki, a former War Minister, was another rival; he was senior to the Prime Minister and had quarreled with him at the start of the China war, when Minister Itagaki had wanted to limit the "incident" while Tojo, his vice-minister, sought to extend it. Itagaki had won the argument—very briefly—and dismissed his vice-minister. Now Tojo took his revenge: his senior was exiled to Seoul, not as governor-general, but merely as commander of Japanese forces in Korea. Tojo was also on bad terms with General Kenji Doihara, a colleague in the early days in Manchuria; with Homma, who conquered the Philippines in 1942 and who was transferred from Manila to China; with Muto, compromised in the Kishi scandal and sent to Sumatra. No one on the general staff now had the Prime Minister's confidence; not even those who had been his strongest supporters could still approach him.

As the situation worsened, Tojo increasingly governed through the military and civilian police, over which the army had gradually extended its control. His policy of police intimidation and repression was revealed in a number of sensational cases—sensational, at least, in political circles, for the censors were again careful to keep the public as much in the dark as possible. One of these cases, the Ozaki affair, broke just after the 1942 elections. An impenitent old liberal, Yukio Ozaki had sat in the House of Representatives since the beginning of the century. During a political meeting before the election he had imprudently compared the reign of Showa (that is, of Hirohito) to the two preceding it. Japan's present rulers, he had declared, were too visibly *sandaime* or "third-generation" men—favorite sons, or grandsons, rather, who skillfully exploited their forebears' success, but who were unable to match them and who were squandering their patrimony. Political spies reported Ozaki's remarks to their higher-ups, and he was accused of having attacked the Emperor himself by comparing him slightingly with his father, Emperor Taisho, and his grandfather, Meiji. This was treason! The old man, stripped of his parliamentary immunity, was arrested. He did not come to trial until two years later, in June 1944; given the foolishness of the indictment, his judges finally brought themselves to dismiss the case.

After this swing at a liberal, Tojo went out after the zaibatsu, the fabulously wealthy business circle that was resisting government control. The army was particularly irritated with the Mitsuis, the great financial barons who had always dragged their heels in collaborating with the military. A black-market case in China gave military police spies a pretext to act. Mitsui agents in northern China had collected 200 million yen worth of wheat to drive prices up and corner the grain market. Speculation of this kind was common in Japanese occupation zones, and it was often engineered by the army. But this was a fine chance to bludgeon the Mitsuis. The army demanded that twenty-five of the combine's directors resign, that the company be reorganized, putting some of its stock up for public sale—and that its head, old Baron Mitsui, make a personal apology. Shaken businessmen added that the military had secretly insisted on millions of yen in fines.

This was the twentieth century's third "Mitsui affair"; the 1914 Siemens scandal had brought down the Yamamoto cabinet, and Mitsui people had been murdered by army rebels in February 1936. The latest incident especially alarmed the trusts by bringing to light a kind of military bolshevism clearly intent, under cover of the war, on confiscating big capital for the State.

Another case cropped up the end of October 1943. A brief newspaper item reported that nationalist leader Seigo Nakano had cut open his belly in accordance with the ancient ritual of hara-kiri. The news caused a sensation: Nakano had long been a powerful and highly popular figure. He was connected with the secret Black Dragon Society, was a member of Parliament and chairman of the Tohokai party which, until political parties were dissolved, had been modeled on the Nazi party. His fiery speeches had largely contributed to Japan's break with the United States in 1941 and with the launching of the war. He had been one of Japan's rare orators and, until 1942, his speeches always drew crowds. For a while, he believed he was the Hitler destined for Japan. The suicide of such a man could not help but stir speculation—especially since nothing was said about why he had killed himself.

I nevertheless learned some confidential details about the circumstances surrounding his death. On the morning of October 28, one of the celebrated politician's servants was housecleaning when she saw a trickle of blood flowing from under the sliding door leading to his bedroom. She opened the door. There was Nakano, lying on the mats in a pool of blood. Everyone in the household rushed to the scene. He had opened his belly, then slashed his jugular vein near the collarbone. He was formally dressed for the ceremony in a black silk kimono emblazoned with his family's coat of arms in white. Near him lay a visiting card on which he had written a short farewell poem, an obligatory part of the hara-kiri ritual. "Tonight, at midnight, I shall cut short my life," it said. Faithful to the conventions, he had calmly dined that evening with his brother and his son, an officer due to leave the next day for China. At dinner he had seemed natural, in good spirits, had given no hint of his intention. To explain his unusual costume, he pretended he was cold.

Technically, his hara-kiri was perfect. Nakano had skillfully avoided toppling over on his side, for the victim kneeling on his mat is expected to maintain total mastery over himself in his dying moments, avoiding spasmodic movements so as to fall directly forward, his head well in line with his knees. To accomplish this, he was careful only to cut his stomach muscle, without touching the entrails. As was fitting, hardly any blood sullied the white silk paper in which he had wrapped his blade, leaving only about half an inch of naked steel showing—just the length needed to pierce the abdomen. The stomach wound could not have been fatal; it was chiefly symbolic, and a second stroke was required to bring things to a quick finish. For this, a devoted friend hacks off the victim's head with a saber or, if he is alone, the suicide opens his own veins. This is what Nakano did, and his success, I was told, was all the more remarkable for the fact that the police had already confiscated his weapons; he had been obliged to borrow his son's military saber on a pretext, and the long, heavy blade was much more difficult to handle than a dagger would have been.

Nationalist circles were much moved, the newspapers said; among the first national figures to rush to the deceased's home was old Mitsuru Toyama, the famous founder of the Black Dragon Society. Toyama and many other superpatriots, including former Prime Minister Koki Hirota, attended the funeral, which attracted large crowds on the following Sunday to the Aoyama cemetery. Nakano was rumored to have left an important political message which was now in Toyama's hands, but its contents were being kept absolutely secret because they were said to attack Tojo.

I was not to know the truth until tongues loosened at the end of the war. Nakano had committed suicide in protest against Tojo's persecution of him and to denounce the general's policy. Although he had violently urged the war against Britain and the United States, he suddenly changed his line when he saw the Reich endangered by its conflict with Russia. After the capture of Singapore, he was one of those who tried to persuade Tojo to negotiate a conqueror's peace; Japan, he argued, could then turn its guns against Russia. On January 1, 1943, Nakano dared to attack Tojo openly in a column in the daily *Mainichi*. He campaigned in political circles for a declaration of war against the Soviet Union to rescue Germany from its trap at Stalingrad. And he stepped up his personal attacks on Tojo and his clique, denouncing them as liars and accusing them of sabotaging the war.

Tojo struck back. Military police arrested Nakano. When the prosecutor assigned to the case dared to recommend that it be dropped, Tojo called in his Minister of Justice and insisted that it be pressed; to rid himself of his overly independent prosecutor, he had the man drafted into the army and sent to China. Nakano was again imprisoned on October 21. But with Parliament scheduled to convene in an extraordinary session on October 25, the law required that he be released. Nakano emerged from prison to find that he was being kept under constant surveillance by Kempetai agents who even occupied his house for the purpose. It was then that he resolved to use the only way open to him to denounce Tojo: to slit his own stomach as a sign of protest.

10

An Imperiled Multitude

Japan was in danger in 1943, but it had not yet been decisively defeated. The war was still being fought thousands of miles from its shores. Yet the euphoria of 1942 was already far in the past; the decline in that one year had been sharp. By this time I had been in the country for five years; each year, each month, almost every day, I had seen it slip a little lower into servitude, restrictions, ugliness. Tokyo had never been a beautiful city, but it was now dirty as well as homely. Every morning the capital awoke a little more sordid, as though stained by the sinister night into which it had just been plunged.

Wartime nights in Tokyo! The raids had not begun and yet, night after night, this city drowned in darkness by the blackout was haunted by a dread that gnawed and worried it more than real enemy squadrons in the sky could have done. I do not believe that any European capital had waited with such a feeling of suffocation for fire to start falling from the heavens. For this braggart metropolis that styled itself the world's second city knew it was built of wood. Seven million people in Tokyo thought nightly of the coming fire. Press, radio, speakers insisted that the inhabitants could control the fires when the time came, but the people were not reassured. They doubted it. Tokyo knew it was an overgrown village of planks. In the streets at night one was, in a sense, enveloped in wood. All those dry beams, all this wood ready to burn, waiting for a spark. Behind those planks, millions of people slept on straw mats.

A rattling steel trolley, vaguely phosphorescent, would surge up at the corner of a deserted avenue. At the stop, cloaked figures hopped down and were swallowed up by the night; for a moment, there was a scuffling of wooden sandals at the entrance to dark passages, then this handful of people went to ground behind walls of wood, of mud, of paper, absorbed into the invisible presence of prostrate multitudes asleep between the planks.

In the morning, the capital stirred in its filth. A Japanese house rots in twenty years. So does a city. Tokyo, rebuilt in 1923 after the big earthquake, was rotten. This thought alone convinced me that this was the end of a civilization. You could imagine no way to save this capital from crumbling in rot and ruin except some catastrophe that would again compel rebuilding —a purifying fire, for example, that would destroy it all.

The ground in Tokyo suddenly gaped with millions of holes, like bomb craters before the bombings and in anticipation of the bombings. Holes everywhere—in empty lots, in gardens, even in the streets, in all the sidewalks, holes every dozen yards. Hole is the only name these shelters deserve, for these pitiful trenches so feverishly dug on orders from on high one fine September day, everywhere at once, all over the city—these trenches were all the government had planned to shelter seven million people from the coming bombs. Each was a maximum of ten feet long and some two and a half feet deep. No roofs—for the moment, at any rate. The volunteers in tattered overalls who dug these shallow tombs dumped the clayey dirt on the sidewalks and in the gutters. The next time it rained, passersby in their ruined shoes would be sucked into the black mud and the holes would fill with water. Meanwhile, to try out their shelters, housewives in pants squatted down in them Japanese-fashion, with their knees against their collarbones, and beamed satisfied smiles skyward; now the bombers could come.

The pox of holes disfiguring Tokyo was only the last stage in its general dilapidation. The subway was a wreck; rusty trolley cars seemed to jounce on square wheels; train windows were broken, baggage racks sagged, seats were eviscerated; public telephones were torn out; bicycles wobbled on flat tires; rattletrap autos were abandoned in the streets. The government had ordered a collection of scrap metal, so stone columns were uprooted along with the grilles they supported, bridge parapets along with their handrails, roofs with their uprights; lamp posts were knocked down, leaving potholes in the sidewalks or steel roots with sharp cutting edges; sections of wall vanished with their radiators. And, since transportation was short, all these radiators and heating pipes and grilles and boilers and scrap metal of all kinds lay rusting for months at a time, ignored on the sidewalks in the heart of the city.

The countryside, too, was affected by this sack of the environment. Cancerous industrial parks burgeoned along the country's north-south communications backbone. Wasting the withered body of agricultural Japan like a fast-spreading disease, the movement generated cellular ranks of hangars in the fields, left rice paddies bristling with pylons and poles, shaved the forests and sapped the bases of nearby mountains that now vomited mud and metallic sand over the green land.

Then the policy of industrial dispersion reached sites farther away; Korean laborers invaded the peaceful countryside, pierced its hills, chopped down its woods, dammed the springs where only yesterday local people had adored the little deities that lived in them, and smeared the floors of devastated valleys with foundations for enormous factories.

Kyoto was ringed with factories to take advantage of what was hoped would be the relative security of that holy city of a thousand temples. Ise, where the Sun Goddess was worshipped at thatch-roofed altars, was surrounded by manufacturing plants. At Chuzenji, a celebrated site near Nikko, the sacred Kegon waterfall was imprisoned in the monstrous tubes of a power plant. The nearby mountains in what had once been a "national park" were dented by giant factories processing light metals for aircraft. And to accommodate the trains chuffing down from these heights, a massive steel bridge crushed the red-lacquered arch of the famous sacred bridge at Nikko.

Surely the eight myriads of Japan's pagan gods would seek revenge for being chased from their mossy rocks and their shady retreats under the Japanese cedars, where straw ropes warned of the presence of a divine inhabitant. Twenty years earlier, the

French poet Paul Claudel was already concerned lest Japan fall
under the curse of the *fong shui*, the Chinese evil spell promised
to those who trouble the peace of the fields and disfigure the face
of nature.

No cosmetic now masked the national poverty. There was a
gaudy, barbarous quality to other Asian countries' misery; ruined
Tokyo was as dreary as the capital of indigence. A new breed of
humanity appeared among that throng of Asiatic faces, the
"green race." These were the skinny, the undernourished, fish
eaters deprived even of their daily sardine. Their stomachs were
upset by the inferior rice and the doubtful mixtures they were
served. These livid faces testified to the chronic diarrhea that dis-
turbed the nation's nights.

All that was pleasing in Japanese life had perished—everything, that is, which much of the world associated with the very
name Japan. For half a century, the dreamers, the poets and the
painters had asked Japan to flatter the taste all men have for
niceness, for prettiness. It's a minor craving that has produced
nothing of genius, but it is more accessible, perhaps, and more
widespread than love of beauty. The thousand satisfactions
Japan had provided for this yearning had vanished: elegant
trifles, artful knickknacks, tasteful, always consciously aesthetic,
decors, good manners, feminine graces.

To be a woman or, at any rate, to affirm one's femininity was
really unpatriotic in wartime. The girls and the honorable wives
who occupied an increasingly important place in the national life
seemed to ask males' pardon for cultivating an ugliness that
resembled their mens'. Kimonos disappeared, not only because
their floating silks would get in the way of war work, but because
they were happy and gay. The masters—so husbands and fathers
were called—wanted austerity. So women adopted pants. But
pleated trousers looked too good on these hipless maidens, flattering their figures and hiding their weak point, their legs. Most
important, pants were European. Women made them a Japanese
invention. A clandestine and touching relic of fashion briefly lingered in a series of experiments: ski pants? golf pants? pajama
pants? None of these were the Japanese pants of which the
women dreamed and their researches finally ended in the most

bastard of forms, something between baggy Turkish pants and a working woman's overalls. And since the lack of cloth meant that this feminine equipment had to be salvaged from worn kimonos, these billowing garments called *monpei,* with their ill-cut legs tied at the ankles, multicolored, striped and flowered, looked like nothing so much as clowns' costumes.

As for the men, they had finally adopted the shoddy, khaki-colored, artificial fabric of the "national costume"—the Japanese expression might better be translated as "patriotic suit" to indicate the spirit in which civilians volunteered to wear uniforms. This unanimity derived far less from a considered sense of discipline than from a gregarious instinct. Men adopted the ways of the herd with frightening ease.

The human herd! I was forever haunted by its unrelieved swarming. Tokyo was a city of crowds, in the streets, the stations, at factory gates, in trains, schools, theaters, at patriotic rallies and national sanctuaries. These were not different crowds after all, but one and the same throng, omnipresent and unvarying. Exotic touches—paper umbrellas, the rare kimonos, wooden sandals, babies slung on their mothers' backs—were lost in the grayness of a multitude to which, from a distance, one could not attribute a specific race or nationality. And, as one drew nearer, the only things that stood out from this image of a human herd, daubed in charcoal on the backdrop of the city, were the thousand faces; not yellow, but dull, dark, often shriveled, which never ceased to fascinate me.

It was incredibly loutish, this crowd, made up of millions of almost peasant gaffes, of clumsy clumpings on wooden *getas,* of lumpish cavalcades down too-narrow stairways and ill-mannered shoving that clogged station entrances, blocked trolley-car doors and prevented passengers from getting off trains. It took them four years to learn to form a line in a period when one had to stand in line for everything. And so extraordinarily passive was the Japanese character that none of those waiting ever dreamed of planting himself anywhere but directly in line behind the person in front of him. Lines of stranded travelers at a ticket window, for example, instead of curving so as not to block traffic, threw impregnable human barriers across railway-station lobbies, neatly sealing off entryways and tracks. Housewives queueing for the daily ration, office workers waiting for their trolleys, people buying newspapers (you had to line up for that, too), customers who arrived too early for the opening of the "workers' beer halls" (one glass of beer a week on presentation of a special ticket)—all these lines were always blocking something, a street, a room, a passage, an intersection. And all these people waited with a patience no other crowd on earth could muster. Late trains, subway breakdowns, trolley accidents, none of these now-daily mishaps drew a word of impatience or a gesture of weariness; not a feature twitched on these dismally impassive faces.

And how much waiting one had to do in this war-mired country! To eat in a greasy-spoon restaurant—this was before the eating places were closed—one had to arrive at four o'clock and wait until the doors opened at five. One spent a night in line to get a train ticket, an hour for standing room in a movie theater, three-quarters of an hour on the sidewalk to finally board the tenth trolley car to go by. Overcrowding grew more alarming every day in public places that were never quickly enough emptied because of the inward rush of new waves of people. To make things worse, this country so anxious to expand to world size had built everything at home, twenty or thirty years before, on the narrow, shrunken scale of a poor society. Overcrowded as few countries on this planet are, it had wedged itself into stingy urbanism and mediocre architecture. Station platforms, sidewalks (when there were sidewalks, which was rare), subway entrances were all too small for this swarming anthill. Tokyo had no places for the public to gather, too few parks, few broad avenues. In the theaters, where the tiny, tightly packed seats seemed designed for children, twice as many spectators were admitted as there were seats. On public transportation, it seemed that even a slight delay in the schedule, a breakdown, a serious accident would make the bottleneck permanent: a few more children, a few trains less and the crush would congeal into a living jelly quivering within the city walls. Unless an alert, a bomb, were to panic the herd, and then what would happen?

But no, the jams were finally dissolved, movement resumed. In fact, despite all the snags, the Japanese seemed possessed by a fever of movement. It was a molecular movement, a clashing, swarming of particles, in which people passed each other, brushed by each other, going who knew where, circulating, stirring. Was it because moving around meant using what little freedom remained to them? Because traveling was one of the last of the authorized pleasures, a last luxury? The regulations limited long trips, rationed train tickets, requisitioned hotels. Never mind! Awesome crowds continued to shove into the rickety trains. Movement had really become indispensable to most people. One of the nuisances of war was that it inordinately lengthened the distances everyone had to cover every day. The housing shortage plunked thousands of people far from their jobs; a lack of schools forced herds of schoolchildren to waste hours on trains every day to attend the schools assigned them. Occupational changes ordered by the government sent thousands of craftsmen off to work in distant factories. And, finally, people moved because the war and its gradually accumulating shortages made life a perpetual chase—after shops that, for today only, had something to sell; after officials who could issue the indispensable papers authorizing every aspect of life; in search of the clandestine counters of the black market and objects that suddenly—momentarily—materialized in unexpected places; after people who, for a day, were offering profitable deals; after the confidential tips that had to be followed up right away. And, of course, the hunt for food sent hundreds of scavengers into the suburbs and the countrysides every morning, especially on Sundays, to return in the evening, after an exhausting round of the farms, loaded with packages and bundles.

This, then, was the tragedy of wartime Japan: that its easy early victories brought its people nothing. Victory didn't pay. What a difference here from what was happening in Germany! The Nazi Blitzkrieg and Germany's ransacking of Europe at least fed and clothed the German people almost up to the country's surrender. Japan's lightning war may have brought the Japanese state the treasures of the South Pacific, it certainly provided the army and navy with the oil and minerals they coveted, but all it meant for the average Japanese was more privation, a tougher life.

This was nothing new. For three-quarters of a century, Japan had been using its conquests not to enhance the lives of individuals, not to raise the citizen's living standards, but for the benefit and increased power of the group. All profit, all change, all expansion was reserved to the nation *as* a nation. The individual kept his place, had no share in any of this enrichment; the sole advantage it brought him was membership in a more powerful group. This, at any rate, is what the State told him. To each of these poor devils who, as individuals, knew they were weak and peaceful and humble, the group proclaimed: "Together you are the strongest, the light of the Orient, the salt of Asia." For all of them, collective pride was their revenge for their petty lives; for their sweat, blood and tears, the crowds were paid with words.

In a secondary swindle within the overall fraud, the State itself was hoodwinked by a few individuals. With each new conquest, an oligarchy of financiers, zaibatsu, politicians and military men usurped much of the profit that should have gone to the community. The big combines reaped the dividends generated by the war and by colonization; the armed forces gained in power. Big business, the army, the navy constantly swelled. Suzuki-san—the Japanese John Doe—stayed as skinny as ever.

Yet even I sometimes forgot to notice how mediocre his life was, how backward his techniques and how frequently primitive his existence; suddenly, in a flash, I would no longer see these famished, ill-housed, shabbily dressed people as individuals, but only as a group. Maybe, I told myself, they are not behind us, but ahead of us, ahead on the road to the human anthill. If humanity is marching toward a worldwide antheap, toward a single termitary, how far ahead they are of us whites with our outdated individualism. Who knew if Japan had not made an invisible but far more solid conquest than its conquest of land: a conquest of time? A century from now, would it have reached a stage of social development that the rest of us might need three or four hundred years to attain? Barely out of its feudal Middle Ages, hadn't it plunged into collectivism with a far more homogeneous mass than Marx or Stalin had ever dreamed of?

How gifted Japan is, in any case, for tomorrow's collective society, if we do come to that. Its Oriental customs, its whole philosophy, have always taught its people never to isolate themselves from the group, never to assert themselves against it but to lose themselves in the culture in which the group is bathed, to render themselves permeable, to melt into their surroundings. Their art taught them to blend into nature, their religion into the nothingness of the great Wholeness, their lives into an anonymous mass.

That mass, united, entirely blended, swept everything before it. Opposition? An unknown phenomenon in psychology or politics. No heterodox theories won prominence, no alternative team was formed to replace the group in power. There was not even any need for active discipline; Japanese discipline was inert. The mass, indifferent to the rare complaints of those it overwhelmed, swept Japan along in a tide with no ebb.

There was an extraordinary mixing of the country's working masses in 1943. The business restructuring voted in June at a special session of Parliament amounted to a death sentence for small firms and a triumph for big manufacturers and heavy industry. Some thirteen million Japanese belonging to two million families had been the nation's shopkeepers and its small, home-based craftsmen. But peacetime trades were unwanted now; the daily stream of purchases flowed through the official rationing outlets, and the shops were empty. The common herd now worked in the munitions factories or was regrouped in middle-sized defense plants. A million and a half artisans employing fewer than five workmen each were also affected by the general upheaval. Their machines were taken away from them for installation in centralized production facilities, and these were followed by their employees. Eighty per cent of the country's industrial labor force had worked in shops employing fewer than thirty people. The army's organizers appeared, moved out their equipment, requisitioned the men, put them to turning out other products, regrouping, amalgamating, suppressing. Another series of measures in 1944 was to make the program still more drastic: closure of the last so-called peacetime firms, student mobilization, renovation of the Labor Service, a ban on production of many items considered useless, and so on.

Finally, and this was probably an even more profound upheaval, an intensive rural recruitment campaign washed over ancient agricultural Japan, wrested from it all the male and female workers it could spare and sent them to work in the cities. One of the most surprising spectacles of wartime Japan was certainly this sudden apparition of an army of the uprooted thrown into the cities like an invasion by a savage horde. Torn from the ancient, primitive structure that had kept it servile and invisible, this army all at once became a dramatically assertive proletariat that submerged everything in its path. Trains, stations, public places were overwhelmed by a bustle of farmers in khaki overalls that served as rumpled hyphens between their shaved heads and the dirty feet in their wooden or straw sandals. The women and girls were less visible merely because they were shut away; they lived in overcrowded dormitories in the factories and usually had only one day off a month. I shall never forget a group of women workers I saw one day along a railroad track as they poured out of a plant: frightened young country girls swathed in ragged uniforms with khaki pants; red-faced, thick creatures with dangling arms and open mouths—a true human herd.

Here again, the brutality of Japan's "progress" was reflected in a myriad caricatures of a modern society gone haywire. The shock of mechanization on the national body was incredibly violent, perhaps unparalleled anywhere else in the world. What made it especially profound was that for many years the political and social structures of old Japan had been so solid that they had resisted the Industrial Revolution. The collapse of a "Japan with feet of clay" had been predicted time and again, but it had never happened; it had been fended off from year to year. The old framework had held fast, absorbing the shock. In the West, the twentieth-century economic revolution occurred in a society that had already broken down its old structures in political revolutions. In Japan, where the Meiji restoration had not deeply affected the country's feudal foundations, modern economics had long accommodated itself to the firm social structures of the past. The war toppled all that. Suddenly Japan had to suffer the consequences of forced industrialization aimed at moving it from the Middle Ages into an ultramodern economy in under half a century.

Japan published no formal banks of statistics during the war; these had been kept secret since 1937. But I would occasionally find significant figures in the newspapers hinting at the savage industrial thrust then taking place, and at its social consequences.

One of the dimly perceived signs of industrial slavery was an appalling rise in the number of work accidents. According to the newspaper *Yomiuri,* the number of workers involved in accidents in the year leading up to the war exceeded half a million. In 1927, the work-accident rate was twenty-five per thousand workers; by 1940 it had climbed to forty per thousand. This was considerably exceeded in heavy industry and machine-tool and steel plants, where accidents were notoriously frequent. In Tokyo, the number of workers killed by machines more than doubled from 1936 to 1939, the *Nippon Times* admitted, citing figures supplied by the police and therefore well below the true numbers.

Trade-union activity disappeared before the war. In June 1939, the last of the unions, long persecuted by the police, had a total of only 315,000 members, or 2.6 per cent of the labor force. In July 1940, the Interior Ministry ordered the "voluntary" dissolution of the Japanese Labor Federation, the Agriculture Federation and the Federation of Maritime Unions, socialism's last three bastions. The Association of State Service by Industry, a kind of Labor Front controlled by the Ministry of Public Welfare and officered by police bureaucrats, was set up in 1938, organizing workers under the surveillance of employers and government-appointed prefects who were automatically directors of local groups. By June 1942 the association had 86,000 branches and nearly 6,000,000 members.

As we have noted, there were no longer any limits on working hours. A twelve-hour day had been decreed in April 1939—the first time a limit had been put on working hours—but this applied only to workers in the five main industries, and even this limitation was abandoned in December 1943. Children went to work in the factories from the age of twelve or thirteen, recruited by the government itself; boys were drafted into the labor service as soon as they finished grade school. Those who were allowed to continue their studies owed the State an increasing number of weeks a year of labor in the fields and factories. Work on the land was sometimes healthful and beneficial; many youngsters, however, merely functioned as unskilled laborers or factory hands.

Newsreel films were sometimes revealing. These were, of course, propaganda films in the Japanese manner, sponsored by the Information Bureau. For example, *Schools in Japan at War:* some forty boys aged twelve and thirteen in a classroom where the desks had been converted to workbenches and the seats removed. The teacher was drawing something on the blackboard— not a geometric equation, but a design from which the children were to fashion pieces of metal into airplane parts. The explanations given, the teacher blew a strident blast on a whistle and all the pupils drew up at attention at their places. A second whistle blast, this time in a series of long shrills like letters in Morse code; at each shrill, the youngsters, all together, in a single movement, bent tensely over their bits of metal and drew a long, plaintive stroke across them with their files. Then, all together, they straightened up like mechanical dolls and ran the files forward with a screech.

Another film: an empty shipyard workshop. A bugle sounded. Some hundred boys aged around fifteen ran in on the double and came to attention at their benches. The bugle sounded again; each picked up his tool, a heavy hammer. Whistle blasts then set the pace for the boys' rhythmic pounding in this children's dungeon.

Hundreds of thousands of women worked in factories, especially in the aircraft plants. By 1939, two years before the war, there were 1.5 million of them on the assembly lines. They did every kind of work, including the hardest; they even worked in the mines. Quarrying and mining by women were banned in 1939 at the insistence of the International Bureau of Labor, but more than 40,000 of them remained in the mines despite the law, according to the *Nippon Times*. In August 1939, the Public Welfare Ministry officially rescinded the ban and called for recruitment of over 20,000 women and children aged fourteen to sixteen to work underground. The government admitted that 78,000 of the 500,000 miners counted in 1942 were women. Women and children were eagerly sought for the labor market because their pay was much lower than men's. In the munitions plants, men earned an average 1.50 yen an hour in 1939 compared with .83 yen for women. According to the *Nippon Times*, no adjustments were made until March 1944 in wages that had been melted away by inflation since 1941.

Public health was calamitous. Tuberculosis raged frighteningly, visibly; one had only to open one's eyes and ears to detect the contagion in the surrounding crowds. The inadequate diet produced stomach and intestinal troubles. Children's health was especially deplorable. Infant mortality was three times higher than in Britain and Germany. "With the present mortality rate," a Population Bureau expert told the newspapers in 1941, "we cannot attain our demographic objective, which is to have one hundred million Japanese in 1960."

Despite this pessimism, statistics testified to a population explosion. In 1941 the number of Japanese grew by 1,070,000. Triumphantly announcing this figure to the Parliament, General Tojo stressed that it represented a reversal—and in wartime—of the population curve over the previous three years, when the annual increases had dipped below 1,000,000. In February 1944, the Public Welfare Minister reported from the speaker's platform in the Chamber that million-plus increases had also been registered in 1942 and 1943. Japan had never before produced so many babies as it did in the midst of the war.

In 1920, the country's urban population had represented only 18 per cent of the total; that figure grew to 38 per cent by 1940. With the 1943 decree reorganizing industry and launching recruitment of rural labor, General Tojo officially stated the principle that the population would henceforth be distributed in the following proportions: 60 per cent in the cities and 40 per cent on the land. Japan's demographic equilibrium had been completely shattered in twenty years.

11

Quarrels, Delays, Reverses

It was increasingly plain in that year of 1943 that the Japanese-German alliance had never been anything but a confidence game. On its side, Japan had hoped to wage a profiteer's war and collect in the East the benefits of the Reich's victories in the West. But Hitler's war was now in reverse; a Nazi triumph was no more than a dream. For its part, Germany had counted, if not on Japan's assistance—it was too proud to ask for help from yellow men—then at least on coordinated operations in East and West and perhaps on their junction. But the junction that was supposed to take place around Suez was a mere bluff by propagandists in Berlin and Tokyo now that Rommel had failed on the Egyptian frontier and Japan had given up the idea of invading India. As for coordinating East-West offensives, the last occasion had been the German push at Stalingrad, when Japanese intervention in Siberia might still have saved the Reich.

But Japan had been careful not to move.

The very principle of Japan's war was its independence. Japan was waging Japan's war, the one it called the "Greater Asia War." The Germans, after all, were white. When the Nazis were winning their first victories, Tokyo feared they might score too brilliant a triumph. By the time they began losing, Japan was already seeing its own victory slip away. It had become important that Tokyo avoid confounding its war with Berlin's.

The staunchest wall sealing off the two conflicts was the Russo-Japanese neutrality treaty. Japan took pains to observe it to the letter. Its only fear was that the Russians might be less scrupulous. A nightmare haunted Tokyo: that the Soviet Union might concede the air bases the United States was vainly demanding in Siberia. If that happened, all would be lost for Japan; its cities would go up in flames. Making war on Russia would immediately expose the Japanese to this mortal danger; it would mean undertaking a second war, one that would benefit Greater Germany, not Greater Asia. So while the propaganda from Tokyo, seemingly playing Berlin's game, derided the threats from London and Washington on the imminence of a second front in the West, the Japanese government denied Berlin a second front in Siberia. During the battle for Stalingrad, the German embassy in Tokyo campaigned frantically for a Siberian war, mobilizing Japanese nationalists behind Seigo Nakano to press for it; the campaign failed because Japan was too busy saving itself to bother saving Hitler.

There was nevertheless a moment when Berlin might have wondered if its efforts had not succeeded after all. Just as the fight was ending at Stalingrad, General Tojo made an ambiguous declaration to the Diet. "Japan," he proclaimed, "swears to fight all the way, shoulder to shoulder, to the common victory by closing ranks with its German and Italian allies and giving them aid and mutual assistance." This aroused great excitement in the Axis colony in Tokyo. Wasn't this an announcement of the Japanese second front demanded by Ambassador Stahmer? But Berlin soon realized that this was just another of the polite bows Tojo made to an alliance that brought him little and could cost him a great deal more.

Italy's woes introduced a comic note into the cacophony of the Axis concert because of the casual way in which Tokyo viewed its Fascist ally's reverses—an airiness that scarcely masked its fury toward a nation of feckless soldiers. When the Americans landed in Sicily, officials in Tokyo arranged for the bad news to be held almost up to deadline time for the evening papers, which published it in short items on the back of their single sheets under such circumspect headlines as "The Axis Falls Back on the Italian Continent" and "The Reich Concentrates Its Forces in the European Fortress." Marshal Pietro Badoglio's overthrow of Mussolini was announced twenty-four hours late by the *Nippon Times* under a modest headline that presented it as a perfectly natural event: "Mussolini Ends His Career as Duce." Italy's surrender on September 8, 1943, was denounced by the Japanese government as a "regrettable act of treason." Official communiqués assured the people that, on this occasion, Japan "reinforced its firm confidence in victory." They also declared: "The Hundred Million, with a tradition three thousand years old, must demonstrate their combative power and, with a single mind and a single soul, attain the sacred objectives of the war, thus bringing repose to the august heart of the Emperor."

The Foreign Affairs Minister, Mamoru Shigemitsu, who had replaced Tani, addressed the Diet with a prediction of a "brilliant future" for the new (Fascist) Italy. Japan formally recognized the Milan "Fascist Republic," whose affairs were handled in Tokyo by the German embassy. For the next six months, the Japanese government would no longer correspond directly with the disappointing Duce, and it resigned itself only after some delay to recognizing a Colonel Omero Principini not as Italy's chargé d'affaires, but simply as custodian of Italian interests in Japan. Rome's Ambassador Mario Indelli and the majority of the Italians in Japan, who backed King Umberto and Badoglio, were clapped into a concentration camp.

To save face, Japan multiplied its shows of cordiality toward the Reich. Tojo sent Hitler a telegram congratulating him for rescuing the Duce, who had been kidnapped from the Americans by Nazi paratroopers. Another exchange of cables marked the third anniversary of the tripartite treaty; Ribbentrop and Shigemitsu were the stars in an exchange of radio programs between Berlin and Tokyo. In a reversal of roles, Japanese propagandists lavished words of encouragement on Hitler and his armies. Once it had been Berlin that cried victory to Tokyo to shake Japanese inertia and draw the Imperial troops into the war; now Tokyo was having its revenge: the slightest local advance on an insignificant front in Burma or China, the sinking of any American skow, was flashed by the Domei agency to the DNB, the German news agency, to console the German public and suggest that discouragement was premature as long as brave Japan was victoriously pressing the fight. In September, the Tokyo government, which was not noted for its sense of humor, gravely announced that, in keeping with the treaty of alliance and to tighten its links to the Führer's government, Japan and the Reich had just negotiated an important diplomatic instrument—a medical treaty.

In fact, a discovery of capital importance made by Japan in 1943 left it little time to worry about the war in Europe: contrary to all its calculations, the two wars, in Europe and in Asia, were not successive but concomitant. They did not compete, they were cumulative. In other words, the long-held Japanese belief that Japan would not feel the weight of the United States in the Far East as long as the war in the West lasted was now shown to be an illusion. Roosevelt had already abandoned the "Germany first" policy he had reluctantly accepted in 1942 in order to rescue Britain.

The United States felt strong enough to fight on two fronts, against Germany in the West and against Japan in the Pacific. Reports from Japanese intelligence agents in the few remaining neutral countries warned Tokyo of this intention at the end of 1943. Particularly telling were the conclusions of two Japanese superspies in Europe, General Makoto Onodera, known as "Egghead," the military attaché in Stockholm, and General Suemasu Okamoto, former chief of Japanese army intelligence who, after working with Marshal Terauchi in Singapore, had been named military attaché in Bern in 1943.

In the event, operations in the South Pacific showed clearly enough that the United States was stepping up its efforts on the Asian fronts without waiting for the European fighting to end. To much of the American public, Japan was Enemy No. 1. In conformity with decisions taken in May at the so-called Trident Conference in Washington, the United States was now fully on the offensive. After the "withdrawal-deployment" from Guadalcanal, Japan had still had a little time in which to consolidate its line of retreat around Munda, in the Solomons; Munda was captured in August, and from then on the American advance kept the Japanese forces permanently on the run. The Americans secured a foothold on Bougainville in October, capturing the island's two airfields and the big naval base on Empress Augusta

Bay opposite Rabaul, Japan's main citadel in the Southwest
Pacific. In September, they were with the Australians on the
north coast of New Guinea; they did not waste time pushing
through the island's headhunter-infested jungles, preferring an
oblique but rapid westward thrust, ricocheting from base to base
toward the Philippines. Before the end of the year, a landing was
made on New Britain, and Rabaul, encircled on the east and
west, was finally neutralized. Japanese pilots reported the appearance of the first giant American carriers, 26,000-ton ships of the
Essex type begun after Pearl Harbor and already in action, as
well as ultramodern battleships of the *South Dakota* class and
new heavy cruisers. American radio reports revealed that new
aircraft carriers were being launched at the rate of one a month.

Japanese resistance in the endangered archipelagos was frenzied. On the tiny island of Tarawa, the Americans were given
their first lesson in how costly a landing can be on a furiously
defended, heavily mined beach swept by a hellish crossfire and
supported from the rear by lines of the fortified pillboxes on
which the Yanks would stumble all along the road to Tokyo. But
the Americans' formidable material superiority did its work.
Japan lost the Gilbert Islands. MacArthur began his progress
from archipelago to archipelago; with each new advance, he left
behind him another island in American hands. On the map, the
Pacific began to look like a miniature pond in a Japanese garden
that you cross by hopping from flagstone to flagstone.

Japan's reply to this alarming American advance was a desperate effort by industry in 1943 to increase aircraft production.
The death of the country's small workshops, the bankruptcy of
thousands of small shops, the hasty regrouping of labor and its
rush to the cities, all these convulsions of the Japanese economy
had a single cause: the impetus to devote all the country's productive energies to churning out the airplanes needed to stave off
disaster. Weakness in the air was the high command's prime concern. Having enjoyed absolute superiority in quantity and quality
in the first months of the war, the air force was now outclassed
everywhere. And American strategy was to attack in all sectors

at once to disperse the Japanese air defense and bring to bear its own growing naval superiority. Aircraft carriers had replaced cruisers as the linchpins in their squadrons, revolutionizing traditional notions of naval warfare.

The magnitude of the campaign kicked off in mid-1943 to reinforce Japan's air power was striking. With a flourish of the pen, General Tojo decreed the transformation of the great textile plants that had formerly enriched Japan into aircraft factories to be operational within six months. Thousands of women employed in the Osaka mills were henceforth to make airplanes. The Mitsubishi trust reorganized itself to concentrate on aircraft production. The Nakajima brothers, who, with French technical help, had become Japan's first airplane makers after World War I, now opened a string of new plants. Factories mushroomed all along the Tokaido line between Tokyo and Osaka; Shimazu, once the country's green-tea capital, and Nagoya, the porcelain-making city, were converted into vast aeronautics plants. The Ayukawa trust brought Manchuria into the campaign.

Japan lacked pilots; so the universities were emptied, examinations eliminated or botched and students routed to the flying schools sprouting throughout the country. All young men from wealthy, middle-class families were automatically marked for pilot training. Intensive propaganda sang the glory of those it called the "flying eagles" as long as they *were* flying and "gods of the air" when they perished at the front after a few months of war. Thousands of youngsters aged fifteen and sixteen were caught up, often over their families' protests, in a "voluntary" recruitment drive in the hope that there was still time to make them into day-after-tomorrow's "gods of the air" before the war ended. Making model planes became the national pastime for millions of Japanese schoolchildren and, by government order, hundreds of shops—the ones that still had something to display in their windows—sold bamboo struts and tissue paper for making the models. With lubricating oil scarce, fifteen million families in the city and the countrysides were given castor-oil seeds to plant in sidewalks and along nearby embankments; they were to turn the harvest over to the authorities.

No country before Japan had ever attempted to conquer empires on both land and sea at the same time. Britain had possessed the one, Germany had aspired to the other, but neither had laid claim to both. Japan was not satisfied with the continent of Asia and the Pacific Ocean; in the midst of its war, it also harbored the mad dream of challenging the United States for aerial dominion over half the world. But the country that for three-quarters of a century had lived by buying or copying Western patents now detected a weakness in itself that horrified Japanese leaders: a shortage of technicians and inventors. It was farther behind in this area than in any other and so its propaganda came up with a new slogan: "Be inventors! Be engineers!"

General Tojo mounted the tribune in the Chamber and told a story. "I sent for my son," he recounted, "who is studying science, and I told him: 'Draw me the plans for a flying machine that will put me down in Berlin in two hours and needs neither gasoline nor coal nor electricity to fly.' My son respectfully laughed in my face and told me this was impossible. Well, if Japanese science had any imagination, this would not be impossible for it.

"'Suppose,' I replied to my son, 'your machine was able to free itself from the earth's attraction; in a few hours the globe would turn under it and I would land in Berlin. And for the fuel, don't you think there must be some kind of gas in the air that can make a motor work?' As long as our scientists lack ideas, we will not be able to use as we should the material riches our victories have put at our disposal."

Innocent Tojo! He was now asking minds saturated in the past, long warned against the audacity of technical imagination and individualism, to strain for flights of fancy, for the great leap forward, to step off the beaten track. Yet it was its lack of inventiveness, even more than the technical gap, that gave the true measure of military Japan's dramatic inadequacy to accomplish the colossal task its leaders had set for it. It belonged to a civilization whose chief concern for hundreds of years had not been to invent, to progress, but to keep the world static, as it had been bequeathed to each succeeding generation. To Oriental craftsmen, creating meant copying. They could not conceive of a made object as anything but a reproduction of a model. A student who invented something was disavowed by his teacher; a disciple who revealed to a layman the techniques confided to him by his master was considered a traitor. Science and secrecy were closely associated, as they were in ancient societies. It was important that secrecy be maintained, first because knowledge gave its guardians a monopoly power they were anxious to maintain, and, second, because the spread of scientific knowledge, a source of revolutions, would sap a civilization motivated by conservatism.

Yet, in this respect, Japan had already betrayed Oriental civilization in the middle of the nineteenth century. It had understood then that it would have to learn from the white race and that any people who lagged behind the whites would be conquered and exploited by the very techniques it tried to reject. But it did things by halves. It adopted hitherto-forbidden techniques, but it bought them ready-made abroad. It borrowed and imitated. For many years, the commercial liberalism of the period eased the way for Japan by making the patents and experts it sought readily available as long as it paid the whites their price. This very facility did the Japanese a vast disservice; it fostered the survival of their routine thinking.

It would be overly hasty, however, to conclude, as the West so often did, that Japan was incapable of invention. True, it began far behind the whites' frightening technical lead, but the experience of a century denied the notion that it was a permanent technical cripple. The time it had in which to accumulate technical experience was very brief by comparison with the West's, and if it imitated rather than invented, the fault—perhaps a lucky fault—lay with the whites, who encouraged it to copy them and who, in fact, were careful to let Japan have only their outdated patents, to sell it their secondhand science. It was only when the West understood, a little late, that it was supplying arms to its most dangerous enemy that Japan was left alone to deal with modern technology—that, in a way, it was condemned to be inventive.

A kind of Japanese individualism does exist after all. I have stressed this people's herd tendencies because they prevailed among the governed classes, which means the immense majority of the people. But military Japan also fostered an elite group, a superior class that in a sense had colonized its own country after rejecting colonization by the West. In many ways, its members resembled what we call individualists. Unlike the mass of Japanese, they were endowed with a general culture, personalized and self-sufficient. They stood out by their broad knowledge of the world and of international life, often acquired in long careers of study abroad. Japanese individualism was different from ours, however, in that it almost always avoided opposing its ideas to the group's. It feared nonconformism, serving its society more often than combating it. Indeed, society itself saw to it that its elite class prospered, provided its numbers remained small. The group needed directors. From these leaders it required initiative, and it systematically cultivated their individuality.

Japan was also distinctive in the Orient for having partly rejected what was passive and nihilistic in Eastern civilization. In a way, it was able to give an offensive point to the principles of renunciation and immobilism taught it by Asia. It had never been satisfied with meditation; finally, it had always ended the artist's meditation with a brusque, spontaneous brushstroke, the warrior's with a sudden saber blow, the Zen philosopher's with a decision that resolved debate and initiated action. In its very history, this hermit people, after three centuries of reclusion, showed itself to be warlike and swaggering. It was no coincidence that Japan was the first of the Oriental countries to adopt Western civilization. Reacting against an Orient discouraged and frightened by materialism, Japan discovered its affinities with the courageous West which instead of believing, as Asia did, in the uselessness of effort and in the world's illusoriness, had taken on the world and mastered it through science.

Did the war, calamitous as it was for Japan, entitle us to consider the Japanese incapable of scientific achievement? Not even the Americans dared go that far. By the time General Tojo made his desperate bid to reverse the progress of the war by a tardy recourse to air power, the country had already showed its enemies the unexpected strength of its modern—and innovative—fleet. For nearly two years, its planes had matched the Americans'. Even when due credit is given to the help provided by German engineers, the fact remains that the Japanese had been able to design useful airplanes that were perfectly adapted to specific needs. Japan's weaponry was good—especially its artillery. The Japanese proved their excellence in designing aircraft and armaments, but they lacked the modern machinery and raw materials to produce the war materiel they needed. They confirmed the advance in torpedo technology they had held since the beginning of the century, at Port Arthur. Even the Americans conceded a four-way superiority of Japanese torpedoes: in speed, range, payload power and invisibility—they left no bubbling wake behind them. The Mitsubishi "0" aircraft (or rather, the "00," since Japanese planes were designated by the last two numbers of the year in the Japanese calendar—2600, for example, for the year 1940) and its successor the "01," were judged excellent and, according to American experts, they were original with the Japanese, not merely inspired by foreign techniques. There is an important fact to keep in mind: in wartime, junk was reserved for the public, but anything manufactured for the State was top-quality. Foreigners were too glib in concluding that the trashiness of everyday articles in Japan extended to materiel produced for the State, which, behind its screen of secrecy, was excellent.

Japan was nevertheless not up to matching America's formidable technological power, nor the inventive and productive capacities of what was then a nation of 120 million people in the vanguard of Western scientific progress. It should be added that some "Japanese inventions" contributed largely to ruining Japan's reputation among its enemies. In this astounding country, an extraordinary mixture of modern civilization and primitive naïveté, everything was well ordered until, suddenly, an essential element exploded, an event that was all the more surprising and amusing because it stood out from such a serious background; this is what might be called the preposterous side of Japanese life.

Germany had its secret weapons, the V1 and V2 rockets. Japan had its own: its paper balloons. One fine day in 1944, press and radio, fresh from a campaign to develop scientific warfare, issued sensational details about the balloon bombs which, they said, were sowing panic all along the United States West Coast.

These amazing paper gadgets, thirty-three feet in diameter and inflated with hydrogen, were simply released into the wind on the coast of Japan; the honorable wind was requested to carry them to the United States, where they would release their charge upon the heads of the terrified Americans. Each carried a payload of some fifty pounds, half explosive and half incendiary; it was calculated that they would reach their destination in thirty hours, when they were detonated by a time fuse.

The first "attack on America" was made in December 1943 in reprisal for the Doolittle raid on Tokyo. Two hundred were released in February–March 1944, but the really massive balloon-bomb offensive took place between November 1944 and March 1945, when 9,000 were cast off, at a cost of 10,000 yen each. According to figures released after the war, 90 per cent of them vanished at sea; those that did reach the American coast exploded over forests and mountains, far from populated areas. And what was the total number of this secret weapon's casualties for the entirety of the war? Six.

The Japanese public, unhappily, was not often treated to such revelations. It heard more about the Americans' ultramodern warfare in the South Pacific, and the news from there at the beginning of 1944 grew steadily worse. Highly confused communiqués indicated a fresh northwesterly advance in the Battle of the Pacific. The war of the atolls was now raging in the Marshall Islands, coral rings scattered under the equator. An American landing was expected in the easternmost islands, which were defended by a network of fortified bases. But these were boldly turned by the Americans who, on January 31, 1944, struck far behind them to the west at Kwajalein, the world's largest atoll and the key to the Marshalls. It was taken in three days of fierce fighting against the fanatical resistance of the 3,900-man Japanese garrison. On February 24, Eniwetok, even farther to the west, also fell to the invaders.

The Japanese communiqués insisted on the fact that most of the fortified positions held by the forces of the Rising Sun were still intact and that the enemy merely occupied secondary islands that the high command had not bothered to defend. But Japanese who took the trouble to figure out what was happening and to follow operations on a map understood that each new hop in this leapfrog offensive brought the Americans closer to the Philippines and neutralized the strong points they outflanked, isolating them with attacks by carrier-based planes.

Indeed, the general public was hearing more and more talk about the exploits of America's *task forces*. The phrase, which was to recur incessantly in communiqués until the end of the war, designated naval attack formations varying in composition with the missions assigned to them. The day of fixed-strength squadrons had long since ended. Flattops no longer functioned as escort vessels for the battleships; now they made up the nucleus of a task force, they were the kings of naval warfare and it was the battleships, more often than not, that escorted the carriers. Refueled at secret mid-ocean rendezvous by its elaborate supply chain, a task force could remain at sea for weeks without returning to base.

Task Force 58, which became famous throughout the Pacific and even in Japan, first appeared on February 18, 1944, before the island of Truk, the most important bastion in these fortified archipelagos that no white man had been allowed to visit for fifteen years. Attacks on two successive days by 450 carrier-based American planes laid bare the weakness of its defenses; Japanese losses in planes and ships were severe.

The next blow fell farther north, on the island of Saipan in the Marianas, on February 23. This was an even more daring move, one that was to have a powerful impact on future operations: the task force had moved 700 miles closer to Tokyo and, once again, the Japanese defenses were shown to be unexpectedly weak at a point of crucial strategic importance, a weakness the Americans would exploit four months later.

At the end of March, the offensive redoubled in intensity. United States naval units attacked in the Carolines, second in importance only to the Marianas as Japanese defense positions between the South Seas and the home islands. At the end of April, after steaming for a week through supposedly Japanese waters, the task force again hit Truk as well as Ponapé; the only opposition met by its bombers, which inflicted heavy damage everywhere they hit, was fierce antiaircraft fire.

The Japanese public may not have followed this series of grave setbacks very clearly, but to the admiralty in Tokyo, the situation was all too obvious: General Tojo's drive to reinforce Japanese air power had not produced the hoped-for results. The navy could not hold in the Central Pacific because it lacked sufficient air support. For the moment, it was the Japanese land positions that were at the mercy of American attackers; the fleet's turn was next.

Navy men declared they could no longer accept the subordinate position assigned to them in the war. Because the Prime Minister was a soldier, they said, the army had the last word in all high-strategy decisions; it had not yet understood that the Greater Asia War was essentially a naval war, and it dissipated the nation's strength in useless operations on distant continental fronts. What was crucial, the navy charged, was that the army grabbed off the priorities in the distribution of armaments, especially in the allocation of new planes; most of these were being dispatched to land fronts just when the navy was critically short of them.

This was not a new quarrel; it was simply the old rivalry between the army and navy, or, as they were described in Tokyo, the star and the anchor, flaring up again in the midst of the war. Once upon a time, it had been the army that complained of the navy cornering supplies. Army men said that after the 1941–42 conquests, the navy, which controlled the ships that brought home the wealth—rice, metals, oil—Japan had just seized in the south, helped itself first; they accused their rivals of stockpiling most of the raw materials needed for national defense and keeping the army on short rations. It was to redress this imbalance that Tojo, while launching his campaign for aircraft production, created a brand-new ministerial department—the Munitions Ministry—which he personally headed.

At the end of 1943, the new department, supplanting the old Planning Bureau and assuming its job of coordinating production, tried to bring all war industry under its control. It only half succeeded. The navy, quite rightly labeling the new ministry a tool of the army, jealously retained its authority over all the factories assigned to it. In principle, the newly created plants were to deliver half the new planes they turned out to the army and the other half to the navy. But the row between the two clans extended into the factories themselves; the example was cited of one plant that had been cut in two and a wall pierced by steel doors erected between the two halves to prevent raids by one side against the other's materials and finished planes.

The navy's discontent was exacerbated by the fact that the nature of the war had gradually boosted officers of the naval air arm into the top ranks. Until Midway, no decision had been reached in the quarrel between the traditional school, that still looked for major fleet engagements in which battleships would play the star role, and the champions of the new naval theories, who said the day of the battleship was over and insisted that the navy's whole effort be concentrated on aircraft carriers and their planes. Now the new men had won, but this did not entirely eliminate friction between the two sides; for one thing, the "orthodox" thinkers were all Naval Academy graduates, whereas few of the naval air officers had gone through this distinguished training school and some had even risen through the ranks. Faced with the defeats in the South Pacific in the spring of 1944, however, the whole navy closed ranks in a unified clamor for more planes. At Truk, the Mitsubishi "0s" were not only inferior numerically, but they were also outclassed by the Americans' new Grumman fighters. The American attacks in the Carolines and at Saipan showed, moreover, that the enemy's air superiority, combined with the mobility of its floating airfields, could now threaten the Japanese coasts, which lacked adequate air cover, and wrest from the Japanese Navy its control of hitherto impenetrable sectors of the Pacific.

Tojo was not the navy's sole target; it also went out after its own representative in the government, Navy Minister Shigetaro Shimada. After three years of work with Tojo, Shimada had become the Prime Minister's devoted aide. This small, dark, amiable man whose austere uniform, bare of braid or decorations, gave him the serious air of a Japanese clergyman, was a weak, characterless man. He was entirely dominated by the general, who increasingly appreciated him as his own irritability grew to where he could tolerate none but obedient servants around him.

Shimada had lost all credit with the navy in an affair that had conclusively proved his weakness. Admiral Soemu Toyoda, respected by the navy and a notable contributor to the creation of the fleet air arm, had urged Shimada early in 1943 to insist on a greater share of new aircraft for the navy. Together they developed a plan under which the army would give the navy half its planes and aircraft factories; Shimada formally promised to secure the government's approval. When the discussion reached the cabinet, Tojo opposed the Toyoda plan and Shimada bowed without further protest. That day the navy lost the only chance it had to redress its position in time to affect the war effort.

In the first weeks of 1944, representatives of the younger naval officers and the naval air arm worked out a plan of action against Shimada, whom they now called "Tojo's geisha." It was almost a conspiracy. They appealed to Admiral Zengo Yoshida, commander of naval forces in China, and asked him to see that the minister was removed at all costs. Yoshida was a man of considerable authority in the fleet and the general staff. He had been an intimate friend of Admiral Yamamoto; they had been in the same graduating class at the Naval Academy, had received the same grades—Yoshida was first in the class and Yamamoto second only for having missed a day of classes because he had the grippe. Yoshida and Shimada had also been classmates, which is why the appeal had gone to him. But Yoshida bungled it. Busy intriguing to become chief of the naval staff, he waited for the situation to develop, giving Tojo time to deal with it. Instead of firing Shimada, Tojo increased his authority. Thus began an acute crisis in the high command that was to paralyze the government when the Americans struck a decisive blow at the heart of Japan's defensive system.

12

Tojo's Fall

A few days after the American attack on Truk, General Tojo abruptly set about reorganizing the army and navy general staffs. Old Marshal Sugiyama, who was to Japan what General George C. Marshall was at that time to the American Army, was dismissed. So was Admiral Osami Nagano, chief of naval operations and Japan's counterpart to America's Admiral Ernest J. King. These men were not only the two highest-ranking officers in the Japanese services, they were also the two most prestigious men in the armed forces and the two great architects of Japan's early victories in the war. Public opinion credited the marshal with having planned and executed the Japanese armies' triumphant advance in the tropics in 1941–42, the admiral with having conceived the blow at Pearl Harbor. Tojo removed them from power by kicking them upstairs to honorary posts on the Imperial Defense Council.

Who replaced them? None other than Tojo himself and his faithful Shimada. Henceforth the Prime Minister and his Navy Minister would complement their governmental duties with direction of the respective general staffs; in other words, they took over both the administration and active direction of operations. Tojo had smelled the storm coming. To parry his growing opposition, especially from the navy, he consolidated his own position and that of the sole naval man over whom he still had authority. In himself he concentrated powers that made his course toward a "shogunist" dictatorship more obvious than ever: at this point he was Prime Minister, Minister for War, Munitions Minister and chief of the army general staff; at various times he had also, and concurrently, held the portfolios of Interior Minister and Education Minister. Because his duties as top soldier and head of government took up all his time, he entrusted the post of deputy chief of the army general staff to General Jun Ushiroku, who was well known as a Tojo yes-man.

The opposition was quick to respond. After the American task force's blow at Saipan on February 23, five admirals and five generals, all retired, met in Tokyo to study the alarming situation. They pinpointed Saipan as the weak spot in Japan's defense. The island, they concluded, must be defended at all costs. Old General Baron Sadao Araki, a celebrated patriot and War Minister during the conquest of Manchuria, was sent to Tokyo to submit the conferees' conclusions to the Prime Minister: Saipan's precarious position, the inadequacy of the island's garrison, the urgent need for infantry reinforcements and all available air power. Tojo rejected the delegation's message out of hand, implicitly telling these elderly pensioners simply to mind their own business, that the Prime Minister was perfectly aware of Saipan's importance and did not need advice on how to defend it.

The populace had no inkling of these internal quarrels and only the dimmest notion of how serious Japan's situation was. Yet it reacted sharply to the radio announcement on May 5 of a fresh calamity: Yamamoto's successor as fleet commander, Admiral Mineichi Koga, had just been killed, like his predecessor, in action in the South Pacific. The second supreme naval commander to vanish in less than a year! Nor was the general consternation appeased by the laconic fashion in which the announcement was delivered. The official version merely stated that Koga "died at his post in the month of March in a plane at the front while directing overall operations."

A rumor circulated that he had died in an accidental crash. This in fact is what happened. Koga had been surprised on March 30 by an American task-force attack on Palau, in the Carolines. He had been able to get his flagship, the battleship *Musashi*, away in time to regain its base at Kure despite serious torpedo damage inflicted by an American submarine. The naval commander and his staff hid out on land, in a concrete bunker, throughout the attack, which lasted from 6 P.M. on March 30 until dawn of March 31. On April 1, the task force moved off to attack Yap, and Koga and his followers decided to fall back on Davao, in the Philippines. They took off in two seaplanes at 9:30 that morning. They never reached their destination.

A few weeks later, Vice-Admiral Fukutome, a member of Koga's staff, was unexpectedly found on the island of Cebu, not far from Davao; he had been recovered from a Filipino guerrilla force that had taken him prisoner. He said the seaplane in which he was traveling with his commander had run into a tornado the day after they left Palau and had crashed into the sea, as the other plane must also have done. Fukutome, rescued by Filipino fishermen, had been turned over to the guerrillas and then delivered to tell his tale.

Back to Tokyo again came a little white box symbolically containing the fleet commander's ashes. There was no national funeral, however, which led public opinion to conclude that Koga's death was not as glorious as Yamamoto's had been. A successor was chosen: Admiral Soemu Toyoda, the man who had made a fruitless appeal to Shimada on behalf of the naval air arm. Toyoda was a fervent advocate of his navy's air force, which he had helped organize as director of that department in the Navy Ministry. Highly popular with the rank and file, he was reputed to favor offensive warfare. In this he differed from Koga, who had thoroughly justified his reputation for moderation and caution during his year in the supreme command; between Yamamoto's death and his own, there had not been a single major sea fight. With Toyoda, it was murmured, there would be some action at last. The thought dismayed some people in Tokyo who preferred Koga's calmness. What perils now faced the great Japanese fleet, or what was left of it? For the moment, it was invisible; part of it was no doubt hiding in Japanese ports, but most of it was probably cut off in the China Sea between Formosa and Singapore, behind the rampart formed by the Philippines and the Dutch East Indies. And where would the American fleet strike next? It was currently prowling unhampered through the whole Central Pacific, only a step to the east of the Philippines.

June 15: a thunderbolt! The Americans had landed on Saipan, in the Marianas. So they had not struck westward, toward the Asian continent, but due north, toward Japan itself. The blow had fallen precisely where Tojo, despite the warning contained in the February 23 attack and the plea of the retired generals and admirals, had maintained that there was nothing to fear.

Tokyo felt the landing as a major disaster. By reaching for Saipan, the enemy, bolder than ever, had again bypassed secondary positions and struck at the heart of the Japanese defensive system. The island was the first stage in a series of archipelagos—the Marianas, the Bonins and the Izu Islands—which, like a rope ladder stretched under Japan itself, reached to Tokyo. Saipan, the Japanese said, was the "gateway to the south," the key outpost south of the Japanese mainland, the first port of call for ships heading toward the equator and an obligatory refueling stop for the airlines which, in better days, had flown as far as Timor, near Australia. The archipelago empire under the flag of the Rising Sun was spread like an inverted fan over the whole South Pacific; its lines of communication—the leaves of the fan—all converged in Saipan, their central relay station. This was the capital of the Marianas, occupied by Japan for the previous twenty-nine years; the island of Guam had been taken from the Americans at the time of Pearl Harbor and so had only been Japanese for two and a half years. Guam is just south of Saipan and was also an extremely important base; its recapture would give the American public its first real taste of revenge for the grim days of December 1941.

Intense attack from the air, followed by forty-eight hours of heavy bombardment by the task force's battleships, had preceded the landing on Saipan. Contrary to Tojo's assurances, the island had been insufficiently and tardily fortified. Its defenses were concentrated in the northern part of the island, but it was on the west side, on a coast the Japanese thought was protected by its coral reefs, that the American assault troops came ashore. The first waves were allowed to get an easy foothold on the beach; then the defenders raked them with furious fire. So badly were the invading infantrymen pinned down on the second day that the American command threw in its reserves to consolidate the bridgehead.

In Tokyo, to reassure an alarmed public opinion and to defend itself against accusations from the navy, the army propaganda machine used the media to develop the thesis that an island like Saipan must be defended on land, not in naval and air battles offshore. Army spokesmen earnestly explained that the proper tactic was to let the enemy land; only then would Japanese artillery and infantry, backed up, of course, by such air power as was needed, show their invincibility and hurl the invaders back into the sea.

The navy replied by outlining its "oceanic" tactic: that the best way to stop a landing was . . . not to let the enemy land. The place to fight was at sea, before the invaders set foot on land—and for that, enough planes were needed to block the invasion fleet's access to the target coasts. Admiral Toyoda attempted to do just that before the Americans landed. On June 19, off Saipan in the Philippine Sea, the biggest naval battle since hostilities began was fought. Conforming to the new developments in modern warfare, the battle was waged without the ships' guns ever coming into play. Both fleets sent their airplanes to do the work.

The Japanese, who had waited so long for their hour to strike, had prepared an American-style task force centered on 9 aircraft carriers with a total of 450 planes. But their attack squadrons, inferior in quality and quantity to the Americans', were unable to pierce the aerial umbrella protecting Admiral Raymond A. Spruance's fleet. Nearly four hundred Japanese planes were shot down and Toyoda's fleet fled; luckily for the Japanese, the American reconnaissance planes anxiously searching for the fleeing ships did not spot them until they were too far away and darkness was falling. Spruance decided against pursuit because his main job was to protect the invasion force.

If the Americans had hoped to wipe out Japan's surface fleet in this battle, they were disappointed and, to this degree, its outcome was undecisive. This was all the Tokyo propagandists needed to announce that the American fleet had been defeated with heavy losses. The "naval victory" came just in time: another Allied landing had been made—in Normandy on June 6. The

Japanese gasped and tried to understand how "fortress Europe" could have been breached when Nazi propaganda chief Joseph Goebbels, whose outpourings were fed to them in massive doses by the German DNB agency, had proclaimed it impregnable.

Organized resistance on Saipan collapsed on July 8. The gateway to the south had fallen, although the Japanese people still did not know it. They had been told that the situation there was desperate, but that the fight was not yet over, that indomitable resistance was still being waged from the island's caves. Tojo knew the announcement of the fall of Saipan might bring about his own fall. He hoped to defuse that bomb by presenting himself simultaneously with the news release at the head of a new cabinet made up of the men who had opposed him in the weeks gone by. His idea was to constitute a government of national union into which he would invite Japan's most famous men, all grouped under his command to carry on the struggle.

But he knew the navy hated him and would certainly try to nullify his plan. So he and his faithful Shimada plotted a typical trick: Shimada, a voluntary sacrifice, would be replaced by a new minister who was popular with the navy, but the general staff's consent would not be sought in advance. The new man would have to be presented as an already functioning minister, would show that he and Tojo formed a united team and so present the admiralty with a *fait accompli*. The new cabinet would be grouped around these two men, the Prime Minister and his sailor.

On July 16, Tojo's emissaries arrived at the naval base at Kure to offer the ministerial portfolio to Admiral Naokuni Nomura (not to be confused with Kichisaburo Nomura, the ambassador to Washington at the time of Pearl Harbor). The admiral was an old sea dog, an expert in submarine warfare who was mainly preoccupied with technical problems; Tojo chose him because he knew Nomura had been too far removed from Tokyo to be involved in its political intrigues. When the admiral was told that he had been requested by the Emperor, he bowed, packed his suitcase and took the train to Tokyo with the men who had been sent to seek him. In the capital, however, the admiralty heard vague reports of the scheme; officers of the navy general staff were rushed to the central railway station to meet the new arrival the moment he set foot in Tokyo and urge him to be on his guard against Tojo's maneuvers.

Tojo had anticipated the counterattack. His men took the admiral off the train a few stops before Tokyo and brought him to the Prime Minister, who was waiting in his limousine. Together they went directly to the palace, where things had been arranged in advance with the Emperor—who knew nothing of what was really going on. In Tojo's presence, Hirohito himself invested Nomura with the navy portfolio. Only after he had left the palace and had gone to the ministry was the admiral finally located by Tojo's opponents and told of the Prime Minister's incredible trick. Reproach and sarcasm were heaped on Nomura, but what could he do? The Emperor himself had been fooled. There was no going back now.

The newspapers of July 17 announced the new minister's appointment. Shimada, however, had only half ceded his place; he retained the functions of chief of the navy general staff. At Tojo's behest, it was explained (exactly the opposite explanation had been given five months previously) that combining ministerial duties with direction of the general staff prejudiced the proper conduct of operations and was too heavy a burden for one man. This now applied to Tojo as well: he kept the War Ministry along with the Prime Minister's post, but he gave his command of the army general staff to the famous General Yoshijiro Umezu, commander-in-chief of the Japanese Army in Manchukuo, the so-called Kwantung Army. It was a shrewd move because it gave partial satisfaction to those who complained that Tojo was grabbing too much power to himself, that he aimed to become dictator.

Now was the time for the maneuver's second phase: assembling a cabinet of notables. Tojo's idea was to call on the distinguished members of the group of elder statesmen called the *Jushin*, or former prime ministers. He particularly thought of offering portfolios to Koki Hirota and Baron Kiichiro Hiranuma, both convinced nationalists, to Admiral Mitsumasa Yonai and General Nobuyuki Abe, both of whom had headed conservative cabinets in 1939, and, finally, to Prince Konoye, with whom he sought a reconciliation. All of them refused.

Tojo had ignored them—even deceived them—for too long to win their support now. Since the previous reign, former prime ministers had met periodically in a council that gradually assumed some of the influence and the function once exercised by the *Genro*—members of the Council of Elders—whose opinion was often sought by Emperor Meiji in matters of high policy. The new council of the Jushin traditionally had been consulted by all the prime ministers in office since Hirohito's reign began, especially when a major crisis arose. Since October 1941, however, Tojo had merely toyed with them; he had convoked them only rarely and then not to ask their advice but to impose his orders on them without discussion.

The group's moving spirit was Admiral Keisuke Okada, an outstanding figure in the naval hierarchy, in which he passed for a Grand Old Man, an experienced and respected counselor. He had been Prime Minister during the 1936 military rebellion and had only miraculously escaped assassination. Liberal and moderate in his views, he had tried in 1941 to avoid the war, and he detested Tojo, who had kept him in limbo since then. His experience in 1936 had bred in him an abiding hatred of extremist soldiers and a profound mistrust of the army. He was closely leagued with Prince Konoye, another mover on the council of ex-premiers; both considered Tojo responsible for the disastrous war in the Pacific and they were determined to get rid of him. Admiral Yonai, second only to Okada as a respected naval leader, had long been fiercely opposed to Tojo, and the trick played on Nomura only intensified his enmity. Marquess Koichi Kido, the Emperor's Keeper of the Privy Seal and chief adviser to the throne in cabinet crises—he was called the cabinet-maker—had been a longtime ally of Tojo, but he now went over to Konoye's camp.

Dictator that he was, Tojo had not gauged how much everyone now hated him. One sign of the times was a plot—a real plot like those that had sent the heads flying from the shoulders of more than one prime minister in the past. The conspirators were nationalists of the extreme right—Nakano's blood cried out for vengeance—and young naval officers. But, in a typically Japanese gesture, some of the navy men warned Okada of what they planned to do. He persuaded them to hold off, formally promising to unseat Tojo.

But the general hung on. Until the last minute, he stubbornly believed he could organize a reform cabinet around himself. Learning that his adversaries were already involved in political horsetrading to put together a new cabinet, he even threw cordons of military police around the homes of Prince Konoye, in the suburb of Ogikubo, and Marquess Kido in Tokyo. Telephone lines to both houses were cut and the two men completely isolated. Tojo nursed one final illusion: that he still had the Emperor's confidence. But Hirohito, after years of being hoodwinked by his Prime Minister, decided after the Nomura business to get rid of him. Having received the former premiers' advice through Kido, he had already determined to put the navy in charge of the next cabinet. The army had made too many mistakes, its chief was thoroughly discredited. And Tojo was now paying for a subtler, more serious mistake than all his conniving, all his responsibility in a war that was heading for catastrophe: he had deceived the throne and offended the Son of Heaven.

Since Tojo refused to leave voluntarily, he was sent a formal notice from the palace: the Emperor no longer wished him as Prime Minister; he would have to go. The general finally bowed and submitted his government's resignation en bloc to the sovereign. This was on July 18, 1944, exactly two years and nine months after the "Pearl Harbor cabinet" assumed power.

In all the commotion surrounding this crisis, only one detail had been overlooked: informing the public of what was happening. Until that July 18, the Japanese people had not even been told of the loss of Saipan. Organized resistance had virtually ended on the island ten days earlier, but the crisis, boiling up under its lid of secrecy, repeatedly delayed public admission of the defeat. Besides, agreement had not quite been reached on the new cabinet. No War Minister had yet been chosen. General Kuniaki Koiso was mentioned, but he was in Seoul; he would have to be recalled to Tokyo at once, which meant that the crisis could not be resolved for another two or three days. Meanwhile, the decision was made to lift the secrecy concealing the fall of Saipan, but to maintain silence on Tojo's ouster. The cabinet's July 18 resignation would not be publicly announced until July 21.

On the morning of July 19, the whole country learned of the loss of Saipan. It was informed that, as was customary, the final Japanese attack took the form of a furious charge at dawn following prayers for the Empire and a last banzai for those who were about to die heroically for their Emperor. It was admitted that the attack had taken place on July 7 and, to cover up what had been happening in the interval, the announcement specified that the battle had continued until the sixteenth. U.S. newspaper reports of the fighting, picked up by radio, were rewritten by Domei and the Information Bureau to sound even more truculent than the originals. The Japanese commander, General Yoshiji Saito, pulling together a force of 1,500 to 3,000 men, almost repeated the feat of the last defenders of Attu. After the customary suicide of their invalids, the survivors hurled themselves into the attack shortly before dawn on July 7, breaking through the American line (no mention was made in Tokyo that on the way they massacred the wounded in an American field hospital), and were finally stopped by artillery batteries firing at them from a distance of some fifty-five yards.

General Saito, wounded in the charge, committed hara-kiri; the Americans reported they found his body in a cemetery; it had been decapitated with a saber wielded by an aide who had helped him in his suicide. The naval commander at Saipan, Admiral Nagumo, also killed himself. He had led the Japanese attack on Pearl Harbor as well as the abortive expedition against Midway; with him disappeared one of the three or four most prominent fleet officers. Admiral Hiichi Hasegawa, the naval air commander at Saipan, died in action, probably in the naval battle in the Philippine Sea. Many officers and men with them also committed suicide, some with traditional ritual, but most of them in a more modern, more expeditious way: blowing themselves up with grenades. Japanese losses (the American figure was not released in

Tokyo) were estimated at 30,000 men on Saipan, plus over 10,000 more on the neighboring islands of Guam, Rota and Tinian, which were taken by the Americans soon afterward. On Guam, U.S. troops took a relatively large number of Japanese prisoners: 86. (Because the rule, as we know, was for a Japanese soldier to kill himself rather than surrender, the number of prisoners taken was usually much lower.)

The most extraordinary scenes connected with the fall of Saipan, revealed with a thundering barrage of Japanese propaganda, involved the civilian population of colonists, planters and bureaucrats who could not be evacuated after the June 15 landing. These ordinary people, including many women and children, had been terrorized by their official propagandists into believing that the Americans were brutes of whom they could expect nothing but rape and murder. So most of the civilians hid in the caves that speckled the island's high cliffs. At the Americans' approach, many blew themselves up with grenades deep inside the caves or at the cave mouths. Mothers strangled their children with their own hands. Girls and women, after donning their funeral clothes and ceremoniously arranging their hair at the edge of the sheer cliffs, threw themselves down before the eyes of American soldiers who watched their bodies break up on the rocks or disappear into the ocean.

One party of U. S. Marines was a distant witness to a grotesque spectacle. About fifty civilians, including some children, were tossing unprimed grenades back and forth, as though they were playing ball, for practice. From a nearby cave leaped a group of soldiers howling guttural orders. The civilians then pulled the pins on the grenades and blew themselves up while the soldiers committed suicide, some using their revolvers, others their rifles. Probably to avoid having their aim spoiled by the guns' recoil, they leaned against the cliff, held their rifles in both hands, put the muzzles in their mouths and pulled the triggers with their toes.

Another scene unfolding at the foot of the high, white walls on this part of the island was watched by American soldiers atop the cliffs. Some one hundred civilians, men and women, undressed among the rocks and bathed, washing themselves meticulously, then put on clean clothes. They spread a huge Rising Sun flag over the rocks, saluted their distant conquerors, then killed themselves with grenades to the last person; the blue waves washed the rocks clean of their torn bodies.

Tokyo Radio and the newspapers accompanied all these recitals with comments designed to raise the Japanese people's morale. The broadcasters, especially, had developed a real technique for reporting disasters. Announcement of the communiqué was surrounded by a kind of solemn din. An orchestra played the poignant "Hymn of the Dead":

> *If I go on the sea,*
> *My corpse will dissolve in the water;*
> *If I go in the mountains,*
> *My body will be covered with moss:*
> *I will have died for the Emperor,*
> *I will have gone with no regret.*

The Imperial General Staff's most celebrated spokesmen recited the news. They were followed throughout the day by countless commentators, orators, retired admirals, police chiefs, former cabinet ministers, famous journalists, etc., parroting the domestic propagandists' prefabricated phrases in those rough voices that give the Japanese language a certain sad weightiness: the "indomitable spirit" of the Hundred Million, "united like a single ball of fire," would finally "rekindle their determination" and they would "launch themselves like human bombs, crushing the despairing enemy with their bodies." The United States, by taking Saipan and daring to come within striking distance of Japan, was "digging its grave"; as its forces approached the "Japanese fortress," their extended lines of communication would leave them at the mercy of the "final blow" to be dealt them by Great Japan's "invincible fleet."

As soon as he arrived in Tokyo, General Koiso agreed to form a cabinet. But he was not to do so alone; the Emperor assigned both Koiso and Admiral Yonai to it. This double investiture was unprecedented. It made for a mixed government in which responsibility would be shared equally by the army and navy. Political circles believed the Emperor had intended to confer full power on the navy after its three years of bullying by the army. But the soldiers were still powerful in the State and Tojo's fall had stirred disquieting unrest in the army. Top military men could not consent to being represented in the cabinet by a mere minister under a navy Prime Minister's authority. So the lame solution of a combined team was adopted and the general, in the final analysis, would preside over the cabinet with the understanding that the navy was no longer to be subordinate to the army.

The public still had to be informed of General Tojo's dismissal and replacement. Things were so well arranged, secrecy aiding, that the political crisis, instead of being revealed along with the military and naval crisis, was not brought to light until two days after the announcement of the fall of Saipan. That made two crises instead of one, and the country felt a countershock after the first upheaval like those that follow major earthquakes.

Koiso and Yonai formed their cabinet. The toughest problem was finding a War Minister. It had been customary since the Emperor Meiji's reign to allow the army to nominate its own man for the post so that it could be sure it was represented in the government by a man it fully trusted. More precisely, it had become the rule that the outgoing War Minister would choose his successor after agreement with the general staff and the military bureaus. General Tojo would have to be consulted, therefore, and asked to nominate someone. Whom do you suppose he chose? Why, Tojo, of course. In a final bid for power, he nominated himself; if he could no longer head the government, he would at least retain considerable authority as War Minister.

This was too cynical. Since the situation had to be spelled out, someone took it on himself to tell the general—for the second time—that the Emperor wanted no part of him, at any price, in any post. He was to propose another name. After consulting with the general staff, Tojo designated old Marshal Sugiyama, whom he had formerly retired. Koiso and Yonai agreed, even though the nomination constituted a final lien on the cabinet for Tojo and his clan.

13

The Fleet Wiped Out

Life in Tokyo was becoming more and more difficult and the future looked increasingly black. We in the French colony knew we were prisoners aboard a sinking ship. The secret exultation aroused in us by the Normandy landings and the gradual liberation of France had partly subsided. The war—the war in Europe, that is—would not be over by Christmas 1944, as we had hoped. Would it even end by the following spring? And our war, the one at world's end? It seemed to us it would go on forever, would last long after the fall of Germany and that it would leave none of us alive, that it already promised us a slow, suffocating death. Completely forgotten, totally cut off from news from outside, would we starve? Constantly tightening restrictions were slowly bringing us to that. Or were we destined for police jails and a concentration camp, a constantly sharpening threat?

In the meanwhile, to subsist, we had to submit to the forced labor of the black market. The key word of the day—*yami,* designating the black market—literally means darkness. It truly portrayed a Japan sunk wholly in darkness, where all of life was shadow-colored. Yami was all the shadowy wheeling-dealing one had to do to find food, clothing, a place to live, a little heat; yami was the furtive commission paid, the trades, cheats, swaps. The other word of the hour was *haikyu*—ration. But rationing had long since been revealed as one of the great swindles of wartime Japan. In Europe, as we have noted, the Nazi regime at least provided enough food for the Germans almost until the end of the war. Japan, on the other hand, from its very first victories, had accustomed its subjects to shortages. Exploiting the people's natural inclination toward a frugal, spartan existence, it preached the slogan of *Yase-gaman*—"strength through skinniness"—to rival the "guns or butter" theory dear to Goebbels. The disorder characteristic of the Japanese administration seemed to have found its natural home in the organization of food supplies. Probably alone among the countries at war, Japan had the admirable idea of a rationing system without cards, tickets or points. Except for the rice ration, which in 1944 dropped below a third of normal requirements, doleful, depleted *Suzuki-san,* the average Japanese, had no right to a fixed allotment of any foodstuff in any prescribed amount. He was never allowed to ask for the pittance granted him from what happened to be available that day; he simply took it as it came from his tonarigumi—his neighborhood association, the official distribution agency.

From the most august levels, lost in the unapproachable mystery of Japan's higher civil service, the rations descended rung by rung to the lowest step, the tonarigumi, and the housewives in their silk trousers could never know in advance what they were going to receive. No need now to make the rounds of the shops, to visit the fishmonger, the fruit and vegetable dealer, the butcher, the grocer; the providential tonarigumi, directed by turns by all the neighbors, served as all of these and easily at that, because it usually received nothing from the higher-ups but enough to provide each family with a dried sardine and a quarter of a cucumber per person every two or three days.

Pilferage was shameless at every level of distribution, so that what reached the average family was so ridiculously meager that, from 1943 on, everyone had to patronize the black market or starve. The smaller people's incomes were, the greater their need to deal in the yami to augment their inadequate resources, and to buy, also on the black market, the food that would barely keep them going, sometimes for cash but usually through complicated barter arrangements.

By 1944, the tonarigumi had long since cut off food supplies to Westerners, except for a few distinguished beneficiaries of special rations—diplomats and the handful of whites who were assimilated into Japanese society, all of whom jealously defended their privileges. Meat, butter, eggs, oil, sugar, fruit, milk completely disappeared for Europeans. Butter, in particular, went to factory workers and soldiers who, for lack of anything else, gradually wound up eating it instead of using it, as they did at first, to grease their boots. All a foreigner in Tokyo received was about ten ounces of bread a day plus a little salt and some soya gruel. All our increasingly scanty supplies of food came from our increasingly frustrating search of the black market.

The same regime of shortages led to the disappearance of the most elementary necessities: matches, soap, thread, coal and charcoal, firewood, shoes, leather, nails, paper. Through carelessness or indifference, speculators were very occasionally allowed to market ersatz materials of the most abominable quality, which the Japanese snapped up: papier-mâché sandals, artificial fibers that one washing would reduce to shreds, powders fraudulently represented as vitamin concentrates to restore children's health. In the second year of the war, with the same indifference, the authorities tolerated shortages of those things that could easily have been kept on the market. One might have supposed, for example, that the 75 million Japanese would always have their two-penny sandals, which left them virtually barefoot anyway, yet wooden *geta* and straw *zoris* were among the hardest-to-find rarities. The world's most maritime country, which before the war netted a third of all the fish eaten in the world, was almost completely deprived of fish. This country rich in forests lacked charcoal even though its millions of housewives had never learned to cook their wretched fare on anything but coals. Acquiring a simple porcelain, wood or clay bowl from which to eat one's rice was a real achievement. Gas and electricity were severely rationed; so was ice, which is almost indispensable in Japan, and refrigerators were banned. Also strictly limited were the honorable hot public baths so dear to the Japanese.

A new wave of arrests struck the French colony, especially in Kobe and Yokohama, where the police guarding the ports and the fleet were particularly ferocious. The charge: espionage, as usual. The real reasons: sometimes mere police resentment or demonstrations of zeal; in other cases, an attempt to erect a legal facade behind which to hide the already complete confiscation of the few French firms that operated in Japan before the war. In all cases, the authorities were preparing the ground for a reversal of the so-called policy of tolerance that had given most of the French colony its conditional and precarious freedom. That France was almost entirely liberated from the Nazis alarmed the Japanese secret police, who prepared a file that would enable them at any time to denounce the French in Japan as a dangerous anti-Japanese Fifth Column. A sign of the times: the newspapers accused Indochina of "insincerity," the Japanese term of opprobrium for resistance to Great Japan. We in the French colony in Japan knew that our fate depended entirely on that of Indochina. We were considered neutrals—and dangerous neutrals —only in terms of the government's Indochina policy and our fragile freedom would last only as long as the Japanese allowed Hanoi to remain under a French administration.

Besides, the police and the people of Tokyo were more convinced than before that strangers were spais requiring unflagging surveillance. The probability of air raids in the near future and the course of the war in Europe made foreigners more suspect than ever and it was important to know exactly what they were doing at every moment of the twenty-four hours of every day. My profession as a reporter, made still more worrisome by the fact that I was for all practical purposes a newspaperman without a newspaper, earned me the honor of being closely watched by the following persons: (1) an ordinary uniformed policeman who visited my home nearly every day; (2) a plainclothes detective of the local branch of the special anti-spy police; (3) a member of the Interior Ministry's secret political police; (4) another policeman specially assigned to foreign newsmen, and (5) the most mysterious of them all, a military police officer of the Kempetai. None of these characters but the first ever showed themselves. Unceasing caution, every day, every instant, plus my ability to speak Japanese, which could smooth over many an incident, saved me from arrest except on two occasions, each of which cost me no more than a disagreeable day in a police station; this does not, of course, include the countless hours I spent with the police while they checked my identity papers or issued some permit or other or renewed my registration, etc., etc.

In all fairness, I should recognize that all the ingenuity of the civilian and military police in poisoning our lives did not manage to squelch the deep desire of many Japanese who knew France to show their still lively affection for things French. For years, during better times, Japan had had the leisure to cultivate its wondrously artistic and aesthetic tastes through its contact with France. These the war now forbade, and they were also being stifled by the rise of an ignorant, brutal proletarian mass. There had been a time when Japan mined the resources of French culture, read all its literature in French or in countless translations, especially the work of its contemporary writers, fervently admired French painting and all other displays of French artistry, kept abreast of developments in French science, medicine, law. Even the common people rushed to watch French films, which they preferred to all other foreign movies.

This was all the more sincere and disinterested for the fact that France never tried to propagandize its culture in Japan; that culture exerted its own, independent influence. Even in wartime, the French escaped the official hatred reserved for Anglo-Saxons, the disdain felt for Italians and the ill-disguised antagonism surrounding the Germans, once too powerful and still too arrogant. From time to time, pro-French sympathies surfaced in sincere and spontaneous gestures. Prewar friends showed they had maintained their secret loyalty, that they were waiting for better days in which the real and deep affinities between their country and mine could be publicly reaffirmed.

But by 1944, contact with foreigners had been made virtually impossible by police persecution. Those who attempted it were questioned, threatened, forced to spy on the foreigner and report on his actions, or they were held at a police station for a day or two. This was usually warning enough; back they went underground.

They knew that Japan had gone its German allies one better in having not one but two Gestapos: the Interior Ministry's special political police and the army's Kempetai. They knew above all that the most powerful, most omnipresent and most inevitable of their police were . . . themselves, the policing they did of each other. This was the national vice of military Japan, spyitis, made paroxysmal by the war; 75 million Japanese spying on each other! They would advise the nearest policeman of the slightest departure from the norm registered in their seemingly inattentive but really vigilant watch over their neighbors. Here again, we see the Japanese assisting in their own servitude, cooperating in their own misfortunes. In wartime Japan, in which we have described the disorder, the factional feuds, the fuzzy ideas and laws, who, then, guarded the herd? In the final analysis, real power was in the hands of the police. It was to them, far more than to the Emperor, the government or even the army that popular sovereignty was sacrificed—assuming it had ever existed at all in this people accustomed for centuries to mandatory cooperation with the policemen who subjugated them.

When General Koiso took power, in July 1944, the people expected his government to be worse than Tojo's. His name, linked to the aggressive beginnings of the puppet state of Manchukuo, his tough-old-bird air (shaggy hair, cold eye, bristling mustache and cruel samurai's face), his past speeches championing Japanese nationalism, all suggested that he would inaugurate his rule with a new turn of the screw. And the backs were already bent.

A specialist in Chinese and Manchurian affairs, Koiso, as vice-minister under the fiery General Baron Araki in 1932 and then as commander-in-chief of the Kwantung Army, had been one of the founders of Manchukuo and among the most dangerous propagators of the New Order in Asia. Retired by the army in 1938, he had gone into politics and was named Minister for the Colonies by Baron Hiranuma in 1939 to try to open the Dutch East Indies by ruse and intimidation to Japanese economic penetration. Governor-general in Seoul since 1942, his energetic methods had earned him the nickname of "The Tiger of Korea."

But techniques of government valid in Seoul were not necessarily suitable in Tokyo. And the empire builder had come to power at a time when, like so many Japanese buildings, the edifice had already begun to rot. Koiso was sixty-five years old; a weary Japan had given itself an old Prime Minister. The Tiger's claws were worn down. He had even stopped deserving the other nickname with which his subordinates once saluted his bravura, in the days when they caroused together in the Japanese tea-houses in Hsinking, the capital of Manchukuo. Koiso was a great sake drinker then, and in his cups he would bawl a warrior's song he had composed himself, *"Oryokko Bushi"*; for his vocal talent he was awarded the gracious name of *Kajika,* the "Singing Frog."

Now the tired old warrior showed he had a reflective side, that he was capable of moderation. Instead of tightening the screws to mark his accession to power, he did just the opposite. More rice was distributed, rationing improved, lying bureaucrats were punished, middle-priced restaurants and theaters were reopened. The press conferences Tojo had eliminated were reestablished with chosen representatives of the big newspapers. Everything indicated a wish to react against Tojo's oppressive dictatorship and to reverse the lowering of the country's morale it had caused. Instead of speaking as a soldier, here was Koiso using the abstruse, hazy vocabulary of Confucianism and Shintoism. In his first proclamation to the country, he gave the watchword in two Chinese characters meaning "Great Harmony." As a program for war it was a little disappointing; the lesson may have taken in ruling circles where the clan feuds continued to rage, but it was lost on the Hundred Million, who failed to understand it.

In other statements, Koiso adopted a simple, good-natured tone. In a press interview on his return from the temples of Ise, where he had performed the customary duty of "informing" the Sun Goddess of his rise to power, he declared: "Going through the railroad stations, I saw expressions in the eyes of the people watching my train that seemed to say, 'Go to it, Koiso; if you don't, who knows what might happen?' I turned to my secretary and told him, *'Makoto-ni moshiwake ga nai'* (roughly, 'Really, I don't deserve this, I am not worthy')." And, dropping back into the mists of Shinto, he added, a little bitterly, as a lesson from a surly and superior schoolmaster to children expected to obey him humbly: "Japan is the land of the gods, but unless the country does its utmost, we cannot count on their protection. The reason for the ordeal they are putting us through now is that the nation failed to understand the true and fundamental meaning of our national policy. . . . The enemy raids will certainly come. If we do everything we can and more, only then will the spirits of the gods give us their divine assistance."

His cabinet was humdrum. Aside from Yonai and Koiso himself, the only figure in it of note was Mamoru Shigemitsu, who had succeeded in reannexing the Greater Asia Ministry to the Foreign Ministry, a complete victory for him in the quarrel between the two departments. The other ministers were unknown to the general public; they were conservatives and at least two, Sotaro Ishiwatari in Finance and Taketora Ogata in Information, were close to the Court.

In short, Koiso's team, instead of being a vigorous government of national union, was just another weak cabinet. That weakness was accentuated by the fact that the Prime Minister remained a retired general, having failed to have himself returned to the active list as his partner Yonai had managed to do. Tojo had been strong chiefly because he was a functioning general and War Minister as well as Prime Minister. Koiso was neither an active general nor War Minister. The army gave him lukewarm support at best because it suspected that he was not a sincere diehard. The navy held aloof because Koiso had refused the navy ministry to a stormy old superpatriot, Admiral Nobumasa Suetsugu. The regime of "Great Harmony" was off to a sour start.

Equally clear was the petulance of the god protectors Koiso had evoked. The sole asset inherited from Tojo was the military situation in central and south China, where, between May and July, the army had recaptured from the Chinese most of the airfields used by the Americans. This was expected to ease the pressure on Japanese vessels in the China Sea; more important, it would eliminate the threat of China-based air raids against Japan. Unfortunately for Tokyo, the fall of Saipan nullified this with an even more dangerous threat. Besides, while the south China operations achieved their main objective of linking Canton and Hankow, that is, south and central China, by rail, what they really revealed were Japanese plans for retreat; the China command quickly reestablished lines of communication between Singapore and Shanghai to provide for future evacuation by land of the Japanese armies in south China whose withdrawal by sea was already partially blocked by enemy submarines and the American presence in the newly won U.S. bases.

In the central Pacific, United States forces had completed mopping-up operations in the region they needed as a springboard for attacks on the Philippines and Formosa. The Turtle's Head in Dutch New Guinea was occupied in July; U.S. forces landed on Morotai, which had a good airfield, and on the smaller islands of Peleliu and Angaur, thus neutralizing the 25,000-man Japanese garrison in the Palau Islands; capture of the island of Ulithi gave the Americans an excellent natural port. Once again they were defying the old rules of naval strategy, jumping off from recaptured weak points to outflank Japanese strong points and neutralize them with air attacks. They refused to worry about the sizable enemy garrisons they left isolated hundreds and sometimes thousands of miles behind them in Rabaul, Kavieng, Bougainville, the Marshalls, the Carolines.

On September 7, Koiso appeared before the Parliament, repeating his magical "Great Harmony" prescription for winning the war. Admiral Yonai declared, a little more precisely: "We have a plan for certain victory: draw the enemy still closer, then defeat him with forces inferior to his." But he added that planes and more planes were needed and that current production was inadequate. The press, less tightly muzzled than it had been by Tojo, cited some of the questions from the members of Parliament that revealed the eternal row between the competing armed services over their shares of munitions; they also disclosed disorder and bottlenecks in industry. A secret session was devoted to airplane production. The government issued a reassuring communiqué boasting that Japan was second only to the United States and ahead of Britain and Germany in aircraft production; Japan's output, it said, had doubled from September 1943 to September 1944, while the number of workers in the plane factories had risen by 50 per cent. The truth, not revealed until after the war, was that monthly plane production, which had been 550 at the beginning of the war, reached a peak in June 1944 that could not be maintained and was certainly never exceeded: 2,857 planes a month and some 5,000 engines.

To rekindle parliamentary enthusiasm, Koiso solemnly promised independence to the Dutch East Indies. A last-minute concession when the game was already lost? Not at all. Koiso knew what he was doing. He was maintaining Tojo's policy: applying a policy of chaos throughout the South Pacific, implanting in the people of those peaceful tropical islands the hatred that would explode when the whites returned there.

Where would the enemy turn next? To the Philippines? In September, the islands were pounded from the air from north to south, especially Manila, where, on September 21 and 22, no warning was even sounded. Or Formosa, where the raids came in October? The Japanese showed a certain zeal in barring the approach to this last outpost of their Central Pacific defensive system. One of their aerial counterattacks east of Formosa caused considerable damage to the American fleet. Tokyo was already making a major victory out of it.

Then, on October 20, the blow fell, in the Philippines—but not where the Japanese were expecting it. They had thought the Americans would reach for Mindanao, at the foot of the archipelago. Instead, they struck in the center of the islands' spine—at Leyte, where Japanese defenses had been depleted to reinforce the south. An armada of six hundred ships entered Leyte Gulf; bridgeheads were rapidly established with only minor losses. And MacArthur broadcast his famous appeal to the Filipinos: "I have returned!"

But, on September 26, the naval section of the Imperial General Staff in Tokyo announced a smashing naval victory. The Japanese fleet, it said, slipping through the southern islands from the Sea of Mindanao, surprised the American vessels at anchor in Leyte Gulf and inflicted heavy damage on them. The battle was not yet over, but enthusiastic commentary was already hailing the extraordinary boldness of the attack and the unequaled daring of the Japanese seamen who had brought their ships at night through the narrow Surigao Straits. Reports described the Americans' confusion when their transports were caught like sitting ducks in the narrow gulf, at the attackers' mercy. On the following day, Tokyo Radio announced a new feat: repeating the Mindanao gambit farther north, a strong Japanese naval force had pushed through the San Bernardino Straits in the central Philippines and attacked the American fleet; again, Tokyo trumpeted, already detailed American losses forecast more to come. In fact, the battle had gone against the Japanese, who ran into a formidable defensive screen. The Imperial Staff's orchestration of the recitals suddenly went pianissimo. Spokesmen abruptly forgot that they had promised the public another installment of the epic. The battle was veiled in a propaganda smokescreen; overall statistics were published that buried details of the operation in vague, general summaries. This obvious sleight-of-hand escaped the notice of newspaper readers and radio audiences. Torpid for long months, deprived of any chance of knowing what the enemy was saying, feeding on hopes and illusions, they swallowed the communiqués whole.

And the Information Bureau, at the orders of the Imperial Staff whose trumped-up reports it distributed, somehow managed the scarcely credible exploit of slipping the biggest naval battle of the Pacific War—the biggest, in fact, ever fought—almost unnoticed past the Japanese public. Japan was not to know that the United States had scored its most resounding victory in the Philippines and that the annihilated Japanese fleet would afterward be unable with what little remaining strength it had to block the final assault on Japan itself. Until the last moment, the leadership's silence, allegedly maintained for security reasons, allowed the people to think that a still-powerful navy was saving itself for the supreme test. Until the very end, the country's leaders dangled the hope of a final triumph when they themselves knew perfectly well that the great fleet of the Rising Sun was now just a phantom fleet.

What had happened in the Philippines? Admiral Toyoda, his offensive spirit intact, thought there was no further point in dispersing and restraining Japan's forces, as had too often been done in the past against an enemy who concentrated his ships in powerful armadas. Better go for broke. So Toyoda engaged nearly three-fourths of the Imperial fleet, organized in three battle groups: one from Singapore, the second from Indochina's Cam Ranh Bay and the third from Formosa. They had a common objective: to surprise the American ships standing in Leyte Gulf and destroy them when the invasion troops began fighting on land. MacArthur would then be stranded and his infantry, without naval support, would be prey to Japanese army counterattacks on Leyte.

The squadron coming from the south did succeed in getting through the Sea of Mindanao and the Surigao Straits, but instead of surprising the Americans, as the premature Japanese accounts had reported, it fell into a trap in the darkness before dawn on October 25. Six American battleships were waiting for it where the straits open into Leyte Gulf, and they slaughtered the unsuspecting Japanese. Among the big Nipponese vessels lost were at least two battleships and a heavy cruiser.

As the central task force emerged from the narrow channels through which it had crossed the Philippines from west to east on October 24, it came under massive air attack that, among other casualties, sank the famous, secret 69,000-ton superbattleship *Musashi*. The Japanese admiral skillfully pretended to retreat to return to the fight later, reappearing to the east in the Philippine Sea. There his squadron encountered units of the American fleet, which had also been divided in three to conform with local geography. Four American destroyers and an aircraft carrier were sent to the bottom, but this time the Japanese maneuvered clumsily, lost time and finally, not daring to attack the enemy's main force, turned tail and raced back the way they had come, pursued by American planes.

The third Japanese squadron, having rounded the Philippines north of Luzon, ran into six American aircraft carriers and a number of battleships. The Japanese launched a vain air attack. Then the Americans counterattacked, sinking all four of the Japanese carriers and two light cruisers. Only two battleships, one of them badly damaged, got away.

Total: three battleships, four carriers, six heavy cruisers and three light cruisers sunk, not to mention a number of destroyers; four more cruisers severely damaged. But the only hint that might have allowed the Japanese people to suspect the scope of the disaster was contained in what was apparently a slip by Tokyo Radio, which announced some time later that Japan lost twenty-two admirals in September and October. The last of them, the report added, died when he crashed his plane into an American carrier.

Highly placed people in the Koiso cabinet and outside of it seriously considered ending the war in the autumn of 1944. Germany, invaded from east and west, beaten in Italy, cringing under Allied bombs, was heading for collapse. A negotiated peace for Japan at that critical moment, before the fall of the Reich and before the bombings began in Tokyo, would save much from the ruins. But the partisans of all-out war had a powerful argument handed to them by the Allies themselves: they knew that the Japanese surrender would have to be unconditional. Army propagandists had been harping on this idea since the end of 1943, after the Allies' conference in Cairo, making it their chief weapon in the army's campaign for a fight to the finish.

Berlin, too, encouraged the "German clan" in Tokyo to support the Axis cause. A whispering campaign spread the notion that terrible "secret weapons" would bring a dramatic reversal of the war in Europe. One day that fall, I learned indirectly from a Japanese source, in great confidence, that wild excitement reigned in the offices of Tokyo Radio. Hitler was about to broadcast an extraordinary announcement to the world that he had a device that could blow up the planet and that he was going to summon the Allies to make peace with him or he would use it. Did Hitler think he had an atomic bomb? Was he trying to make the Japanese think he had it? At the appointed hour, Tokyo Radio's monitors were on the alert. But the speech was never made.

Besides, what difference did it make what discussions for or against peace might have taken place then in Tokyo? Japan's slide toward catastrophe was picking up speed, and the only active force in the country—the army—was relentlessly pushing the country down the slope. The Koiso cabinet was no longer in control of events. And among all the forces overwhelming it and obliging it to continue the struggle was the frenzy to die for the

Emperor that had now reached paroxysm in the army. How could Koiso have dared to sue for peace when thousands of soldiers were rushing to their deaths? The clamor of their ultimate banzais reverberated in Tokyo itself and even generated a last surge of vitality in the faltering government.

In mid-November, an Imperial General Staff communiqué, issued with maximum fanfare, informed the nation that suicide was being used systematically as a combat technique. For the first time, it exalted the exploits of the *kamikaze* or "special attack corps" of the Japanese Air Force. The annals of Japanese military heroism were already full of individual cases of infantrymen transforming themselves into human bombs; the navy had had its "special submarines"; but never before had official policy envisaged the training of large numbers of volunteers pledged to destroy themselves on their targets.

The term "kamikaze" means "wind of the gods" and it touched deep chords in Japanese imaginations. It evoked the defeat of Kublai Khan's Mongol invasion in the thirteenth century, against which, according to legend, the divine guardians of the sacred soil whipped up a violent tempest, hurling the invincible Mongol armada back into the sea just as it was about to land. But the "wind of the gods" no longer meant the fury of the elements; now it signified the heroic fury of those twenty-year-old pilots who, in the battle for Leyte Gulf, dived from the skies into American warships and transports with the idea of paying for the life of each suicidal flier with the loss of an enemy ship and its entire crew.

The Imperial Staff announcement and the flamboyant comments that surrounded it were not designed merely to reveal the heroism of Japan's fliers; they were also a maneuver for combating defeatism in the government, and they kicked off a campaign to persuade the Hundred Million that everyone would shortly be called on to commit national suicide for the Emperor. Nine aviators in their twenties, members of the "Banda special attack corps" under the direction of a Captain Iwamoto, were the first to sacrifice themselves, the communiqué specified, sinking an American battleship. Thousands were to follow them; there were more volunteers than there were planes for them. Systematic training in suicide bombing had been going on for months and was now about to bear fruit. The great majority of kamikaze pilots were university students, the cream of Japanese youth whose studies Tojo had brutally interrupted in 1943–44 to send the boys to war. And the newspapers all carried, at length, the official instructions given by the inspector general of air forces to the first special attack corps, whose members perished in the Philippines:

> The Empire is at a crossroads between triumph and a fall. The success of the first suicide unit, which is resolved to win victory through spiritual force, will bring other units in its wake, one after another. Your mission is certain death. You will die physically, but your spirits will not die. The death of any one of you will be the birth of a million others. Let no negligence affect your training or your health; you must leave behind you no cause for regret that will remain with you for eternity. One thing more: no excess in your haste to die. If you do not find the desired objective, turn back; you will have good luck the next time. Choose a death that gives maximum results.

14

Tokyo Aflame

On November 1, 1944, at 1 P.M., the sirens howled their brief warnings in Tokyo. Millions of throats tightened: this was the first real alert since the Doolittle raid. And with the Americans on Saipan, half a day's flight away, this would certainly not be an isolated raid like the one in April 1942, but the start of a period everyone foresaw as tragic. They had waited long enough for it, this first invasion of the Japanese sky. From month to month, week to week, the capital had been upset by fire-fighting drills that sometimes involved the entire civilian population and almost completely interrupted the city's life.

The latest move in anticipation of the coming raids was the clearing during the summer of 1944 of broad fire-trails everywhere in the city, especially in the northern and eastern sectors. Grids were traced in straight lines running through flat, densely overpopulated neighborhoods where thousands of houses were marked for demolition. The people living in them were given a week at most—sometimes only two or three days—to get out with their meager possessions, their bedding, their rags. Then the troops arrived and, often aided by schoolboys and older students, embarked on a kind of brutal, rapid sack of the city. Lined up for miles, khaki-clad soldiers smashed buildings, chopped at them with axes, pounded them with battering rams, pulled them down with ropes; in less than three hours, the old wooden houses crumbled into dust. When everything was broken and flattened, the tonarigumi descended on the ruins like a plague of locusts. In two or three days they cleaned everything out and the fire-paths opened broad, empty vistas through the city; those whose houses were untouched carried home their neighbors' houses, now reduced to a heap of rubble or to splinters that would supply housewives for months with the dry wood they so sorely needed.

Then, on that November 1, the alert finally came. It is difficult to recall now which predominated, relief or fear of the B-29s, the giant Superfortresses, far more powerful than any of the planes that had ever attacked Germany. The city waited. Millions of lives were suspended in the silence of a radiant autumn afternoon. For a moment, antiaircraft fire shook the horizon with a noise of doors slamming in the sky. Then—nothing; the all-clear was sounded without sight of a plane. The radio announced that a single B-29 had flown over the capital without dropping any bombs.

That invisible visit was repeated morning after morning. One day the visitor finally appeared, flying at 35,000 feet; he even left his signature chalked on the blue sky: a line of pure white like some living thing that seemed to nose an almost imperceptible silver fly ahead of it. Then they started coming in twos and threes, soon five or six at a time, always above 30,000 feet, undisturbed by the antiaircraft fire, which was sparse and could not carry over 25,000 feet. To the people's amazement, Japanese pursuit planes did not even bother to go after them. The Japanese began to murmur when what they called the "photographic raids" were followed by the first bombing runs somewhere in the north. But people nevertheless seemed absolutely blind to their frightening lack of shelter and fire-fighting equipment.

Nothing had been done since the summer of 1943 to improve the shelter holes dug all over the city except to give them flimsy roofs made of bits of wood salvaged from houses demolished for the fire-paths and hastily covered with dirt. The tonarigumis had only a few hand pumps, filled from buckets or cisterns, that emitted a feeble, finger-thick jet of water. To fight ultramodern incendiary bombs, the populace's basic weapons were straw mats soaked in water, little paper sacks of sand and, in quantity, water buckets that had to be filled from the cisterns at each house; bucket brigades were made up of women and girls and retired elders. It was officially drilled into them that with speed and order their equipment was adequate to put out even the most violent fires. Air-raid warnings were obviously still considered devices for controlling the population and stimulating its morale; no thought seems to have been given to the danger involved.

The newspapers constantly prattled about government plans for massive evacuation of all nonessential citizens, but except for sending schoolchildren to the country or the mountains, nothing had yet been done on that score. Instructions posted in each home by the tonarigumis urged people not to wander off during raids and to be sure there were shelter holes near their homes. Tokyo would be saved, they said, if each family stayed put and defended its own home. The police systematically discouraged public shelters; with large numbers of people concentrated in centralized locations, houses would be left empty and undefended. People could not reach their homes soon enough after the all-clear to save them because fire could consume a Japanese house in minutes.

In short, it was as though the government during the first raids still could not believe that the bombings could be serious or, if it did concede this, its policy seemed to be to leave large numbers of people deliberately unprotected in the city to encourage immediate, mass action to fight the fires, even if this meant heavy loss of life.

The first big raids occurred before the end of November: some forty Superfortresses appeared regularly at noon like big silver flies in Japan's sparkling autumn sky, dropping both explosive and incendiary bombs. On several occasions I was away from my own neighborhood when the warnings sounded. Each time, the street crowd—hundreds of people caught, like me, far from home or work—found most of the shelter holes occupied by local families; all we could do for "shelter" was to stand or crouch close to the plank walls or in the narrow passages between the wooden houses. If a bomb fell near us . . . Besides, foreigners had been advised by the police not to move around during the raids because the authorities had reason to fear—one cop said so flatly to a Frenchman in Tokyo—that in case of a serious raid, white people might be lynched.

Then, on the night of November 29–30, the sirens sounded: the first night raid. Millions of people learned for the first time what it was to scramble up from the padded quilts stretched over their mats, rush out of doors in the icy rain and huddle in crude, muddy holes already ankle-deep in water. It was an exercise they would shortly be performing every night and, soon, several times a night. All around them were the wooden houses, massed like piles of dry wood at a building site. Light planes flew over in gusts, very low: so there *were* Japanese night fighters after all. Clusters of bombs exploded, shaking the ground.

Suddenly there was an odd, rhythmic buzzing that filled the night with a deep, powerful pulsation and made my whole house vibrate: the marvelous sound of the B-29s passing invisibly through a nearby corner of sky, pursued by the barking of antiaircraft fire. It was announced on the radio that half the bombs dropped were incendiaries. I went up on my terrace roof, where I was to spend so many nights during the coming winter, because to fight a bomb falling on a house you had to see it coming; you could not be huddled in a hole and still race to douse the bomb in the brief interval before it erupted in a geyser of flame. In the sky, the B-29s caught in the sweeping searchlight beams went tranquilly on their way followed by the red flashes of ack-ack bursts which could not reach them at that altitude. A pink light spread across the horizon behind a nearby hill, growing bigger, bloodying the whole sky. Other red splotches lit up like nebulas elsewhere on the horizon. It was soon to be a familiar sight. Feudal Tokyo was called Edo, and the people there had always been terrified by the frequent accidental fires they euphemistically called "flowers of Edo." That night, all Tokyo began to blossom.

The next day I rode a streetcar through the stricken districts to assess the damage. This was the first of those sinister blemishes that would spread like leprosy across the capital. A Japanese neighborhood, even a city, then, could vanish without a trace— none, at any rate, but a sort of underbrush of roasted sheet-metal and reddish-blackish iron and heavy shards of gray tile! It was almost impossible to see where streets and alleys had run between the burned-out squares that once were houses. In the surrounding districts, life went on more busily than ever in the little wooden houses destined to fuel the fires in coming raids. The homeless had already moved in with their neighbors, invading their homes with the few scraps they could save: muddied, cinder-smeared padding bulged from their quilts, making them look like soiled bandages, but their owners handled them as though they were precious antiques. All indications were that the people had not panicked under the bombs. Their attitude toward foreigners was still hostile—it had been for a long time—but it was also courteous, although the surprise of a sudden, specially brutal raid could touch off a violent reaction. Fortunately, the intensity of the bombings increased gradually, so that people were progressively accustomed to the danger.

Nevertheless, a mass exodus began in early December. The city was electrified by the rumor that a giant raid was planned for December 8, the anniversary of Pearl Harbor. Thousands left hurriedly, besieging the railroad stations and mobbing trains. On December 7, warnings sounded four times, but the bombs fell farther south, on the city of Shizuoka. This former green-tea capital, completely razed by a fire in 1939 and newly rebuilt, now went through twenty-four hours of tragedy: a violent earthquake shook it at 1 P.M., two hours after it was fire-bombed by the Superfortresses; another shock was felt at midnight. In Tokyo, however, December 7 and 8 went by peacefully, by the standards of the times.

I had moved to another house in October, just before the raids began, abandoning the Japanese house on Parliament Hill as too tindery in case of fire and too close to the ministries for safety. Now I was living in a European-style house, solidly built of stone, surrounded by gardens and endowed with one of the extremely rare cellars in Tokyo. The housing crisis gave me no choice of neighborhoods, however, and the one I was in was—or seemed to be—distinctly unpleasant. Not far away, at the foot of a hill, began the belt of big factories that stretched for a dozen miles along Tokyo Bay to Yokohama. On December 12, the adjacent slum districts were hit by explosive bombs, some of which fell within two hundred yards of my house. I was off to a decidedly bad start. But the following raids reassured me. It was clear that the Americans' bombing schedule called for priority concentration on the northern half of the city; my house was located near the southern city line.

The winter of 1944–45 was one of the clearest, and the coldest, Tokyo had experienced in twenty years. For forty-five straight days, the thermometer hung below freezing and there was no fuel at all for heating. The city was sluggish; it came to life only during the raids. Day or night, I could not help exulting over them. They meant the war was no longer a matter of blind and impotent waiting; being in it and under it was already a kind of liberation. And how could I be as afraid as my neighbors were of the fire from the sky when the sky was filled not with the enemy, but with the Americans I had been waiting for so long? In the daylight raids, the beauty of our terrifying liberators made me want to cry out. When they rushed through the blue sky in the frozen light of those glittering afternoons, flying fairly low as they doubled back after their bombing runs—they banked down fast then and flew right over my head—they were translucid, unreal, light as fantastic glass dragonflies. In each of those machines were twelve free fighting men who had come to liberate us. They had flown 1,500 miles over the ocean to get here, or roughly the distance from New York to Chicago, and they had to do it again on the return. In 1944–45, such distances seemed fantastic.

The Japanese defense, so inadequate at first, gradually improved. There were more Japanese pursuit planes. During daylight raids you could watch the dogfights in which these barely visible little insects buzzed around the giant B-29s, sometimes approaching them with extraordinary daring. Inspired by the kamikaze fliers, the newspapers said, fighter pilots flew straight into the Superfortresses, which broke up on impact. I didn't really believe these tales until the day I saw it happen with my own eyes: a lone, laggard B-29 was dived on by a swarm of fighters. Suddenly, there was an explosion: a fighter had rammed the giant bomber's left wing head-on. The small plane, linked to its

victim by a ribbon of white smoke, zigzagged down and crashed
in the city; the big, flaming American bird lost altitude, made a
few desperate tries to rise again, then suddenly heeled over and
went down, probably into Tokyo Bay.

January 1945 was calm; the Americans were kept busy by
their campaign in the Philippines. There was one terrible raid on
Tokyo, on a day of low-hanging clouds—the kind of weather the
Japanese most feared because the newly invented radar, they
said, enabled their assailants to see through clouds or in semi-
darkness. The raid took place on a Saturday at 1 P.M. A siren
went out of order and began to wail and the crowds in the central
city, thinking this was the all-clear, poured out of their holes just
as fifteen Superfortresses flying in formation dropped their full
loads of explosives on the Ginza and Nihombashi districts. Thousands died, especially in Owari-cho, in the very heart of Tokyo,
where a bomb landed directly on a crowded subway station near
the *Asahi* newspaper plant; hundreds of people were slaughtered
by splinters and the shock wave tearing under the station arches.
I visited the scene two days later, after the police cordon was
withdrawn; what I saw was an awesome tangle of wreckage.
Ginza, the racketing, multicolored center of the capital, haven of
restaurants and bars, city of theaters and geishas, with its willow-
lined streets and its thousand shops where silks and tortoiseshell
and pearls were sold before the war—Ginza was an ash-strewn
ruin. A huge throng of the curious came from all over the city to
stare in amazement at the debris. It was from that raid that the
people of Tokyo knew the war was lost.

The pace of the raids speeded up, day and night, with the biggest a week or two apart. The warning system worked with remarkable efficiency, in contrast to the disorder in everything else.
Well before the sirens sounded, the population was warned by a
radio voice that was calm if the planes were still far away, excited if they were close; enemy attack formations, it announced,
had been seen over the "South Sea" heading for Japan. Comments and explanations continued throughout the raid, with the
announcer reporting the arrival and departure of successive
waves of bombers in the various defense sectors. The island network extending toward the Marianas was extremely useful as an

early-warning system for the capital; usually, an alert was sounded a good half-hour before the planes appeared. Mount Fuji was accused of betraying the Japanese because its snow-covered summit, always visible above the clouds, functioned as a beacon and rallying point for squadrons bound for nearby Tokyo.

A new element heightened the danger in mid-February: an American task force had been seen cruising impudently along the coast of Japan. Then, on that luminous winter's most radiant day, no fewer than two thousand carrier-based planes blackened the sky over Japan, pinpointbombing the airfields and the big factories between Tokyo and Yokohama. They returned the next day, eighteen hundred of them according to Tokyo Radio, and this time they also attacked the city, zooming in at rooftop level to machine-gun the streets under their wings. Normal life in the capital stopped completely for forty-eight hours.

On the last Sunday in February, the annual snow miracle occurred. Filthy houses, blackened streets all awakened that morning transformed by its enchantment into a world of purest white where what remained of beauty in this afflicted city stood out like jewels against a setting of Oriental magic: pagodas with horned roofs, zigzagging pines, temple roofs with upswept eaves, a whole antique Japan reappeared, lined and mantled with ermine. Then the war came to shatter the spell.

Over two hundred Flying Fortresses were already overhead when the radio announced the arrival of an unexpected reinforcement from the U.S. task force, which had returned to the waters off Tokyo under a cloud cover. Superfortresses and carrier-based bombers rained explosive and incendiary bombs on the snow-clad city. Whole districts were set ablaze and, with the wind carrying smoke, sparks and ash from the fires, the day ended with a new wonder: black snow.

The city was paralyzed for the next two days by the fires, the bomb damage and the thick coat of snow that refused to melt. Streetcars were marooned, trains blocked almost everywhere and whole sections of the city isolated. Kanda, the university district, was among the affected zones. The trace of the carpet-bombing rolling toward the center almost reached the edge of Azabu, where most of the foreigners lived. Several French had already lost their homes; the Swedish colony was particularly hard-hit.

Life was just beginning to resume a week later—a Sunday—when the snow and the bombs once more made a combined onslaught on the city. There was an unreal, nightmarish quality about that raid in prodigiously heavy snow that made it hard to believe there were enemy planes above. The raiders were probably above the clouds and operating on radar. Falling endlessly in the absolutely still afternoon air, the flakes smothered the throbbing of the B-29s in a plume of white, muffling the shrouded whine of the bombs. Suddenly, the slowly descending snow was lit up by a mysterious inner light—huge, invisible fires that I judged to be near my neighborhood. The half-light veiling the city gradually took on a luminous yellow tint shot with a wondrous pink gold that pulsated weirdly, fading slowly, then flaring anew. At last, in the total silence that returned at the end of the day, everything bathed in a final raspberry-colored glow that flickered and dwindled, disappearing in the snow-filled air behind a curtain of bluish twilight.

Four days went by and then it was March 9—March 9, 1945, a date Tokyo will remember as it remembers that of September 1, 1923, the date of the great earthquake. On that March 9, spring made a surprise entry into the city, as the seasons do in Japan. But the fine weather in this time of bombing raids alarmed rather than cheered people. Still more worrisome was the wind, which had been rising since morning, turned gusty in the afternoon and brought the clouds back in the evening; that night it was almost as violent as a spring typhoon. The wind was to blame for the coming tragedy. A single thought haunted the city: it could be terrible if *they* come in such a wind. And *they* knew what the weather was like in Tokyo, for a lone B-29, flying at 35,000 feet, had flown over the capital that day, obviously on reconnaissance. And at eleven o'clock that night, *they* did come, heralded by the sirens and a radio announcement of large formations.

They set to work at once sowing the sky with fire. Bursts of

light flashed everywhere in the darkness like Christmas trees lift-
ing their decorations of flame high into the night, then fell back
to earth in whistling bouquets of jagged flame. Barely a quarter
of an hour after the raid started, the fire, whipped by the wind,
began to scythe its way through the density of that wooden city.

This time again, luck—or rather, the American command's
methodical planning—spared my district from direct attack. A
huge borealis grew over the quarters closer to the center, which
had obviously been reached by the gradual, raid-by-raid unroll-
ing of the carpet-bombing. The bright light dispelled the night
and B-29s were visible here and there in the sky. For the first
time, they flew low or middling high in staggered levels. Their
long, glinting wings, sharp as blades, could be seen through the
oblique columns of smoke rising from the city, suddenly reflecting the fire from the furnace below, black silhouettes gliding
through the fiery sky to reappear farther on, shining golden
against the dark roof of heaven or glittering blue, like meteors, in
the searchlight beams spraying the vault from horizon to horizon.
There was no question in such a raid of huddling blindly underground; you could be roasted alive before you knew what was
happening. All the Japanese in the gardens near mine were out
of doors or peering up out of their holes, uttering cries of admiration—this was typically Japanese—at this grandiose, almost theatrical spectacle.

The bombs were falling farther off now, beyond the hill that
closed my horizon. But the wind, still violent, began to sweep up
the burning debris beaten down from the inflamed sky. The air
was filled with live sparks, then with burning bits of wood and
paper until soon it was raining fire. One had to race constantly
from terrace to garden and around the house to watch for fires
and douse firebrands. Far-off torch clusters exploded and fell
back in wavy lines on the city. Sometimes, probably when inflam-
mable liquids were set alight, the bomb blasts looked like flaming
hair. Here and there, the red puffs of antiaircraft bursts sent dotted red lines across the sky, but the defenses were ineffectual and
the big B-29s, flying in loose formation, seemed to work unhampered. At intervals the sky would empty; the planes disappeared.
But fresh waves, announced in advance by the hoarse but still

confident radio voice, soon came to occupy the night and the frightful Pentecost resumed. Flames rose nearby—it was difficult to tell how near—toward the hill where my district ended. I could see them twisting in the wind across roofs silhouetted in black; dark debris whirled in the storm above me.

Already the word was being spread: the fire was nearing, it had reached the neighboring district of Sarumachi—the name means "Village of Apes." People came running down the adjoining street and we could hear a crackling like the sound of bonfires—the noise, it seemed, of houses collapsing. On the hill above us, a wide boulevard stretched across the fire's path, and there were parks and gardens closer in that would help to stop it. The Village of Apes was partly burned, but again the blaze spared the flank of the hill on my side. So the anxious scouting for sparks went on while the night slowly receded before a black-and-pink day and the whole city pumped smoke obliquely into the sky.

All this, however, was just the terrifying lighting for the real tragedy that was taking place farther away, on the capital's northeastern and eastern rims. I will transmit the accounts as I heard them in the days that followed and later on. The target district was the Tokyo flatlands, the endless working-class zone huddled among its factories. It contained not only the big plants and the homes of all who worked in them, but countless small workshops as well, where craftsmen and their families worked—often at home—for the national defense. It was called "the plain side" as distinguished from "the mountain side," the hills to the west and south dotted with residential districts. The plain was a jungle of tightly packed towns that were themselves compact masses of overcrowded districts fused into a single urban crust slashed by narrow streets. Aside from a few straight avenues and a tangle of stagnant canals, only the Sumida River cut a broad swath through these thousands of wooden houses. On the left bank were the Fukagawa docks facing Tokyo Bay, along with the Honjo and Mukojima factory districts; along the right bank stretched Asakusa, Shitaya and the outskirts of Kanda and Nihombashi. These were the areas hardest hit by the holocaust. Around midnight, the first Superfortresses dropped hundreds of clusters of the incendiary cylinders the people called "Molotov flower baskets," marking out the target zone with four or five big fires. The planes that followed, flying lower, circled and criss-crossed the area, leaving great rings of fire behind them. Soon other waves came in to drop their incendiaries inside the "marker" circles. Hell could be no hotter.

The inhabitants stayed heroically put as the bombs dropped, faithfully obeying the order that each family defend its own home. But how could they fight the fires with that wind blowing and when a single house might be hit by ten or even more of the bombs, each weighing up to 6.6 pounds, that were raining down by the thousands? As they fell, cylinders scattered a kind of flaming dew that skittered along the roofs, setting fire to every-thing it splashed and spreading a wash of dancing flames every-where—the first version of napalm, of dismal fame. The meager defenses of those thousands of amateur firemen—feeble jets of hand-pumped water, wet mats and sand to be thrown on the bombs when one could get close enough to their terrible heat—were completely inadequate. Roofs collapsed under the bombs' impact and within minutes the frail houses of wood and paper were aflame, lighted from the inside like paper lanterns. The hur-ricane-force wind puffed up great clots of flame and sent burning planks planing through the air to fell people and set fire to what they touched. Flames from a distant cluster of houses would sud-denly spring up close at hand, traveling at the speed of a forest fire. Then screaming families abandoned their homes; sometimes the women had already left, carrying their babies and dragging crates or mattresses. Too late: the circle of fire had closed off their street. Sooner or later, everyone was surrounded by fire.

The police were there and so were detachments of helpless firemen who for a while tried to control the fleeing crowds, chan-neling them toward blackened holes where earlier fires had some-times carved a passage. In the rare places where the fire hoses worked—water was short and the pressure was low in most of the mains—firemen drenched the racing crowds so that they could get through the barriers of flame. Elsewhere, people soaked them-selves in the water barrels that stood in front of each house before setting off again. A litter of obstacles blocked their way; telegraph poles and the overhead trolley wires that formed a dense net around Tokyo fell in tangles across streets. In the dense smoke, where the wind was so hot it seared the lungs, people struggled, then burst into flames where they stood. The fiery air was blown down toward the ground and it was often the refugees' feet that began burning first: the men's puttees and the women's trousers caught fire and ignited the rest of their clothing.

Proper air-raid clothing as recommended by the government to the civilian population consisted of a heavily padded hood over the head and shoulders that was supposed chiefly to protect people's ears from bomb blasts—explosives, that is. But for months, Tokyo had mostly been fire-bombed. The hoods flamed under the rain of sparks; people who did not burn from the feet up burned from the head down. Mothers who carried their babies strapped to their backs, Japanese style, would discover too late that the padding that enveloped the infant had caught fire. Refugees clutching their packages crowded into the rare clear spaces—crossroads, gardens and parks—but the bundles caught fire even faster than clothing and the throng flamed from the inside.

Hundreds of people gave up trying to escape and, with or without their precious bundles, crawled into the holes that served as shelters; their charred bodies were found after the raid. Whole families perished in holes they had dug under their wooden houses because shelter space was scarce in those overpopulated hives of the poor; the house would collapse and burn on top of them, braising them in their holes.

The fire front advanced so rapidly that police often did not have time to evacuate threatened blocks even if a way out were open. And the wind, carrying debris from far away, planted new sprouts of fire in unexpected places. Firemen from the other half of the city tried to move into the inferno or to contain it within its own periphery, but they could not approach it except by going around it into the wind, where their efforts were useless or where everything had already been incinerated. The same thing happened that had terrorized the city during the great fire of 1923: under the wind and the gigantic breath of the fire, immense, incandescent vortices rose in a number of places, swirling, flattening, sucking whole blocks of houses into their maelstrom of fire.

Wherever there was a canal, people hurled themselves into the water; in shallow places, people waited, half sunk in noxious muck, mouths just above the surface of the water. Hundreds of them were later found dead; not drowned, but asphyxiated by the burning air and smoke. In other places, the water got so hot that the luckless bathers were simply boiled alive. Some of the canals ran directly into the Sumida; when the tide rose, people huddled in them drowned. In Asakusa and Honjo, people crowded onto the bridges, but the spans were made of steel that gradually heated; human clusters clinging to the white-hot railings finally let go, fell into the water and were carried off on the current. Thousands jammed the parks and gardens that lined both banks of the Sumida. As panic brought ever fresh waves of people pressing into the narrow strips of land, those in front were pushed irresistibly toward the river; whole walls of screaming humanity toppled over and disappeared in the deep water. Thousands of drowned bodies were later recovered from the Sumida estuary.

In Asakusa, the crowd sought sanctuary around the old Buddhist temple, one of the loveliest in Tokyo. It was a temple to Kwan-yin, Goddess of Mercy, who drew as many as 60,000 visitors a day in peacetime. The haven was considered absolutely safe; the seventeenth-century building had survived all the big fires in Tokyo, including the one that followed the 1923 earthquake, because the bonzes allowed only refugees without baggage to enter the temple grounds. This time, however, Kwan-yin could not save her people; ignited by flying firebrands or by the bombs, the vast wooden structure burned, bringing down the immense gray-tile roof. The great gingko trees in the park went up in flames, along with the gardens—and the people.

Frightful scenes were enacted at every one of the rare open spaces that beckoned like oases among the tightly packed houses; people perished in them by the hundreds—in the Garden of a Hundred Stones, so dear to Japanese poets, in the Kiyozumi park in Fukagawa and other such places. In the inner courtyards of the Kameido temple, famous for its wisteria, people died within the circle of flaming buildings; it was there, or in their tiny houses nearby, that the girls of the neighboring red-light district perished, a fiery end to the hell of nocturnal vice I described earlier. The celebrated Yoshiwara district, near Akasaka, saw a repetition of what had become a classic drama in the great fires in Tokyo's history: before the raid really got under way, the tenants slammed shut the great iron gates isolating the area to keep the precious herd of girls from escaping. The houses were doing a lively business on that first evening of spring and many of their customers perceived their danger too late: by the time they did, their escape was blocked. Most of the women died in the flames with their night's lovers.

In Nihombashi, police directed refugees to a modern, well-built high-rise, the Meijiza, or Meiji Theater. As the fire neared the building, dense clouds of smoke entered on the wind; the suffocating refugees lowered the theater's big electric-powered steel curtain. But burning air seeped into the structure from the conflagration raging all around it. When the occupants tried to flee, they found they could not raise the curtain. All were roasted alive.

But what is the point of continuing this catalogue of horrors? Sirens sounded the all-clear around 5 A.M.—those still working in the half of the city that had not been attacked; the other half burned for twelve hours more. I talked to someone who had inspected the scene on March 11. What was most awful, my witness told me, was having to get off his bicycle every couple of feet to pass over the countless bodies strewn through the streets. There was still a light wind blowing and some of the bodies, reduced to ashes, were simply scattering like sand. In many sectors, passage was blocked by whole incinerated crowds.

Some time later, I learned the first official casualty figure; it was supposedly confidential, but it was soon whispered throughout Japan: 120,000 dead. And after the war I was told that some official Japanese records estimated the dead and missing at 197,000. I repeat that the enormity of the holocaust, comparable to that caused by the atomic bomb, is to be blamed on the terrible wind blowing on the night of March 9–10.* Tokyo was to suffer even more intense raids in terms of the number of planes

* The 1923 earthquake, which brought Japan sympathy and aid from the rest of the world, claimed 59,065 victims in Tokyo.

and bombs that finished razing the city, but none of the subsequent raids seems to have claimed more than 20,000 lives, at the most.

According to information released by the Americans, over three hundred Superfortresses—only two of which were lost—took part in the March 9 raid. Each carried a specially heavy load of bombs, seven to eight tons per plane. The bombs were of a new type, cylinders filled with a mixture of incendiary jelly and gasoline. In that one night, between midnight and approximately 3 A.M., 700,000 bombs fell on Tokyo. Their total weight was ten times that of the bombs dropped by the Luftwaffe during the "Great Fire of London" in September 1940, and the area razed in Tokyo on March 9–10 was fifteen times larger than that flattened in the British capital in the 1940 bombings.

And all this happened five months before the atomic bomb fell.

15

The Invaders Are Coming

Early in November 1944, with the Americans bogged down on the east coast of Leyte, the Imperial General Staff in Tokyo made what it treated as a sensational announcement: General Yamashita had taken command of Japanese forces in the Philippines. In this hour of danger, Koiso had remembered the hero of Singapore and recalled him from the exile on the Siberian frontier to which Tojo had consigned him. In a statement to the press, the "Tiger of Malaya" adopted an optimistic tone: "The Philippines are a vast field of operations; the place is big enough to give our forces freedom of action. I am going to show you what can be done when maximum use is made of these forces." And he added: "In Singapore, when I negotiated the surrender there with Sir Robert Percival, the only words I spoke to him were 'Yes or no?' I intend to ask MacArthur the same question."

It took less than two weeks to prove to Yamashita that this was easier said than done. He did indeed send reinforcements to Leyte, but by then the Americans were definitely taking control of the air. Kamikaze raids inflicted severe losses on the invaders, but since the Japanese squadrons' defeat at the end of October, United States warships cruised freely in Philippine waters. In the first half of December, a large American force landed on the island's west coast, taking the Japanese defenders from the rear and definitively reversing the situation in MacArthur's favor. Leyte was captured. Now anything was possible, beginning with a strike at the head of the Philippines: Luzon, the archipelago's main island, and its capital, Manila.

In Tokyo, the Information Bureau continued to distill its false optimism and its exhortations to all-out war for home consumption. Hitler's unexpected counterattack at Bastogne toward Liège and Antwerp offered the propagandists a welcome diversion. Bureau spokesman Sadao Igushi proclaimed on December 31: "The efforts by the Axis have laid the foundations for victory. We will ultimately crush the enemy and we will bring the world a new era of peace, prosperity and happiness." Speaking of the Pacific situation, he developed the main line the newspapers would henceforth chorus daily: "By drawing the war within the inner Japanese defense lines, the enemy has put his head in a noose and we are going to strangle him in it."

He failed to impress the Japanese public. The B-29s were more eloquent than Igushi, and everyone knew that the government's statements were always denied by the facts a few days later. This time was no exception. On January 9, the great event everyone feared finally happened: the Americans landed on Luzon, the main island in the Philippines, at the northern end of the archipelago. The invasion came at Lingayen Gulf, only 125 miles northwest of Manila. There was not a whisper in the Tokyo communiqués of the much-bruited counterattacks promised by Yamashita. By mid-January it was becoming clear from these vague, brief announcements that the "vast field" the general thought to exploit in fact worked to the advantage of American armored units, which seemed to meet no organized resistance. MacArthur's Blitzkrieg swept the plains of Luzon and on February 3, less than a month after the landing, the Americans entered the suburbs north of Manila. Instead of withdrawing to save the city from destruction, the Japanese waged a ferocious house-to-house defense. Tokyo newspapers, probably to cover up the atrocities the cornered Japanese troops committed, blamed the "American barbarians" for Manila's evisceration. Radio and newspapers carried an incredible communiqué declaring—I am reproducing this from memory: "To protect Manila, the Japanese command declared it an open city. It therefore completely evacuated all troops and military installations from the city. But because the false Americans, indifferent to the city's fate, infiltrated by fighting in the northern suburbs, our troops were forced to counterattack at once and they will defend the city to the end."

Manila fell in a week, the famous fortified island of Corregidor in two weeks; the last Japanese defenders blew themselves up in a terrible explosion in the fort's tunnels. In two months the Americans recovered the use of Manila Bay, an objective that had cost the Japanese six months of fighting to achieve in 1942. The Tiger of Malaya disappeared into the mountains in northern Luzon with the remnant of his troops and was being tracked by the Americans. In Japan, people kept only a weary eye on operations. No Japanese would yet let himself say the forbidden words *Nippon maketa*—Japan is beaten—but one could see the thought lurking behind the wooden faces. More clearly than the news from the Philippines, the Superfortress raids showed the population what the official news was worth.

Another line of propaganda began to take shape, a very different line in which the army progressively, methodically magnified the violence at the front, the kamikaze missions, the troops sacrificed, the fanaticized defenders. Now, at the beginning of 1945, the question was no longer one of winning the war but of how Japan would lose it.

The answer came from the most frenzied of the fascist superpatriots, Colonel Kingoro Hashimoto, leader of the youth brigades of the Imperial Rule Association, a ferocious nationalist, swollen with pride, who in peacetime had ordered a British gunboat shelled on the Yangtze River in China. "The time has come," he now declared in a broadcast, "when, like the soldiers at the front, the people in the rear must also transform themselves into human bombs. The Hundred Million must all resolve to die for the Emperor!" This was the kickoff of the propaganda campaign for national suicide.

On February 19, the Americans, who no sooner ended one operation than they launched another, landed on the Sulfur Island—Iwo Jima—in the Bonin Archipelago (*Ogasawara* in Japanese), midway between the Marianas and Tokyo. And a now-familiar phenomenon was repeated: the Japanese people, who had taken only a moderate interest in the fall of the Philippines, were suddenly filled with zeal for the defense of this eight square miles of volcanic ash and rock. True, its strategic importance was obvious: the Americans wanted to use it as a base for fighter planes to escort the B-29s on their Tokyo raids. But what chiefly fascinated the Japanese was the heroic defense put up by its 30,000-man garrison under General Tadamichi Kuribayashi, whom the Americans themselves admired. The Japanese allowed the invaders to land and to bring their equipment on to the beach, then pinned them down with a hellish fire, mainly from mortars that included big 320-caliber mortars used for the first time in the Pacific. Kuribayashi sent a last message to Tokyo that was published in all the papers; it ended, "I will die here."

As usual, direct communications with the island failed after a few days, and American broadcasts were Tokyo Radio's source for the tales of heroism the Japanese loved so much. In the first days of the invasion, 40,000 Americans were concentrated in less than two square miles; at every step forward they encountered pillboxes, blockhouses and trenches. A furious Japanese charge on the fourth day of fighting almost threw a whole division back into the sea. The invaders nevertheless advanced. Hill 382, on the mountainous half of the island, was taken and retaken six times. Stubborn fighting raged for Mount Suribachi, the island's volcanic summit; thousands of Japanese were annihilated at its foot, some of them roasted in their holes by flamethrowers, others walled alive in the approximately 180 caves they refused to leave when summoned to surrender.

The fight officially ended after four weeks; an average of two tons of explosives per defender, the Americans said, had been dumped on the tiny island. Ten days after the end, 200 Japanese surged up out of nowhere and staged a night raid on an air base; the banzai charge caused many casualties.

On one Japanese soldier's body the Americans found a diary like the logs most Japanese troops carefully kept until just before they died. The last page said:

> Today, facing north and prostrating myself reverently in the direction of the Imperial palace, saying good-bye to my parents

and my wife, I solemnly swore to go on to the end. I am only twenty-six years old. I owe having lived to this day to the Emperor and to my parents and I am profoundly grateful to them. My life is like a flower whose petals scatter to return to the earth. I am very happy. By the sacrifice of my body, I am going to become the white crest of an ocean wave.

Elsewhere he had written:

Corporal Yasuhira was wounded in both legs. He asked, "I beg you, cut me right." Lieutenant Masumai, sweat pouring down his brow, struck one blow, two blows and with the third magnificently cut the head off.

And his last line:

Happy to die on the anniversary of the battle of Mukden. . . .

In Tokyo, the March 10 raid once more smothered the people's interest in faraway happenings, including the last days of Iwo Jima. It was not there they were being defeated, it was here, and Tokyo showed it dramatically. In the burned-out quarters, people searched for their dead, gathered shapeless debris, poked through the ruins. To uncover a dented pot, a few knives, a broken bowl, they worked patiently from morning to night, camping out, fetching water over long distances from shattered mains, sleeping in their shelter holes. Theirs was almost a happy resignation: for them, the nightmare was over. They had already accepted the defeat and they did not much care what happened now as long as they were still alive. Many moved gamely into the razed districts, hoping the lightning would not strike in the same place twice. In those deserts of wreckage studded with the vague smudges of blackened, twisted tree-trunks, they built tin huts lashed to charred beams with wire or straw ropes for lack of nails; heavy stones weighed down the roofs in anticipation of high winds in the rainy season. In the city—that is, in the districts still standing—they went around in rags blackened and tattered by the fire. Some made hideous sights: wretches with burnt limbs who showed fleshless hands or feet or bloody masks that once were faces peering through filthy bandages.

There was a sort of scramble to leave what was left of the city. Hundreds of thousands of people wanted to get away before the flames devoured everything. There was still no panic, just a kind of dull, obsessive "save-yourself" attitude that drove people to struggle against the thousand obstacles impeding hasty flight. The most serious of these was a severe shortage of transportation. Fortunes were paid on the black market for the illegal hire of a truck, usually an army or navy vehicle that uniformed hoodlums secretly diverted from its regular service. A bicycle cart or an old bike with no inner tubes but with a baggage rack was worth its price in gold—or, more precisely, a heavy sack of unfindable rice. Hundreds of people, mostly women, carried heavy bundles on their backs that sometimes contained all the household's silk bedding wrapped in ordinary cloth. Suitcases, trunks, baskets were, of course, unobtainable.

There was a shortage of everything—even and especially wood —but Japanese houses were a mine of unpainted wood, and people wrenched the boards they needed for making crates from closets, doors, corridors, roofs. With cotton curtains and women's old clothing, they made square containers that they stuffed with kimonos, underwear, cushions and, above all, mattresses and quilts, a family's most precious, most indispensable possessions; without these *futon,* they would have to sleep on bare boards or mats wherever it was they found refuge.

There was no question of sending baggage by rail; only travelers were allowed into the trains, with no more possessions than they could carry. Around the stations, motionless hordes waited for whole days amid their packages, parcels and bundles before they could get inside. They waited hours longer, spent the night squatting or lying in the station halls, stiffening in fear when the air-raid sirens went off, but keeping their places. Finally they reached the platforms, waited some more, then rushed the trains that would evacuate them toward peaceful countrysides.

In the streets, everyone was selling what he had. Rather than abandon their remaining furnishings and utensils to the next fire, people became sidewalk vendors, swallowing their pride and ignoring what others might say. Tokyo was a vast flea-market in which all the articles unobtainable for months, even on the black market, suddenly reappeared: sets of porcelain, chests of drawers, European furniture, new and used sandals, charcoal, straw mats and the thousand knickknacks that adorned prosperous homes: silk paintings, luxurious cushions, vases, lacquered boxes, Japanese books, incense burners. And all of it went for a pittance.

Despite the departures, the population in the intact districts was no less dense—more so, if anything. Housing abandoned by its tenants was immediately invaded by twice as many people, burned-out parents or friends who could not or would not leave Tokyo, or refugees from the demolished zones who moved in, two and three families to a floor. Those who left were the huge crowd of nonessential people whom the government should have evacuated months before. But the evacuation orders came too late; the prevailing slackness and disorder saw to it that they were not applied. Then, too, many who could have left had boasted that they would hold out to the end; they were now the ones in the greatest hurry to flee. Finally, there were the industrial workers, office staffs and bureaucrats—mostly men—whose presence was required in Tokyo. They carried on their work as best they could in often ghastly conditions; their calmness, coolness, their frugality in the face of defeat were a kind of vindication of this people's virtues.

The threat of more air raids could not in itself explain the size of the exodus. What drove these crowds was the secret fear, not that the whole city would burn down, but—and this was new— that this plain of roasted debris would probably be a battleground within a matter of months. The public now clearly understood where things were heading, and the fall of Iwo Jima dispelled any lingering doubts: it was in Tokyo itself that the final battle would be fought when the Americans, striking into the heart of the Empire, landed on the nearby beaches to confront the Japanese Army.

Meanwhile, the Superfortress raids continued their inexorable buildup: always more planes at shorter and shorter intervals, attacking over ever-larger areas. The Japanese command hoped for a respite of a week or two after the March 10 raid. But the construction of new airfields on Saipan, Guam and Tinian now enabled General Curtis LeMay, the American Air Force commander in the Marianas who directed the bombings, to speed up the raids. In the forty-eight hours following the March 10 action, Nagoya came under heavy attack, Osaka burned on March 14, Kobe on March 17, then Nagoya again. In ten days, half of four of Japan's six largest cities was burned to ashes.

The U.S. task force was back on the prowl along the Japanese coast. On March 18 it launched 1,400 bombing planes against Kyushu, Shikoku and central Japan. This was repeated on March 19 and amplified by strikes at the port of Kobe and the naval base at Kure. And, once more, all Japan asked the same question: where was the fleet? As though to answer this and to confess indirectly that the fleet was at the bottom of the sea, the government undertook a reorganization of the defense establishment that gave away the situation and showed those willing to understand that an invasion was henceforth inevitable. Marshal Sugiyama, Minister for War and the senior man in the army's top echelons, resigned his ministry to take command of the First Metropolitan Army, comprising all the troops in the northern half of Japan, the sector most exposed to invasion; command of the southern half of the country went to another figure of comparable prestige, Marshal Shunroku Hata.

The usual stir whenever the War Ministry was left vacant naturally occurred this time too. Koiso wanted to take the post himself in addition to his Prime Ministry, but this the army resisted. Army support had been reluctant even when he formed his government nine months earlier, and he had not been allowed to return to active military service. This was now used as a pretext to oppose a retired general as War Minister. In fact, the army brass considered Koiso too weak to command the country in the supreme crisis they saw looming. They wanted to overthrow him and replace him with an energetic figure wholly committed to all-out resistance: General Koreshika Anami.

A secondary but highly significant incident helped discredit

Koiso. As though to provide a distraction from the secret desire for peace with America developing in ruling circles outside the army, even in his own cabinet, he clumsily let himself be drawn into serious consideration of a peace offer supposedly tendered by Chiang Kai-shek. No such attempt had ever succeeded since the China war began, but relations with the puppet Nanking government had always covered intrigues organized by private go-betweens with ephemeral contacts with Tokyo and Chungking. The Chinese were said to be in a perpetual "state of negotiations"; Japan, at any rate, was in a perpetual state of illusion about the solidity of China's resistance, which Tokyo imagined was forever on the brink of collapse.

This time the intermediary was a Chinese known to Tokyo under the name of Wang Pin, a former Kuomintang official who collaborated with the Japanese in north China. Declaring that he had been assigned to a liaison mission between Chungking and Nanking, he arrived in Tokyo and affirmed that, by offering generous peace terms, Japan could reach a compromise with Chiang's government, which was exhausted by eight years of war. Army opposition, as well as the lack of substance of both the negotiator and the negotiation, cut the business short. What was interesting, however, was that highly placed people had become involved, with Koiso's consent: Ogata, the head of the Information Bureau; Prince Toshihiko Higashikuni, and even Prince Takamatsu. Ogata was very close to court circles, Higashikuni was the Emperor's first cousin, Takamatsu the sovereign's younger brother.

At the same time, a more serious diplomatic problem was worrying the government: the deterioration of relations with Russia. Germany's weakness after its defeat at Stalingrad had led to a gradual stiffening in Moscow's attitude toward Tokyo in obedience to the Russian Empire's laws of physics, which demanded that it make its weight felt more acutely in the East when it was not harassed in the West. The most recent Russo-Japanese agreement dated from March 1941; at that time, Moscow had insisted on cancellation, twenty-five years before the lease would normally have expired, of concessions to the Japanese to work the oil wells and coal mines in the Russian zone of Sakhalin. Fishing rights were renewed for five years, but quotas were eliminated in several sectors off the Siberian coast and in Kamchatka, newly designated as strategic areas. In addition, Japan had to agree, despite German protests, to allow regular passage of American lend-lease arms and equipment for the Soviet Union, which Soviet freighters loaded in U.S. ports and carried home via the Kurile Straits, in what were definitely Japanese waters. Tokyo, then, had consistently overpaid for an increasingly fragile commodity: Soviet neutrality.

In the autumn of 1944, Russia's attitude emerged all too clearly. In a speech on November 6, Generalissimo Stalin denounced Japan, which he had hitherto conciliated, as an aggressor, and hinted that the Japanese, whom Russia had so long refrained from attacking despite the urging of London and Washington, must in the long run share the fate of their German partners. Finally, on April 5, 1945, Japan's ambassador in Moscow, Naotake Sato, told Tokyo that the Kremlin had informed him it wanted to annul the Russo-Japanese neutrality pact. Under the terms of the agreement, cancellation was to take effect one year later. The denunciation was accompanied by excuses, delivered in an acerbic tone, which merely came down to an ambiguous declaration that the situation must now be considered as having "radically changed."

On that same April 5, Koiso handed the Emperor his cabinet's resignation. Did Sato's dispatch have something to do with this? In fact, Koiso had received the final blow four days earlier: on April 1, the Americans gained a foothold on the island of Okinawa, in the Ryukyus, their first invasion of a part of metropolitan Japan, their first trampling of the nation's "sacred soil."

16

Kamikaze Days

A month before the Koiso cabinet fell, grave developments occurred in Indochina. On March 9, 1945, the Japanese Army suddenly swept away Admiral Decoux's French administration and took power in its own hands. It was then that the Vietminh, systematically encouraged by the Japanese, began operations, and the destruction of France's work in Indochina got under way. Just what provoked the move is unclear. In Tokyo, the Foreign Affairs Ministry seemed to want to avoid violence and deal circumspectly with France in the Far East as the price of French indulgence after the defeat the ministry saw coming; France was the only white nation whose friendship it thought it could eventually regain. The sweep, therefore, seems to have been planned by the army in Hanoi, which knew that resistance was being organized by the French in Indochina and feared the kind of French complicity there in case of invasion that had eased the American landing in North Africa in 1942. The Japanese command also saw defeat as inevitable, but its policy was the opposite of the Foreign Ministry's: it sought to plant the seed of racial hatred to promote Indochinese rebellion against the returning French.

In any event, the Indochinese situation immediately kicked back on the French colony in Tokyo. It seems we had at first been destined for a concentration camp, but this was softened to simple internment in Karuizawa, a mountain village north of Tokyo, under the guard of the redoubtable Kempetai. This eliminated the need to find internment quarters in Tokyo, where the bombings had made housing critically scarce. Karuizawa had once been the foreigners' summer colony, and although it had already been invaded by a number of European refugees of various nationalities, there were enough empty houses left for us. The French were evacuated at the end of March, practically under the bombs. We could take with us no more than we could wear and carry; anything left behind us that we had not had the foresight to store away when transport was still available would now be destroyed in the air raids. For in the next three months, all of Tokyo was to be razed except for its outer suburbs and part of the business district, where most of the buildings were modern brick-and-stone constructions.

We were forbidden to leave Karuizawa—military police patrolled the town's boundaries—and this at once presented us with a serious food problem. We were denied access to the surrounding countryside, poor as it was, but our food ration consisted entirely of a daily seven-ounce cube of black bread and a little soya gruel. We had to buy virtually all our food on the black market that profiteers had organized with the aid of the police—who took their cut of the receipts. Money had lost all value to the local peasant population; reduced by the war to going barefoot and dressing in rags, they accepted no currency but old shirts, worn clothes and used shoes.

Even so, our daily diet consisted mainly of boiled potatoes, rice and soya. Few vegetables were available in those mountains before June. We learned to distinguish which herbs and wild plants were edible; I personally gathered at least a dozen kinds as soon as the late spring brought them out: mountain onions and rootstocks, white dead-nettles, wild garlic, etc., not to mention watercress and waterdock gathered in a nearby pond. Butter, meat and sugar—White Russian specialities on the black market—had almost disappeared, and their barter value was fantastic.

Coinciding with our transfer to Karuizawa, more French were imprisoned in line with the continuing police policy of severity toward a few individuals and half-measures for the rest. The outskirts of the village crawled with police, most of them in plainclothes, and with police spies. Their primary job was to segregate the various nationalities who lived side by side there without the right to communicate with each other. Next to the French was a group of voluntary refugees—mainly Swiss and White Russians—for Karuizawa had long been one of the few places in Japan authorized for non-Axis whites. There was even a large number of closely watched Japanese exiles, most of whom sheltered in their own summer homes and, as members of a liberal, wealthy bourgeoisie, were quite rightly suspected of hating the war and liking foreigners.

For the time being we were housed individually and allowed to live in families, or in groups of two or three bachelors. In the strange miniature Babel of this small mountain village where the houses were isolated in the woods, not even the strict police surveillance could prevent clandestine meetings, chiefly to exchange information, with people we were forbidden to see. In the final analysis, this was fairly benign internment; in view of the horrors of Nazi persecution suffered by so many French in France and Germany, I would not dream of trying to darken the picture of our stay in Karuizawa.

The difficulties we faced nevertheless increased with every passing day, while our insecurity grew steadily more alarming. If the war went on another year, as it might if Japan resisted to the end, not only would shortages leave us all but dead of starvation, but the country's political and military disintegration would place us in a critical situation. The Japanese Army was leading the way toward a final, colossal disaster on the very soil of Japan. And what we could then expect—growing popular and police hostility left us few illusions on this score—was already being pictured for us by the beleaguered Japanese Army's atrocities against and massacres of foreigners in the Philippines.

Admiral Baron Kantaro Suzuki, General Koiso's successor in the Prime Ministry, was seventy-seven and long retired. From Tojo to Koiso and from Koiso to Suzuki, direction of the government seemed to fall into less and less energetic hands as the situation grew more and more desperate. This appearance was a little deceptive, however, because the old man to whom the Emperor had entrusted Japan's destiny was to show in time of crisis that he had not lost the qualities that had carried him through a distinguished naval career. He belonged to the old generation formed in the days of the Emperor Meiji in another mold than the one that had fashioned the figures in public life in the past twenty-five years.

Born in 1867, he had distinguished himself in the navy during the 1895 Sino-Japanese war and again in 1904 against Russia before becoming supreme commander of the fleet during World War I. Although Japan was then in the Allied camp, it was already dreaming of dominating the Pacific, and Suzuki was popularly believed to be the man who would lead the fleet in case of war with the United States. He was already retired by the time Japan launched itself on the imperialist adventure that would finally thrust it into conflict with the American colossus. Appointed an Imperial chamberlain, Suzuki tried to use his influence with the throne to neutralize the pressure of the military. The clan he belonged to was that of the conservative nobility which also included, for example, Count Nobuaki Makino and Baron Kijuro Shidehara. A breach opened between these men trained in the Meiji school, in the shadow of the palace, and the younger generation of militarists and superpatriots spreading the new ferment of violence and revolt among the Japanese masses. This earned Suzuki a place on the list of "reactionaries" drawn up by the army rebels in 1936; on the day of the uprising —February 26—he narrowly escaped death when armed soldiers invaded his home. He tried calmly to dicker with them, then, seeing that he was getting nowhere, he broke off the discussion and exclaimed, "Kill me, then!" The troopers immediately opened fire; riddled with bullets, Suzuki crumpled before their eyes, but doctors saved him. He then joined the Emperor's secret council with the newly bestowed title of Great Chamberlain.

When Koiso fell, the ex-premiers of the Jushin, whose moderating influence and heightened importance became clear when Tojo was ousted, made the admiral their candidate. They thought a Suzuki cabinet, though it would not be called on to conclude the peace the Jushin believed was not yet that near, would at least constitute a good transitional government; it would inevitably be followed sooner or later by the creation of a real peace cabinet, probably led by Prince Konoye. Since there was no question of openly admitting such plans for the time being, they outlined the sense of his mission to him in general terms and promised their support. "If you accept," they told him, "we will help you *in all circumstances.*" Suzuki agreed. But, while awaiting an opening toward peace, he had to carry on the war. General Anami, the army's candidate for the Prime Ministry, was given the key post of War Minister, giving the new cabinet a two-headed Suzuki-Anami aspect resembling the late Koiso-Yonai government.

Like Suzuki, General Anami stood out from his entourage as a strong personality. Aged fifty-seven, able and enthusiastic, he was one of the few military leaders of his generation who had remained completely outside of politics. His habit of shunning personal glory-hunting and holding himself aloof from power struggles finally paid off after Tojo's fall. Commander of the army in Manchuria at the start of the war and later transferred to command in the Celebes, he was recalled to the War Ministry under Koiso as Inspector of Military Education, a highly influential post in the army. There he made his weight felt as a new man respected by everyone. He was known to be an ardent partisan of a fight to the finish, and his presence in the government seemed an assurance that the war would continue even if it had to be fought on Japanese soil.

Any doubt that this was the intention of General MacArthur and Admiral Nimitz, the supreme commander of the U.S. Pacific fleet, was dispelled by the American landing on Okinawa on April 1. It was now evident that the United States was not going to waste time, as might have been thought only weeks earlier, on campaigns in Indochina or even in central China. The extraordinarily bold American plan was to strike straight at the heart of Japan. To lose Okinawa would not only be a staggering blow to Japanese morale—since, as we have seen, the Ryukyus were administratively part of metropolitan Japan and considered Japanese soil—but would also open a disastrous gap in the country's internal defense system. For the American Navy, with its badly overextended lines of communication, the island provided a staging area near the Japanese coast for the accumulation of an invasion force. It would give U.S. ground forces a vital springboard for a landing in southern Japan—probably on Kyushu, less than four hundred miles to the northeast. And it would offer the American air forces an ideal base from which to send bombers and fighters of all sizes and ranges against Japanese factories, cities and communications systems.

The Americans mounted a formidable attack. An armada of 1,400 ships, including, for the first time, a British task force of two battleships and four aircraft carriers, covered the ocean around the island to the horizon. Eight divisions were poised for the landing. Defenses on the small island—it is some sixty miles long and sixteen miles across at its widest point—were softened up by nine days of intensive pre-invasion air and naval bombardment. The Japanese had around 77,000 men in that narrow corridor, but their movements were hampered by the presence of over 400,000 civilians and, of course, they were virtually without naval support. Their best chance to hold on was to make another stab at the maneuver that had failed in Leyte Gulf: to let the enemy land and then cut him off from his seaborne communications. This time, Japanese fliers would have to do the job assigned to the fleet in the Philippines; while units ashore were saving their strength, all available planes would be thrown into the fight with a single mission: to destroy as many American capital ships as possible. Now was the time for massive use of the kamikaze corps, to convert everything still flying into a kamikaze plane, launch every pilot on a one-way trip, commit the nation's total air power to an all-out battle. It was not even a question of winning or dying, but of dying in any case and winning if possible.

To the American command's surprise, its assault troops landed on Okinawa's northern beaches practically without firing a shot and moved inland virtually unresisted. The defenders had evacuated the whole northern sector to concentrate in the southern half. On April 6, the Japanese air attack began: wave after wave came in, although in dwindling numbers, as long as the battle for the island continued. During the first weeks, the waves included some modern bombing planes that made the round trip. Slowly, however, the proportion grew of kamikazes bound for suicide.

They took off from airfields on Kyushu or in the northern Ryu-kyus, halfway to the target area. Day after day, these fanat-icized young pilots saluted their officers, said good-bye to com-rades who would leave later on, boarded their planes alone and took off to accomplish their mission: a ship sunk for every plane lost; a crew drowned for every pilot killed. A suicide's value was measured by the importance of the enemy unit it destroyed; it was wholly justified when the "hero-god of the air" blew himself up on the biggest game, an enemy carrier or battleship.

As it happened, many of the planes failed to reach the target areas. They were intercepted by fighters from the American car-riers, far superior to the often outmoded Japanese planes. Per-haps half the number that took off broke through the Allied de-fense to reach the stretch of sea around Okinawa, with its thick cover of Allied ships. They still had to get past the heavy an-tiaircraft fire spitting from every vessel, spot the most attractive of the potential targets, dive at it and crash into the deck in a final explosion—unless they were hit by an ack-ack blast or sim-ply missed their mark and dived into the ocean a hundred yards away.

How costly were the kamikaze planes to the American fleet? Tokyo's communiqués, while exalting the pilots' heroism, admit-ted that the Japanese command's estimates were vague. When they could, the pilots radioed back, "Carrier spotted, I'm div-ing . . ." But this was their last message and there was no way for the Japanese to know if they scored a hit. Observers on the Okinawa coasts also followed the fighting through telescopes and the peculiar Tokyo communiqués would simply specify that "Twelve columns of flame were observed, indicating that twelve enemy ships were sunk or seriously damaged. . . . Three col-umns of fire rose from the deck of a vessel believed to have been an aircraft carrier. . . . Columns of flame broke out in an enemy warship, a battleship or heavy cruiser. . . . After an ex-plosion, a transport was seen to be sinking." American radio re-ports picked up by the Japanese monitors prominently featured the suicide planes, but scoffed at their effectiveness and gave no indication of the damage they did; military censorship here was tight.

With good reason, it would be learned after the war. The damage inflicted by the kamikaze planes on the American fleet was heavy enough to worry the naval command. In one month of fighting, the famous Task Force 58 was halved. The carriers *Bunker Hill, Ticonderoga, Hancock,* and the old *Saratoga* as well as Britain's *Intrepid* were among the big ships sunk or put out of action. Losses among transports of troops and equipment were alarming. Drydocks on the American West Coast soon were so overloaded with work that the most heavily damaged vessels were sent around to the Atlantic coast for repair. The fleet was melting away.

Yet the progress made on land by American Marine and infantry units left no doubt of the battle's outcome; the stake was worth the continuing Allied sacrifices. The Japanese savagely defended the deep line of fortifications barricading the way to the southern half of the island, but they were being forced back step by step toward the central bastion of Naha and Shuri. American ships, planes and ground forces were using a new type of rocket. The Tiny Tim, biggest and most modern of the missile-armed planes and the last word in the development of rocket-propelled weapons introduced after Pearl Harbor, made its appearance at Okinawa; it launched a giant missile nearly ten feet long and weighing almost 400 pounds. Rocket ships, which went into action in March, fired 30,000 rockets in the following twelve weeks. And planes were already taking off from new bases in the northern part of the island to attack Japan.

The Japanese Navy took no part in the battle, except for the large number of kamikaze planes it contributed. Indeed, the sole sortie of the only modern Japanese battleship still in operating condition, the *Yamato,* one of the country's two 69,000-ton superbattleships, ended in disaster. It was spotted on April 6 heading southwest out of the Inland Sea either to attack the Americans off Okinawa or, more probably, to find a safe harbor away from the constant bombing of the naval base at Kure. It was attacked at high noon on April 7, less than sixty miles from the southern tip of Kyushu. Escorted only by one light cruiser and a destroyer squadron and lacking any air cover, it came under attack by 400 American bombers. Hit by at least twenty aerial torpedoes and countless bombs, it blew up in a gigantic explosion that sent debris flying 1,800 feet into the air and sank within half an hour. This was a re-enactment of the sinking of Britain's *Prince of Wales* and *Repulse* in similar circumstances in 1941, but this time at the expense of the Japanese.*

At the end of May, the admiralty in Tokyo issued a drum-beating announcement of a new suicide weapon being used by navy planes at Okinawa. Without revealing exactly what it was, the admiralty asserted that Hitler's V1s and V2s paled by comparison with the Japanese weapons, which were given the name of *ohka* (cherry blossoms). And since 450 young pilots in the first consignment were cited in an order of the day by fleet commander Admiral Toyoda for having died while using these mysterious ohka, it can be inferred that the weapon was a kind of piloted V1. The Americans confirmed this later on. Japan's secret weapon, famous among Yankee soldiers as the *baka bomb* (*baka* is an insulting Japanese slang term meaning "idiot"), was a twenty-foot-long wooden plane that carried a pilot sitting on nearly a ton of T.N.T. Towed like a glider by a medium bomber, it was released just before it reached the battle area, propelled by three rocket engines until its pilot could dive into his chosen target at up to 550 miles an hour. The craft had no landing gear; it was on a one-way flight.

On land, the defenders of Okinawa, continuing their lopsided struggle against a powerfully armed enemy who was supported by air and naval bombardment and whose infantry advanced behind flamethrowing tanks, died in the holes and caves of their last line of resistance between Naha, the island capital, and Shuri, the ancient castle of the lords of Okinawa. An attack by Japanese commandos parachuted into American air bases in the last week in May gave Tokyo material for an inflated publicity campaign, but in fact the results were practically nil. In mid-June, the commander of Japanese forces on the island, General Mitsuru Ushijima, rejected a surrender ultimatum and, with a

---

* Of the three other "secret superbattleships," the *Musashi* was sunk at Leyte, the *Mutsu* mysteriously blew up in port in Japan and the *Nagato,* damaged in the Philippines and half destroyed by the bombing of Yokosuka, ended its career at Bikini, under the third atomic bomb, in 1946.

handful of frenzied men, launched a final attack on American
Marine and infantry detachments. On June 21, all organized resistance ended on Okinawa.

The Japanese lost more than 100,000 men and 7,830 planes,
ohka included, at Okinawa. The campaign, which lasted twelve
weeks instead of the ten projected by the Americans, cost the invaders 12,500 dead and missing: the highest casualty total of any
of the Pacific operations. Between March 18 and June 20, the
Allied fleet lost 4,900 men killed and almost as many wounded.
For the first time since the war began, fleet casualties in an am-
phibious operation exceeded those of land forces.

Official figures published by Washington after the war showed
that naval losses to the kamikaze and ohka planes and standard
Japanese bombers were greater than had been supposed. From
the time they went into action until the atomic bomb fell, the
kamikazes sank 36 ships, including 3 aircraft carriers, and damaged 369, among them 36 carriers of various classes, 15 battleships, 15 cruisers, 87 destroyers. At Okinawa alone they sank 16
and damaged 185: 7 carriers, 10 battleships and 5 cruisers.

While this drama was being played out on "Fortress Japan's"
forward esplanade, as the Tokyo papers called it in imitation of
Goebbels, the debacle was spreading over the forgotten fronts of
Asia. Fighting ended in the northern Philippines before the end
of April; in the south, American troops landed in Mindanao and
pushed to Davao, once the capital of a vast Japanese colony. In
Burma, three armies—Chinese in the north, British in the center
and Indo-African in the south—mopped up Japanese forces trying to invade India, but halted before Imphal. British fleet units
recaptured Rangoon on May 3. Australian planes were bombing
the Dutch East Indies. The Chinese were counterattacking in
central China.

At the height of the battle for Okinawa, the Japanese public
was momentarily fascinated by the Reich's last stand. The fall of
Berlin . . . Hitler dead . . . Germany's unconditional surrender
on May 7—it was as though the headlines burned the paper they
were printed on in Japan's single-sheet newspapers. How believe
the unbelievable? Yet there it was, in print and therefore true.
And Japan's last foreign correspondents, in their last refuges in

Lisbon, Zurich and Stockholm, the men whose dispatches had for so long asserted the invincibility of "fortress Europe," now cabled their stories of the war's finale.

Unconditional surrender! Ill-disguised rancor welled up against Japan's last Axis partner, a sullen anger at its total defeat, which, on the evidence, now undeniably prefigured the fate stalking Japan. For months, people in trains and in the streets had been glaring at the Germans in Tokyo, reproaching them in language that was sometimes insulting and informed with hatred. The police suddenly reinforced their surveillance of the Nazis, treating them like any other whites, while the people reported on them as vulgar spais, taking their revenge for the arrogance they had long suffered in silence. A few newspapers, such as the *Asahi,* hailed the conquered ally. But many others kicked the fallen Reich. *Mainichi,* and others with it, found base and bitter terms for contemptuous criticism of the "lack of fighting spirit" in the remnants of the German Army. And at a time when Japanese troops were committing well-publicized atrocities in the Philippines and elsewhere, the Tokyo papers blamed Germany's defeat on its lack of *bushido.* With bushido, the Japanese code of chivalric honor, one never dies, never surrenders unconditionally. A country with bushido shows its fighting spirit to the end and never gives up the fight. But Japan had bushido, along with another unique gift, an imponderable quality incomprehensible to foreigners: the *yamato damashii*—spirit of Yamato —that is, of old Japan; consequently, it would never surrender as Germany had. The Hundred Million would rather commit suicide to the last Japanese to preserve their honor.

The B-29 raids slackened at the start of the Okinawa campaign. Kyushu, Japan's southern island, was bombed, but by carrier-based planes from the task force that attacked the kamikaze bases on April 26 and again on May 12 and 14. In April, the American command finally gave up its old plan of bombing Japan from bases in central China. The giant Chengtu base was abandoned and its men and materiel transferred to Guam and Tinian. Up to 800 Superfortresses could now reach Japan from the three bases in the Marianas (Saipan, Tinian and Guam), escorted by the 350 fighters based on Iwo Jima. A daylight raid on

May 14 brought 500 B-29s over Nagoya, dropping 3,300 tons of incendiary bombs on that wooden city and its factories and starting fires that burned until the following day; the city, virtually wiped out, would suffer no more big raids.

Tokyo came under another giant assault on May 24. The radio announced 220 B-29s, but its figures were always too low; the number announced by the Americans was 550. Carpet-bombing was resumed exactly where it had left off in the devastating March raids. Hardly had the great fires begun to subside when, at midnight on the night of May 25–26, terror reappeared in the capital with 500 more B-29s in successive waves guided by brilliant moonlight. The carpet unrolled with pitiless regularity, spreading its mat of fire over the flat districts between the port and the hills, the heights crowned with foreign residences and embassies, Shinagawa and its suburbs, Gotanda, where I lived before leaving Tokyo, the whole belt west of the city, the huge industrial zones, Ueno, Nippori, suburbs such as Nakano and Sekiguchi, the pleasant countryside around Omori.

The sheer number of the bombs was incredible. The former French embassy, which burned that night, stood alone in a big garden; it nevertheless received 35 bombs on its roof. Under the steel wings reflecting the inferno's glimmer, the whole sky, witnesses said, blossomed with bouquets of flame. As soon as they touched the ground, the cylinders spewed flames that leaped, the newspapers said, "like bounding tigers."

Shortly after midnight, all Tokyo firemen were summoned by a special alert: the palace was burning. For the first time, a heavy load of bombs had fallen inside the forbidden city—hitherto spared by the raiders—that marked the center of Tokyo. The Emperor was quite safe in his personal shelter in the vast reinforced-concrete cellars where general-staff headquarters had recently been dug alongside His Majesty's underground redoubt. But on the surface, the fire was spreading everywhere among the buildings of this complicated palace, a baroque tangle in which the pure and austere Japanese style coexisted with the bad taste of monumental German-style galleries and red-brick-and-pumice-stone wings in the bizarre style of American architect Frank Lloyd Wright's Imperial Hotel. The firemen deliberately abandoned several Tokyo districts to the flames—including the sectors around the central railroad terminal and the city hall—to try to save the palace. Reinforced by troops of the Imperial Guard, they struggled vainly against a fire that was no sooner squelched in one sector than it sprang up in another under the rain of sparks and debris carried on the wind raised by other fires. Hastily summoned units of the First Infantry Regiment were late in arriving: the vast Azabu barracks were also aflame.

The last of old Tokyo's architectural treasures—the ones that had survived the 1923 earthquake—were burned to the ground: the Shiba pagoda; the Yoyogi temple where "the ashes of the true Buddha," given to Great Japan in 1942, were kept; the black-and-gold-lacquered tombs of the Tokugawa shoguns; all these perished in the tragic forty-eight hours from May 24 to 26. Some 4,500 tons of incendiaries were dropped in the first raid, 4,000 on the following night. This represents over 2.5 million bombs, any one of which could set a Japanese house on fire.

Of the six biggest Japanese cities, Kyoto, with its thousand temples, was still intact, and so was Yokohama, which seemed miraculously spared; half of Osaka remained; the rest were leveled. An American broadcast said that Kyoto, the ancient Imperial capital, would be preserved along with its neighbor, the museum-city of Nara, to save the artistic and architectural treasures of old Japan. It was rumored that the Americans were interested in protecting what was left of the big-business center of Osaka for exploitation after the war, as well as the port and the old European concession in Yokohama that they would need when they landed. No one doubted that there would be a landing.

Four days after the giant Tokyo raid, on the night of May 28, the skies over Yokohama were suddenly filled with 600 planes, 500 of them B-29s and the rest fighters from Iwo Jima. The ferocity of the raid was unexampled. The city, a third the size of Tokyo, was razed in two hours; 3,200 tons of incendiaries, the Americans would report. Here again, the density of the bombs was such that any building, even those isolated in gardens or the fields bordering the nearby rice paddies, received its share of flaming liquid. People did not even attempt to save the wooden

districts, but, like the inhabitants of Tokyo in the latest raids, fled
to the hills and the open spaces; what was important was not
being hit on the head with a bomb and escaping, if the heavens
willed it, the heavy slugs spit by the P-51 fighters' machine guns.
Osaka's supposed immunity also ended in tragedy: what remained of the Manchester of the Orient, which had been converted into a vast munitions and aircraft factory, went up in
smoke on June 1 under 3,000 tons of bombs. This seemed to be
the bomb ration now reserved for a day's or a night's bombing of
a Japanese city; it represented a million of those six-pound cylinders of incendiary jelly.

But there were no more big Japanese cities. Fifteen million
people were homeless. Now it was the turn of the middle-sized
cities, with populations of 100,000 to 300,000, to receive the fire
from the skies. Hamamatsu, for example, with its big factories,
burned on the night of May 24, along with Tokyo; only about
forty B-29s were needed for the job.

From the Tokyo region to Kagoshima, on Kyushu, at the
southernmost tip of the Japanese archipelago, there was no one
in that late spring of 1945 who did not know that the war was
lost and that defeat would be total. The population had only to
contemplate the black deserts where once their cities had stood.
Country people had seen the terrifying flying machines over
their rice paddies a hundred times, and they had watched the
dogfights over the fields in which the victims were more often
wooden birds bearing the Rising Sun insignia than the steel mas-
todons flaunting the American star. And they heard the stories
told by refugees from the cities detailing their days and nights of
horror; the invasion by the homeless, the immense reflux of an
urban population that had lost everything but the rags on its
backs, had overflowed into the remotest countrysides, even the
frigid, mountainous north—the only part of the country that was
still relatively safe.

Yet the Hundred Million remained absolutely obedient to the
leaders who had brought them to this. The propaganda ceaselessly inundating this docile herd remained unchanged. Indeed,

the exhortations to national suicide had never been so clamorous. The army, reacting in its agony as the Nazis did in Germany, was being swept along in the catastrophe it had caused and could no longer turn back; it wanted the whole people to share its ruin. The Japanese Army? It had suffered far less than the navy and air force. There were still 2.6 million men under arms who had never seen action and who were frenetically training across the country, cultivating a fanatic violence in anticipation of the battle for their "sacred soil."

Thousands of officers and the horde of militarized army bureaucrats yearned to put off, to refuse, defeat until the last possible moment because they sensed the coming of an unknown world in which they would surely be the pariahs. And the army maintained iron control over the country's propaganda machine, which gave it a means of total exploitation of the Emperor's pronouncement and, even more, of the Imperial silence. Hirohito had never rescinded the orders he gave in his August Proclamation on December 8, 1941, Pearl Harbor day, when he called on his brave and loyal subjects to wage total war for the sacred goals of Japan. Everywhere in the country, on the eighth day of every month, "Greater Asia Day" was still solemnly celebrated with a public reading of the revered text: "We, by the grace of Heaven Emperor of Nippon, sitting on the throne of a line unbroken through ages eternal . . . rely upon the loyalty and courage of Our subjects in Our confident expectation that the task bequeathed by Our forefathers will be carried forward. . . ."

Kamikaze heroism was another media favorite. The cream of Japanese youth, the thousands of university students torn from their classrooms to attend the suicide schools, could not have died in vain. Millions of men and women believed what had been drilled into them daily, that their lives too would be required and, in truth, they were ready to make this gift to their Emperor. They were not told that the supposedly voluntary sacrifice by the first of the kamikaze pilots had in a matter of months become obligatorily voluntary—if we may so term the forced consent wrested from any Japanese when the pressure from his superiors and the contagion of his peers were strong enough.

Their leaders counted, moreover, on the fund of guilelessness their supposedly modern education had always carefully preserved in the people's minds. How many Japanese in wartime, even in the cities, were merely slightly derusticated peasants! Their thousand names revealed it—those equivalents of Farmer and Smith and Greenfield, names adopted by their peasant great-grandparents on government order because there were no family names in ancient Japan. And now, having believed for so long that they could save their cities from burning by tickling the fires with buckets of water, they enrolled for mandatory service as "popular volunteers" to defend Japan with bamboo spears. Men and women from north to south were drilling in the still-standing towns and villages, training for "banzai charges," uttering the savage yells that were standard in combat and stabbing bales of hay representing American soldiers with those bamboo spears with sharpened edges, like halberds.

One simplistic but amazingly effective line of reasoning was this: "To make Japan surrender, it must be vanquished, and to vanquish it, the Hundred Million in Japan must be killed one by one. No army in the world is capable of such a task; it is physically impossible, even for the American Army. Therefore, we *cannot* be beaten." The argument spread by word of mouth, was always repeated word for word by the Hundred Million—who had never been more than seventy-five million—so faithfully that it seemed to stem from an officially primed whispering campaign. And there was another argument, this one a crusher: the military police were everywhere, threading through every town, every village, some in uniforms and brassards, most disguised as ordinary civilians. Martial law was never proclaimed, not even at the height of the raids, but Kempetai headquarters in Tokyo let it be known that, in the name of the army, the military police now had authority over the ordinary police attached to the Interior Ministry. The old rivalry of these two mainstays of the regime again came into play to see which, on the eve of the final battle, could best tighten its network of gold-toothed, eyeglass-wearing cops, of minute and omnipresent espionage, of aggressive control over all of national life.

17

Toward Peace

Nourish the people on the myths fitting their ignorance, reserve awareness of reality to the inner leadership circle—these had been the unavowed principles of Japanese policy before the war. Relics of the Japanese Middle Ages, they presupposed a servile disposition in the masses and, in their leaders, mistrust of the people and a taste for tyranny. But secrecy, the first rule of state, divided even those in command and robbed them of part of their power; first, because the lies fed to the nation often rebounded to mislead the very governments that fabricated them, and, second, because secrecy fostered factional struggles within the closed world of power. The end result of all this was that no one ever knew all the elements in a situation; each clan promoted its own fragment of the truth to carry its position over that of its rivals. This was the mechanism which, in 1940–41, thrust Japan into aggression. Through four years of war, the machine was never allowed to go into reverse. In 1945, it succeeded in grinding the country more completely into its defeat.

In 1942, the myth of lightning war, bred by fanatic hope, promised the country immediate victory; in 1945, the myth of the "final battle," born of despair, bemused the people with a new illusion, that of an eleventh-hour victory. Secrecy concealed from them precisely that essential fact they needed to know: that this war was a naval war and that Japan no longer even had a fleet to fight that final battle. And, again and inevitably, the clan struggle ended in triumph for the army, since the defeat had physically eliminated the navy that alone might have learned the lesson taught by defeat and so worked for peace.

Peace? Japan could and should have offered it first after Singapore, when it was at the peak of its success. This would have been Tojo's peace. Koiso could have sought a compromise peace a year later, after the fall of Saipan. And Japan was still passing up its main chances for a peace of the vanquished: before the German surrender, it might have negotiated less disastrous conditions than now seemed probable; afterward, it could still have proposed a cease-fire. But nothing seemed to have presaged Admiral Suzuki's peace, for it was predicated on a new element—the most invisible, the most hidden of all—that was helping to shape Japan's fate. This was secrecy within secrecy, an unseen influence that would not be revealed until the last moment, when defeat was so obvious that it could at last be openly conceded. For the new factor was the Emperor's gradual awakening to the uselessness of continuing the fight.

Hirohito's desire for peace probably dated back to General Tojo's fall in July 1944. For three years, Tojo had jealously barred access to the throne by anyone who was not a vassal of his clan. So important a figure as Prince Konoye, for example, was not allowed a single private conversation with the Emperor. For this he or others like him would have had to be summoned, since protocol formally forbade them to solicit an audience or to appear before the throne uninvited. The Emperor did not summon them.

This was a grave responsibility: the sovereign, after all, could have freed himself from the army clan's hold, could have called in his former advisers, who would have opened the palace to fresh air from outside. He remained cloistered only by his own consent. His entourage would later try to excuse this with the argument that he was restrained by his concern to conform scrupulously, minutely, with the letter of the Constitution; this provides for access to the sovereign by ministers of state and the members of the secret council, but says nothing about the Emperor's right to receive anyone else.

Hirohito's attitude during the Tojo cabinet crisis plainly showed, however, that he was weary of the control to which he had submitted. When the name of Koiso was proposed to succeed Tojo, the army objected, but the Emperor nevertheless chose Koiso. More: he insisted that Koiso share responsibility with Admiral Yonai, known to disagree with the army's conduct of the war, as a counterpoise to the army in the cabinet. Yonai was the same man who had stubbornly opposed the Axis agreement in 1939, who had done his best to avert war in 1941. The reports the sovereign, and those advisers he could assemble, received thereafter were no longer confined to the deceptive data long imposed on him by the army. A number of officials, including such men as Ogata, the Information chief, and Finance Minister Sotaro Ishiwatari, tried to keep him honestly informed, at least on conditions within the country.

In this new climate, the group of advisers the Emperor had long avoided organized secretly to work out ways to meet the crisis they saw approaching. In 1943, four Jushin, Prince Konoye, Admiral Okada, Baron Reijiro Wakatsuki and Admiral Yonai, met almost weekly to study the progress of the war and internal affairs. They were particularly anxious to collect accurate information on what was happening on the various fronts and in Europe and on the international diplomatic scene. The problem was to crack the wall of secrecy and censorship that the army, even more than the war, had raised around Japan. In this quest for information, a young diplomat, Toshikazu Kase, played an important part. Even for the powerful, however, it was a risky business, requiring infinite precaution to avoid attracting too much attention from the political police and the Kempetai.

A whole clan, still secretly alive, coalesced again—the conservative and moderate politicians who had lost out in the 1935–40 period and whose weaknesses, mistakes, whose collusion, too, had cemented the army's triumph. They included old Baron Shidehara, for example, a convinced middle-of-the-roader who would be Prime Minister after the capitulation; Baron Seihin Ikeda, the Mitsui combine's man and former Finance Minister under Konoye; Shigeru Yoshida, an energetic and upright diplomat who secretly tapped diplomatic sources of information;

Ichiro Hatoyama, a politician with a keen sense of which way the wind was blowing and who regretted his former sympathies for foreign fascism and for General Tojo. All these people kept each other informed, discussed problems; they had already realized where the war was heading.

These breaths of fresh air were sniffed at court. Prince Higashikuni, an army general, had been deeply marked by long residence in Paris, where he had adopted his liberal ideas and where he had left his heart, and he was now actively pro-peace. His Royal Highness Prince Takamatsu, who had made his career in the navy and held the rank of commander, exposed the wreckage of his illusions to his illustrious brother. And there was another figure at court, an unseen figure whose role was unsuspected even in official circles, who campaigned actively to inform and persuade the Emperor that the time had come to shed his timid reserve and to act. That person was the Dowager Empress Sadako, the daughter-in-law of Emperor Meiji. Then in her sixties, she was an intelligent, enlightened woman. Her marriage in 1900 had brought her into a liberal court in a democratic Japan allied with Britain. After the death of her husband, Emperor Taisho, in 1926, she had retired from active court life, but her influence over Hirohito remained strong. In the blindered, reactionary atmosphere of her son's court, she, at least, clearly saw the danger threatening not only the country, but also her dynasty, the soul of Japan. In the nation's agony, the line descending "unbroken through ages eternal" from the Sun Goddess might very well be swept away and with it would go Hirohito and little Prince Akihito, the dowager's grandson and heir presumptive to the throne, to whose education she devoted much of her time.

A line of communication was opened between the Konoye-Okada group and the dowager empress. It was maintained by an elderly survivor of the brilliant Meiji era, Count Makino, then over eighty years old. He was the son of one of the founders of modern Japan, Marquess Shigenobu Okubo. After his father's assassination, Makino was raised by another major figure of the day, old Marquess Kido. The young man became an intimate of and secretary to Prince Saionji at Versailles in 1919 and later served as adviser to Emperor Taisho, whose Keeper of the Privy Seal he became. He had lived long enough to know a third reign, the tormented era of Hirohito, and had almost died for the liberal ideas he embraced in his youth. Makino figured on Prime Minister Tsuyoshi Inukai's murder list in 1932; in 1936, the February 26 rebels thought they had finished him off with a volley of revolver shots, but, miraculously, he survived. Now he lived retired in his pleasant residence in Kamakura, near Tokyo, seldom straying from his beloved beaches and pines, but he was secretly in liaison with Empress Sadako and he received frequent messages and visits from Konoye and his friends. Despite his age, his sight and hearing were perfect, his mind clear and his hand still firm enough to execute fine calligraphy. In his retirement, as Saionji once did, he kept abreast of political developments and knew all the important men of state.

It was in mid-February 1945, I was told, six months before the atomic bomb, that the Emperor first indicated the change in his thinking. He had been impressed by the incredibly rapid collapse of Japan's defenses in the Philippines. On February 12, six days after the fall of Manila, he sent word to Prince Konoye to come to the palace on February 14. The prince was living on one of his properties outside Tokyo, at Odawara; there, at the foot of the Hakone Mountains, he was safe from the air raids but close enough to the capital to maintain his communications with it. Because he knew he was being watched—even he!—by the shadowy military police, he gave out that he was going to Tokyo to attend a Sino-Japanese conference on science. Count Makino was also summoned to the court, as indeed were all the Jushin. This would be the Emperor's first confidential talk with these old political wheelhorses since Pearl Harbor. He received each of them separately. In measured, respectful terms, all except Tojo spoke of the danger facing Japan.

Konoye stayed with his sovereign longer than the others.

Alone among Japanese dignitaries then, he knew how to talk to Hirohito. Only he could adopt the easy, almost familiar manner, authorized by his rank and princely fortune, that put the Emperor himself at ease. The others fell over themselves like schoolboys before their teacher in their reverence for the Son of Heaven. So Konoye outlined his pessimistic view of the situation. He told his intimates afterward that he had been astounded at how clogged the Emperor's mind still was with false ideas and faulty information.

To clarify his sovereign's thinking, Konoye gave him a written memorandum summarizing the Jushin's arguments and conclusions. Count Makino had a copy of the memo, and so did Yoshida, who had helped write it. This ex-diplomat, who would be the great Prime Minister of postwar Japan, had been ambassador to London until the eve of the war. There he had tried boldly but vainly to reverse the trend of Japanese policy and channel it toward a renewed alliance and economic cooperation with the British in the Far East. In 1939 he fought the opening moves in the campaign for the tripartite agreement his colleague in Berlin, General Oshima, was then negotiating with Ribbentrop. Accused of Anglophilia, violently criticized by the military clique in Tokyo, Yoshida returned home and resigned. He retained considerable influence at the Foreign Ministry, however, and until Pearl Harbor he used it unstintingly to oppose the war. Even afterward, he remained active in the background at the ministry, organizing resistance there to military control following a personnel purge by the army and its men, notably Toshio Shiratori, former ambassador to Rome and co-author with Oshima and Ribbentrop of the Axis alliance.

When Tojo fell from power, Yoshida secretly campaigned for a prompt end to the war, to which he remained bravely opposed. But he was under close watch by the military police who, early in 1945, planted an agent among his servants. In one of her regular searches of Yoshida's papers she came across the secret memorandum drawn up for the Emperor. She reported it to her superiors and Yoshida was summoned to Kempetai headquarters for a grilling. The report was unsigned: who wrote it? for whom was it written? Yoshida claimed sole authorship, but refused to reveal for whom it was intended. He was thrown into a windowless cell closed at one end like a cage with heavy wooden bars (the iron bars had long since gone for scrap); in a neighboring cage was a Protestant bishop named Sugai, a regular victim of police persecution. Yoshida was constantly routed out for long interrogation sessions in which he was questioned about conversations spied on and reported to the authorities. A particular charge was that he had recommended that the cabinet put out peace feelers when Allied leaders held a scheduled conference in San Francisco. Instead of denying the allegations, the ex-diplomat proclaimed his convictions, which, he asserted, had never changed and which he had never disguised. Finally brought to trial in mid-April, he insisted that Japan should end the war, pleading his cause so passionately that he carried his judges with him. They acquitted him, which spoke loudly in his favor—and showed how singularly the prevailing atmosphere had changed.

The increasingly punishing air raids on Tokyo from early winter on impressed the Emperor even more than the pessimistic reports he was getting. He had refused to leave Tokyo despite urging by the army, which sought to isolate him in one of his provincial palaces—the one at Nikko, for example, where a number of princes of the blood had taken refuge. He courageously insisted throughout the war on remaining in his capital. An absolutely secure underground shelter was built for him; he went there during raids, but not until the last minute, according to reliable sources, and then with a reluctance that was not at all to the liking of his security men.

On the day after the great March 10 raid, rumors of the frightful fire toll reached the palace. The sovereign sent for his Interior Minister and found that the official report, minimizing the loss in lives and property, did not square with the information he was receiving from private sources. He confessed to his intimates a desire to make a personal inspection, to see the extent of the catastrophe for himself. An elaborate intrigue developed to persuade him to give up the idea; the army command, which had a pipeline into the palace, feared that the spectacle of a flattened Tokyo would have a baleful effect on His Majesty's outlook. But other advisers, including Marquess Kido, who detected the change in the wind, favored the Imperial inspection. Finally, the Emperor expressed a formal wish, which had the weight of an order, and the visit took place.

With a smaller escort than protocol usually dictated, he went to Fukagawa and beyond, a district that was to Tokyo what the East End is to London and the East River docks are to New York. Hirohito was appalled when, beginning at Nihombashi, the city's commercial center, now almost entirely razed, his limousine rolled through an endless desert of ash and wreckage. He left the car to walk through the most devastated areas, beyond the Sumida River, stopped at a temporary shelter for the homeless and talked to people who were camping in holes. This was several days after the raid; the charred bodies had been removed and the streets reopened. But the Emperor had seen enough to understand the terrible evidence his ravaged capital presented. Later he was given the awesome casualty figures; preliminary official estimates placed the number of dead at between 120,000 and 150,000—killed in a single raid, on a single night—and even these figures were probably too low.

That visit to Fukagawa and northeastern Tokyo was to have a profound influence on the sovereign's conduct and on the war itself. From that moment, resolved to end the hecatomb as quickly as possible, he displayed a new boldness, the temerity of the timid, that made up for his former weakness, and he stuck to it despite all the obstacles placed in his way. It was then, too, that a new feeling grew up between the Emperor and his people, born of that meeting amid the ruins. To understand fully what this meant, one must have felt the dreadful aridity of the climate enveloping the Japanese catastrophe. This people had experienced only the inhumanity of its leaders whipping the herd forward into its collective agony. For the first time, it was soothed by compassion, its sovereign's compassion; Japan would not forget the fatherly pity that was to rescue it from despair and allow it a glimpse of a future beyond the defeat.

At the beginning of April, old Admiral Suzuki, former Imperial Grand Chamberlain known for his devotion to the throne, took over the Prime Ministry from General Koiso. All indications are that he was informed of the Emperor's attitude by the sovereign himself. The secret history of the Suzuki cabinet reveals an undeviating course toward peace. Almost at once, Suzuki appointed a committee to investigate and report on Japan's economic and military ability to carry on the war. The report was submitted in mid-May. It was deeply pessimistic. The Japanese navy had only three battleships left, not one of them seaworthy: *Nagato* was laid up at Yokosuka with heavy damage; *Haruna* and *Ise* were out of action at Kure. Of the six surviving carriers, only two were operable. The fleet that was once the third largest in the world now had only six cruisers, some thirty destroyers and about fifty submarines. By the time Japan surrendered, its merchant marine, with a total displacement of nearly 7 million tons at the time of Pearl Harbor, would be down to 1,280,000 tons including damaged vessels. Rail freight shipments in 1945 were half what they had been in 1941. Aircraft production was barely more than a thousand planes a month. The battle for Okinawa and the kamikaze campaign had devoured all Japan's good pilots. Gasoline was so scarce that trainees' flying time had to be drastically reduced; fighter pilots now received their wings after only 120 hours of flight instead of 500 hours at the start of the war. Gasoline imports from the Dutch East Indies were down to zero, as were all other imports from the inaccessible South Pacific. Steel production was dropping because of the air raids to a fourth of its prewar level. Food supplies for the civilian population were entering a period of acute crisis with rice imports cut off and stocks in the big cities destroyed.

To fight the "final battle" which, according to the fight-to-the-finish faction, would end in an eleventh-hour victory, over 2 million green troops were available, ready to fight fanatically, but poorly equipped; tanks, especially, were inadequate in number and quality. Against them, American plans for a landing in Japan—plans that were not published before the war, but of which the Japanese general staff must at least have had a general notion—called for an army of 7 million men, 800,000 of them in the first wave. MacArthur would have 11,000 planes. The American war fleet would have a total displacement of 15 million tons;* it would include around one hundred carriers and it would be backed up by two hundred British warships in the Pacific.

What was more, the danger from Russia was growing monthly more acute. In concluding its analysis of the international political situation, the report said the Soviet Union was likely to enter the war soon and would probably attack around September, when the American landing was expected. Suzuki's Foreign Minister was Shigenori Togo, who held the same portfolio in Tojo's first cabinet. As soon as the admiral took power, he informed his minister obliquely but purposefully that he would give him "full power in the diplomatic area." He did not speak to him expressly of peace, but his words carried a tacit recommendation that Togo explore the diplomatic terrain with a view to ending the war. The vice-minister's post was given to Shunichi Matsumoto, a coming man in the Foreign Ministry, but Suzuki authorized Togo to work in absolute secrecy, without even informing his deputy of what he was doing.

Togo, a skillful diplomat, a former ambassador to Moscow who had prepared the Matsuoka-Stalin neutrality treaty, was ardently pro-Russian and an expert Kremlinologist. If only, he thought, the dying treaty could be kept alive a few more months. Or even, more daringly, be replaced with a Russo-Japanese agreement that could fix Russian and Japanese spheres of influence in that part of the world in the coming postwar era. Japan would be willing to buy such an agreement with vast territorial and political concessions.

Another device might be Russian mediation in ending the war, an even more tempting solution. Ambassador Sato, in Moscow, thought this would be difficult, but not necessarily impossible if Japan was willing to pay the price. His reports to Tokyo had always stressed what he saw as the fragility of the alliance between the Russians and the Anglo-Saxons. Moscow, he said, mistrusted its capitalist partners and feared that the peace after Germany's fall would not endure. Its attention had long been riveted on the

---

* On August 15, 1945, the American war fleet consisted of 23 battleships, 20 heavy aircraft carriers, 70 escort carriers, 8 light carriers, 2 battle cruisers, 23 heavy cruisers, 48 light cruisers, 273 destroyers, 365 escort destroyers, 240 submarines.

West; a compromise in the Far East that would secure the Soviet position in Siberia might be worth trying for.

The Supreme War Council met in Tokyo in May. Its function was to coordinate the work of the military command, in charge of operations, and that of the cabinet, which administered the country's war effort. It was usually called the Council of Six because its working sessions were attended almost exclusively by the six men chiefly responsible for the conduct of the war: the chiefs of the army and navy general staffs, the Prime Minister, the Foreign Minister and the Army and Navy ministers. At this session, the council considered Japan's position after the German surrender on May 7. Togo reported on the international situation, dwelling at length on the Russian problem. He believed, he said, in the possibility of Soviet mediation between Japan and the Western Allies with a view to a peace that would at least spare the country a foreign invasion. He asked the council to authorize him to begin negotiations with Moscow. The council agreed.

At that point, three members of the council were apparently already agreed on the desirability of peace: Suzuki, Togo and Admiral Yonai, then the Navy Minister. Did General Anami, the Army Minister, and his chief of staff, General Umezu, endorse Togo's proposal, so different from the all-out resistance for which they were vigorously campaigning throughout the country?

A Russian attack! The fear haunted the military command. After Stalin's speech denouncing Japan as an aggressor, the military thought Moscow might launch a winter offensive across the frozen Siberian rivers. But oddly, in a way that scarcely jibed with the Kremlin master's warning, the Red Army had relaxed its guard over the Manchurian frontier and Japanese patrols observed, with an ease unknown for several years, that everything looked quiet on the Soviet side. It was as though Stalin had felt obliged to give verbal satisfaction to the Allies then fighting in Normandy although he neither could nor would take action.

Since the end of the winter, however, Japanese observers and intelligence agents had detected major movements of troops and equipment; most disquieting was the arrival near the frontier of large quantities of materiel for building pontoon bridges, an indication that the rivers and streams would be crossed after the current winter but before the next—in other words, during the summer of 1945. The Japanese had transferred large contingents of the Kwantung Army to General Yamashita's command to reinforce the troops defending Leyte and Luzon, in the Philippines. The gap they left, it was calculated, could be filled in 1945 by troops evacuated from the southern fronts—south China, Thailand, Burma, Malaya—via the Canton-Hankow railway. Until then, Manchuria would remain so weakened that the general staff had to adopt a new defense plan: only the strongly fortified southeastern quarter of Manchuria—the part, including Korea, that was closest to Japan—would be defended. The rest would have to be abandoned to the enemy. A Soviet attack in Manchuria, then, would be the last and greatest of disasters. This is why General Anami raised no obstacles to Togo's proposal; he could always return to his role as the archchampion of a fight to the finish when events proved that mediation was a false hope.

It was in anticipation of such a setback that the army—of which only a few top officers were even aware of the negotiations—worked to stimulate the propaganda campaign for national suicide. The fight for Okinawa, the air raids on Japan, the burning of the palace—any occasion was seized on to prepare the Hundred Million to follow the kamikaze pilots' example. The media played up the heroism of the youngsters of Kerama, one of a small group of islands near Okinawa captured by the Americans early in the Ryukyus campaign. They told how all the island's young people, inflamed by the governor's exhortations, enlisted in the small local garrison and died like real soldiers. The American version: some two hundred local inhabitants, convinced that they were going to be massacred by the invaders, committed suicide; before they did, many of them murdered their children with their own hands.

An agitated communiqué issued on May 29 proclaimed that the hour had struck for the decisive battle of Japan itself:

> We must be prepared for the worst, and renew our resolution to win or die. We must make our bodies into human bombs against the enemy. Let each male subject imitate the hero Masashige, who once wrote to the Son of Heaven: "If the news that

your humble servant is no longer alive should reach Your August Majesty, deign graciously then to consider that Your Majesty's fortunes will flower anew. . . ." Let each woman be a feminine shield for the Emperor, like those women who gave their lives for the Imperial Family in the time of the Restoration. May the young imitate the heroic Byakkotai troop [young heroes of Japanese history who died for their emperor], who perished in the cause of justice. The human-bomb suicide of the Hundred Million must not be purely verbal. The Hundred Million must be like the kamikazes. Braving death—this is what will decide whether we do or do not leave behind us a heritage of ignominy for thousands of years and whether we will commit the sacrilege of being unfaithful to our glorious three-thousand-year-old tradition.

At the same time, however, negotiations to secure Soviet mediation began in maximum secrecy. To establish contact with the Soviet ambassador in Tokyo, Jacob Malik, Togo used an intermediary, former premier Hirota. Meetings took place in the Hakone Mountains, where the Soviet embassy, to protect its staff from the bombings, had rented a large hotel in Gora, above the much-frequented spa at Miyanoshita, the German embassy's refuge.

In outlining Japan's proposition to buy Soviet mediation, Hirota stressed that one condition was essential: the Emperor must remain on his throne. Malik reported on the talks to Moscow, which acknowledged them but did not react. Togo thought the tone of the conversations was promising. He preferred not to press Malik for an answer, deciding instead on a change of tactic: after the fourth meeting in Gora, he turned the negotiations over to the able Ambassador Sato in Moscow.

A race was on between peace and national suicide. The disastrous turn taken at the beginning of June in the battle for Okinawa encouraged the Emperor and the partisans of peace to pursue their efforts, but it also excited the advocates of a fight to the finish. Decisions taken at the highest levels reflected the struggle between the two camps. On June 8, a secret Imperial conference was held. Such sessions, as we have seen, were held only in exceptional circumstances and always marked a great moment in Japanese politics. But, as so often happened, this one ended am-

biguously. The peace party, including Togo, emphasized a passage in the final summary of the meeting that called on the government to "safeguard the national structure and preserve the
country's territory." They saw this as an endorsement of efforts
for peace because, for the first time, this very abstract language
really defined the conditions any peace agreement must satisfy.
"Safeguard the national structure" meant preserving the monar-
chic principle after the war and maintaining the Sun Goddess'
dynasty on its throne. "Preserve the country's territory" was a
way of insisting that the sacred soil of Japan not be desecrated by
foreign occupation after the guns fell silent.

But to the advocates of a fight to the finish, including General
Anami and Admiral Toyoda, the language was a green light to
all-out resistance. At a meeting of the Council of Six held two
days before the Imperial conference, they had even won consent,
subject to the Emperor's approval, for a new mobilization plan
and for emergency measures designed to throw the entire Japanese population into the supreme fight to hurl the invader back
into the sea. They presented the plan at the Imperial conference.
When the sovereign said nothing about it, they had Suzuki call a
short extraordinary session of the Diet to vote the laws the high
command needed. For the moment, despair had prevailed. The
Emperor's desire for peace was not enough to stop the war. All
Japan was being rushed by its leaders toward the catastrophe of a
final battle and the sovereign controlled no brake powerful
enough to stop its course. America would supply the brake, and
a tragic one it would be: the atomic bomb. But this was still two
months away.

For the time being, then, the fight-to-the-finish camp, backed
by the public opinion it controlled, was very strong and ready if
necessary to fight the cabinet openly. Their orders came, as so
often in the past, not from the army's official commanders, but
from the military bureaus, the young colonels on the general staff
and in the War Ministry. Other incendiary slogans came from
the kamikaze training schools and army camps. The southern
provinces of Japan, long a hotbed of militarism, prepared fanatically for the invasion. Agitators from the nationalistic secret
societies spread out over the country. Women did not escape

conscription; they were finally ensnared by a series of measures—census, labor service, biannual mobilization in the factories—they had long struggled to evade. "People's volunteer corps" were organized everywhere for elementary training in handling weapons and guerrilla combat. Antique carbines from the Russo-Japanese War, wooden rifles and bamboo spears were about the only arms they had. But they were fed on savage stories of Nazi *Wehrwolf* exploits before the German surrender, and they were readied to do even better when the time came for murder and vengeance against the invaders.

New batches of kamikaze fliers were being hurriedly trained in the flying schools. These were no longer the brilliant young men of the program's beginnings; the university students had long since perished at Leyte, Okinawa and Iwo Jima; now it was the turn of the crude youngsters of the war years who were ripening into maturity in time for the harvest of suicide. There was nothing voluntary about the program but its name now; the consent of future human bombs was no longer required. The most optimistic estimates gave Japan barely ten thousand planes; only three thousand were modern, the rest a sort of flying flea market of planes of every age and model. They were spread as thinly as possible to escape bomb destruction on the ground. In southern Japan, the navy was training men in great secrecy to handle other suicide weapons: torpedo launches that would explode with their occupants against the flanks of American battleships; diving rigs that would provide underwater protection for the coasts under attack and would enable the divers to dynamite enemy hulls.

North of Tokyo, in the Nagano Mountains in the heart of Japan, the last redoubt of future resistance was being organized. At the start of winter, Imperial headquarters had chosen a site on which to fall back when the Americans landed. The place was near the village of Hanishina, close to an ancient battleground of the feudal wars. Not far away, near the ruins of the castle of Sanada, hundreds of Koreans were at work on a shelter for the Emperor. On the surface, peasants were evacuated from farmhouses that were rebuilt in concrete under the thatched roofs left on as camouflage; the Emperor would live there on mats, amid simple furnishings.

On June 21 the Americans announced the cessation of Japanese resistance on Okinawa. Now they had a jumping-off place for the invasion that was less than four hundred miles from Japan proper. The Japanese command did not think they would attack Tokyo directly; the distances over water would make transport risky and supplies difficult to funnel to troops thrown ashore too far from their bases. The attack was to be expected, then, in southern Japan, and Tokyo reckoned it was still at least two months off. We now know that these forecasts were reasonably accurate. The Americans had planned a two-phase invasion after Okinawa. "Operation Olympic," as MacArthur's staff dubbed the first stage, would be launched in the autumn of 1945 at three points on Kyushu. "Operation Coronet," scheduled for the early spring of 1946, would put nine infantry divisions, two armored divisions and three Marine divisions on the beaches northeast of the capital for an assault on the plains of Tokyo. Japan's surrender was envisaged for the summer of 1946. Naturally, these plans were formulated in ignorance of the A-bomb, an ignorance in which the American planners, including MacArthur, would be kept until the last moment.

On June 22, the Emperor personally attended a meeting of the Supreme War Council in the Imperial shelter under the ruins of the palace. He interviewed the six men present, heard their reports and insisted on the importance of finding ways to end the war as soon as possible. As they emerged from the meeting, the Prime Minister told the Principal Secretary of the Cabinet: "The Emperor said what we mere subjects cannot say openly." After that the Council of Six met several times to discuss the proposal for Soviet mediation and finally decided to stimulate the Moscow negotiations. To persuade the Kremlin to take a stand at last, an envoy extraordinary would be sent to Moscow with authority to speak for Hirohito.

On July 12, Prince Konoye was summoned to the palace and, to his great surprise—he had not foreseen the purpose of this audience—was asked by the Emperor to leave for Moscow. Konoye agreed. According to what he told me confidentially two months later in an interview following the surrender, the Japanese Army had approved his mission. War Minister Anami had made clear, however, that the army would never agree to surrender; it would accept only an armistice on satisfactory terms arranged through Soviet intervention. What terms? In fact, the government and the Council of Six were sharply divided on the subject. Togo's idea was to press the Kremlin for authorization for Konoye to fly to Moscow. The cabinet would be given twenty-four hours in which to discuss the proposals he would take with him; the time limit would ensure that they would be botched. But it was understood with Hirohito that Konoye could ignore them. As the personal envoy of the Emperor of Japan, he would have full power to accept any terms with one and only one condition: preservation of the Imperial regime after the defeat.

Immediately after the prince's audience with the sovereign, Togo cabled Moscow asking Sato to obtain urgent right of transit for the Imperial messenger. Stalin was about to leave for Potsdam, where Churchill and President Harry S Truman were awaiting him. He delayed his departure a day to ask Tokyo for details on the aim of Konoye's mission. Moscow put the question twice to Tokyo, both times receiving the simple and evidently unsatisfying answer that Konoye would go in the Emperor's name to solicit Russia's good offices in obtaining an armistice and that the Japanese government's specific proposals would be revealed only by the prince himself on his arrival.

Stalin did not bother to wait for the second reply. On July 14, accompanied by Soviet Foreign Minister Vyacheslav M. Molotov, he left Moscow for Potsdam, leaving not only Sato dangling, but also China's T. V. Sung, who was in Moscow as Chiang Kai-shek's envoy to negotiate a major Sino-Soviet treaty. The Kremlin therefore informed Tokyo that because of Stalin's absence, Russia's answer concerning Konoye's trip would be delayed for several days. This did not worry Togo, who believed with stubborn optimism that Stalin would agree. In the event, Moscow's reply would be a Soviet declaration of war on Japan, communicated to Sato by Molotov on August 8—a catastrophe, but already a secondary catastrophe beside a far more stunning one that had occurred two days earlier: the bomb at Hiroshima.

18

Hiroshima

On July 25, 1945, from Potsdam, where the Allies held their supreme and final conference for ending the war, came an ultimatum announcing the tragic climax. It was prefaced in the two weeks preceding it by a terrible concatenation of naval and aerial bombardment. For the first time, the American fleet, liberated by the fall of Okinawa, appeared off Tokyo and bombarded the Japanese coast not with its planes, but directly, with its guns. A fever of horror ran through the country when it was learned that the city of Mito, a name recalling the struggle for the Restoration, had been annihilated by a brief storm of steel spewed from the horizon. This was the first of a series of bombardments reaching as far north as the naval base at Muroran, on Hokkaido. Less than a century earlier, Commodore Perry's "black ships" had forced feudal Japan to allow "foreign barbarians" to go ashore. Now a vastly greater array of "black ships" and still more terrible "black birds" sought to impose a shameful surrender on the nation.

Northern Japan was no longer immune from air raids; one after another, its cities were beginning to flame under the B-29s: Niigata, Sendai, Aomori and others. The fleet turned back toward the capital, appeared out of the fog at the mouth of Tokyo Bay and shelled coastal installations at short range with radar-directed fire. Twenty aircraft carriers stood before the city, the Americans announced, and for the first time their planes attacked the naval base at Yokosuka, where they finished off the battleship *Nagato* as it sat helpless in the roads. This was followed a few days later by a raid on Kure, the navy's second biggest base, and on central Japan.

The anguished month of July was drawing to a close when the government, closely following developments at Potsdam, learned by radio at dawn on July 27 of the solemn proclamation just issued by Truman, Churchill and Chiang Kai-shek. An ultimatum. Japan was summoned to surrender unconditionally before it was struck, the proclamation enigmatically warned, by "an infinitely greater power than that which devastated Germany." The three Allied leaders listed the implacable terms laid down to Japan: dismissal and punishment of the men responsible for the war, military occupation of the country, reparations, dismemberment of the Japanese Empire, total disarmament, institution of a democratic regime. Not a word about the fate of the Emperor and his dynasty.

Tokyo noted that Stalin had not signed the Potsdam ultimatum. This was a good sign, in which Togo saw proof that he was right to keep hoping for Russia's good offices. But could Stalin really have been no more than a spectator? Even if he intervened on behalf of Japan, would the resulting peace terms really differ from those drawn up in his presence? Another subject of embarrassment for Admiral Suzuki: extremists in and around the government found excellent fuel in the ultimatum for their campaign for all-out resistance.

Should the enemy proclamation be made public? Most important of all, should it be rejected? It was decided to release a shortened, censored version. The cabinet, after lengthy discussion that reflected its divisions and its disarray, thought it would be useful to play for time, to try to get around the problem. The Information Bureau put out a communiqué saying that Japan had decided to "ignore" the ultimatum—the exact word used was *mokusatsu,* which literally means "to kill with silence." This, it was thought, should satisfy the extremists while reassuring the pacifists, since it left the government a free hand for the future. But its ambiguity aroused very different reactions from those expected. Extremists were outraged and insisted on a categorical rejection of the ultimatum. The newspapers derided the proclamation. The Allies, on the other hand, interpreted the communiqué as a flat and final "no" from Tokyo.

On July 16, President Truman was informed of an epochal event, the highly satisfactory explosion of the first experimental atomic bomb in New Mexico. The news reached him in Potsdam the day after his arrival. Preparations for using the device against Japan were already under way when the explosion occurred. Before leaving for Germany, the President had ordered two versions of the bomb—one working on plutonium, the other on uranium—dismantled and taken to Tinian, in the Marianas, to be dropped on Japan, less than 1,200 miles away. And, by July 25, everything was in place: two bombs, two crews. As soon as he heard Suzuki's "mokusatsu," Truman confirmed his earlier order to Tinian: drop the bomb as soon as possible after August 2.

Monday, August 6, 1945, in Hiroshima. A few seconds after 8:15 A.M., a shattering flash of light, brighter than a thousand suns, shredded the space over the city's center. A gigantic sphere of fire, a prodigious blast, a formidable pillar of smoke and debris rose into the sky: an entire city annihilated as it was going to work, almost vaporized at the blast's point zero, irradiated to death, crushed and swept away. Its thousands of wooden houses were splintered and soon ablaze, its few stone and brick buildings smashed, its ancient temples destroyed, its schools and barracks incinerated just as classes and drills were beginning, its crowded streetcars upended, their passengers buried under the wreckage of streets and alleys crowded with people going about their daily business. A city of 300,000 inhabitants—more, if its large military population was counted, for Hiroshima was headquarters city for the southern Japan command. In a flash, much of its population, especially in the center, was reduced to a mash of burned and bleeding bodies, crawling, writhing on the ground in their death agonies, expiring under the ruins of their houses or, soon, roasted in the fire that was spreading throughout the city— or fleeing, half-mad, with the sudden torrent of nightmare-haunted humanity staggering toward the hills, bodies naked and blackened, flayed alive, with charcoal faces and blind eyes. . . .

Is there any way to describe the horror and the pity of that hell? Better, probably, let a victim tell of it. Among the thousand accounts we read in Japan was this one by a Hiroshima housewife, Mrs. Futaba Kitayama, then aged thirty-three, who was struck down 1,900 yards—just over a mile—from the point of impact. We should bear in mind that the horrors she described could be multiplied a hundredfold in the future:

It was in Hiroshima, that morning of August 6. I had joined a team of women who, like me, worked as volunteers in cutting firepaths against incendiary raids by demolishing whole rows of houses. My husband, because of a raid alert the previous night, had stayed at the *Chunichi* [*Central Japan Journal*], where he worked.

Our group had passed the Tsurumi bridge, Indian-file, when there was an alert; an enemy plane appeared all alone, very high over our heads. Its silver wings shone brightly in the sun. A woman exclaimed, "Oh, look—a parachute!" I turned toward where she was pointing, and just at that moment a shattering flash filled the whole sky.

Was it the flash that came first, or the sound of the explosion, tearing up my insides? I don't remember. I was thrown to the ground, pinned to the earth, and immediately the world began to collapse around me, on my head, my shoulders. I couldn't see anything. It was completely dark. I thought my last hour had come. I thought of my three children, who had been evacuated to the country to be safe from the raids. I couldn't move; debris kept falling, beams and tiles piled up on top of me.

Finally I did manage to crawl free. There was a terrible smell in the air. Thinking the bomb that hit us might have been a yellow phosphorus incendiary like those that had fallen on so many other cities, I rubbed my nose and mouth hard with a *tenugui* [a kind of towel] I had at my waist. To my horror, I found that the skin of my face had come off in the towel. Oh! The skin on my hands, on my arms came off too. From elbow to fingertips, all the skin on my right arm had come loose and was hanging grotesquely. The skin of my left hand fell off too, the five fingers, like a glove.

I found myself sitting on the ground, prostrate. Gradually I registered that all my companions had disappeared. What had happened to them? A frantic panic gripped me, I wanted to run, but where? Around me was just debris, wooden framing, beams and roofing tiles; there wasn't a single landmark left.

And what had happened to the sky, so blue a moment ago? Now it was as black as night. Everything seemed vague and fuzzy. It was as though a cloud covered my eyes and I wondered if I had lost my senses. I finally saw the Tsurumi bridge and I ran headlong toward it, jumping over the piles of rubble. What I saw under the bridge then horrified me.

People by the hundreds were flailing in the river. I couldn't tell if they were men or women; they were all in the same state: their faces were puffy and ashen, their hair tangled, they held their hands raised and, groaning with pain, threw themselves into the water. I had a violent impulse to do so myself, because of the pain burning through my whole body. But I can't swim and I held back.

Past the bridge, I looked back to see that the whole Hachobori district had suddenly caught fire, to my surprise, because I thought only the district I was in had been bombed. As I ran, I shouted my children's names. Where was I going? I have no idea, but I can still see the scenes of horror I glimpsed here and there on my way.

A mother, her face and shoulders covered with blood, tried frantically to run into a burning house. A man held her back and she screamed, "Let me go! Let me go! My son is burning in there!" She was like a mad demon. Under the Kojin bridge, that had half collapsed and had lost its heavy, reinforced-concrete parapets, I saw a lot of bodies floating in the water like dead dogs, almost naked, with their clothes in shreds. At the river's edge, near the bank, a woman lay on her back with her breasts ripped off, bathed in blood. How could such a frightful thing have happened? I thought of the scenes of the Buddhist hell my grandmother had described to me when I was little.

I must have wandered for at least two hours before finding myself on the eastern military parade ground. My burns were hurting me, but the pain was different from an ordinary burn. It was a dull pain that seemed somehow to come from outside my body. A kind of yellow pus oozed from my hands, and I thought that my face must also be horrible to see.

Around me on the parade ground were a number of grade-school and secondary-school children, boys and girls, writhing in spasms of agony. Like me, they were members of the anti-air-raid volunteer corps. I heard them crying "Mama! Mama!" as though they'd gone crazy. They were so burned and bloody that looking at them was insupportable. I forced myself to do so just the same, and I cried out in rage, "Why? Why these children?" But there was no one to rage at and I could do nothing but watch them die, one after the other, vainly calling for their mothers.

After lying almost unconscious for a long time on the parade ground, I started walking again. As far as I could see with my failing sight, everything was in flames, as far as the Hiroshima station and the Atago district. It seemed to me that my face was hardening little by little. I cautiously touched my hands to my cheeks. My face felt as though it had doubled in size. I could see less and less clearly. Was I going blind, then? After so much hardship, was I going to die? I kept on walking anyway and I reached a suburban area.

In that district, farther removed from the center, I found my elder sister alive, with only slight injuries to the head and feet. She didn't recognize me at first; then she burst into tears. In a handcart, she wheeled me nearly three miles to the first-aid center at Yaga. It was night when we arrived. I later learned there was a pile of corpses and countless injured there. I spent two nights there, unconscious; my sister told me that in my delirium I kept repeating, "My children! Take me to my children!"

On August 8, I was carried on a stretcher to a train and transported to the home of relatives in the village of Kasumi. The village doctor said my case was hopeless. My children, recalled from their evacuation refuge, rushed to my side. I could no longer see them; I could recognize them only by smelling their good odor. On August 11, my husband joined us. The children wept with joy as they embraced him.

Our happiness soon ended. My husband, who bore no trace of injury, died suddenly three days later, vomiting blood. We had been married sixteen years and now, because I was at the brink of death myself, I couldn't even rest his head as I should have on the pillow of the dead.

I said to myself, "My poor children, because of you I don't have the right to die!" And finally, by a miracle, I survived after I had again and again been given up for lost.

My sight returned fairly quickly, and after twenty days I could dimly see my children's features. The burns on my face and hands did not heal so rapidly, and the wounds remained pulpy, like rotten tomatoes. It wasn't until December that I could walk again. When my bandages were removed in January, I knew that my face and hands would always be deformed. My left ear was half its original size. A streak of cheloma, a dark brown swelling as wide as my hand, runs from the side of my head across my mouth to my throat. My right hand is striped with a cheloma two inches wide from the wrist to the little finger. The five fingers on my left hand are now fused at the base. . . .

Nagasaki's martyrdom three days later—I will discuss it in a moment—was no less tragic. For an account of that second A-bomb I chose the testimony of Dr. Takashi Nagai, the author of several books that made him famous, including one called *The Bells of Nagasaki*. Here are the notes he scribbled in a copybook a few days after the bombing. They were found after his death six years later, an end to his long ordeal of pain from what the Japanese call "atomic sickness."

> There was a flash of light. We were all under the ruins of the hospital. We couldn't see anything. Everyone thought it was a bomb. I did not seem to be injured, but if fire broke out, it was all over. . . .
> Soon, hospital patients and people from outside began flowing in. They were all injured, naked, bloody and as though their skin had been peeled off. There were charred faces, ashen or nearly black, under grilled, shaggy hair. They looked as though they had come out of hell. They crawled along the ground; they could no longer stand. . . .
> One of my assistants arrived from the city and said there were dead people in the streets everywhere. Fire was raging everywhere, he said, but there were so many dead and injured in the streets that you couldn't get through. I looked outside. Everything was burning. The city had completely disappeared. . . .

People scattered like panicked sheep when the growling fire reached the hospital. Dr. Nagai tried to lead them toward the hills, where there were open fields. The whole city was emptying of everyone who could still run.

> It was a frightful sight. All those still capable dragged or carried the bodies of wounded or inanimate relatives or friends. Children carried their fathers or mothers on their backs. Mothers climbed the hill clutching their children's bodies in their arms. The bodies of all these people were torn, bloody, and everyone, without exception, was naked.
> As they climbed, they looked back to see if the fire had caught up with them. They dragged themselves toward the open

spaces, hoping to revive there. Cries for help were heard everywhere. People searched, pleading, for someone to save them. In that endless throng mounting the hill, I saw more and more people grow breathless, collapse and die on the slope.

But the fire was getting closer. We could hear the frightful cries of people calling for help from the burning houses. On every side the cries came from caved-in dwellings. Even on the hill and on the valley's paths I saw countless dead. You didn't know where to step. And people were calling ceaselessly for help.

By my estimate, there must have been around 20,000 dead and between 60,000 and 70,000 injured in the part of the city around me. Toward evening, a frigid crescent moon rose, but gassy clouds still hung in the sky and shone in the light from the burning city. In the valley we heard the fleet's dirge being sung and farther along, where there was still grass, a choir of Nagasaki Christians sang hymns. The wounded cried, "Water! Water!" An enemy plane flew over our hill, that hill where, in a fearful state, the living bivouacked with the dead.

Nagai then noted escapees' first reactions to the bomb:

People first perceived a strange noise, then an intensely bright and absolutely white light. Some report, however, that at the same instant there were scarlet flames on the ground. Those who were near the center felt their skin burn and then, a second later, intense atmospheric pressure, as though a typhoon had knocked them down and crushed them.

In a flash, everything on the ground was destroyed and the earth was completely bare. Within a radius of six hundred yards all the wooden houses had been pulverized and even those of stone or brick were flattened. Leaves and grass disappeared and even the biggest trees were down. Animals, from insects to cattle, had perished, and people were buried under the wreckage of their obliterated houses, all in an instant, in hardly the time it took to cry out. . . .

I try to shut my eyes to that terrible and lamentable vision, but I cannot. If I can sum it up in a few words, it was, exactly, the end of the world as the Ancients described it, or perhaps it was the image of hell.

I myself saw Hiroshima after the bomb, saw it with my own eyes, but that was three months later, when peace had returned.

Let me anticipate for a few pages here and skip to this immediate postwar period. Nothing had changed in the circle of desolation since the bombing; I saw the city just as it was right after the cataclysm—minus the dead and dying.

I saw the city? Let's just say I saw the city's absence. It had vanished almost without a trace. The details are blurred in my recollection now, more than thirty years later, but this somehow clarifies my memory of the shock, my heart-stopping first look at the sight. This city had been conjured away, wiped off the map, wiped off the face of the earth. The sensation of emptiness was all the more striking because the ground on which Hiroshima had lived is an absolutely flat plain, the delta of a river with five or six branches spreading far into the gray hills around it. As far as the eye could see around point zero, where there had been a city with streets and crowds there was now nothing but this horizontal pedestal, this gray and reddish desert on which hardly any ruins stood.

I had seen many other destroyed Japanese cities, including Tokyo. After the big incendiary raids, one at least found the corpse of a city, made of bits, of remains. At Hiroshima, nothing. The bomb's hurricane and the fire that almost immediately consumed the city's pulverized substance had effaced everything in a circle two or three miles across. It was so empty that our plane simply landed in the heart of what had been the city. A little sweeping and cleaning had cleared a short airstrip, just long enough to take the tiny military observation planes that brought the few visitors allowed in by American occupation forces. In other cities, life had resumed almost at once. Here there wasn't a soul, not a shack to house survivors, no witness to talk to, to tell about it. The escapees had fled this accursed land in fear of radiation. Only on the periphery, toward the hills, was a zone reborn —shacks built of debris.

Something was missing under that Japanese autumn sky and its absence was frightening: there was no grass, not a trace of vegetation. All Japan wondered then if grass would ever grow again, if a flower would ever bloom in the earth of those two atomized cities, Hiroshima and Nagasaki. Reassurance did not come until the following year: Dr. Nagai told in one of his books of how moved he was when he saw a seed he had planted thrust a slender green sprout toward the sky, a fragile resurrection of hope.

I was with James de Coquet, special correspondent for the Paris morning daily *Le Figaro*. Our feeling was one of stunned consternation, mixed for me with a heavy feeling of shame—and I think my companion shared my remorse. "I'm ashamed for the West," I thought. "I'm ashamed for science. I'm ashamed for mankind." Curiously, the few American reporters who came on the same plane with us had crossed the phantom plain without stopping, as though it did not interest them at all. We two stayed behind, alone. We scratched at the ground, looking for some twisted or vitrified object, as at Pompeii, to call up the city, but we found nothing. It was as though the A-bomb had atomized everything, reduced it to the tiniest of particles. It had even pulverized the ruins. There was still one ruin in the landscape, however: the remains of a phantom building crowned with the skeleton of a dome that was once an exhibition hall; its carcass was preserved as a memorial. And at a bend in the river there was a wrecked bridge that supposedly marked the blast's point zero.

The lucky ones were those who died vaporized in the circle of total death, the approximately five hundred yards around point zero. Those beyond that line faced the horror of slow death, of bodies transformed into sponges, endlessly dying, or stricken with radiation sickness; its victims would lie under death's shadow for months, even years, before expiring.

How many died at Hiroshima? The official figures—78,150 dead, 37,425 injured and 13,983 missing—are not worth considering. They are far below the real numbers; they were issued at a time when, apparently, the Japanese could not and the Americans would not publish a true count. It is in any case a difficult figure to arrive at for several reasons: first and foremost, because tens of thousands of victims were counted as injured who died soon afterward; because whole families disappeared, leaving no survivors; because the exact population of Hiroshima on the day the bomb fell is unknown—it had been reduced by the number of those evacuated against the air raids, but swelled by troop movements in preparation for the defense of southern Japan. The figures given today are approximate, cited in round numbers: between 200,000 and 250,000 dead, including those killed on the spot and those who perished later. Shinzo Hamai, who until his premature death was Hiroshima's famous postwar mayor, gave me a figure at the time of "over 200,000 dead" and later published the figure of 240,000. The Japanese Red Cross advanced the figure of 250,000 dead and 150,000 injured, these representing survivors more or less gravely sickened by the bomb. It's the same story for Nagasaki, where the official figures were 73,884 killed and 74,904 injured, versus unofficial estimates of around 120,000 and 80,000.

In any case, the A-bomb, or rather, the two bombs dropped on Hiroshima and Nagasaki, continued killing long after August 1945. During one of my visits to the Japanese Red Cross "atomic hospital" in Nagasaki, in 1962, there were 246 bed patients, including two dozen youngsters, and some 600 outpatients suffering from ailments caused by the bomb.

"When was your last atomic death?" I asked Dr. Motoichiro Yokota, the hospital's director.

He looked at me in silence for a moment, then said softly, "Why . . . yesterday."

Could he mention any particularly remarkable cases? Plenty of those, he said. For example, the thirty-five-year-old man exposed to the bomb who had lived for thirteen years in apparent good health and then died in six months with all his vital organs destroyed. Or the boy who lived with macrocephalia for sixteen years; he had been irradiated in his mother's womb and was born with a skull as big as an ape's. Or the child born fifteen years after the bombing to a mother who had been exposed to radiation but not sickened by it; the baby was born without a head.

"Can this be blamed on the bomb?" the doctor commented. "In some cases, we cannot be sure, and all we can do is collect data. But in many cases there is no doubt: seventeen years later, the bomb is still killing." And over thirty years later, it still isn't over.

Can the use of the atomic bomb against Japan be justified? People will probably still be debating it for a long time to come. If

I may digress briefly, I would like to offer some information I gathered after the war. In the United States, before and after Hiroshima, a major argument in favor of the bomb was that, had it not been used, an American landing would have been far more wasteful of human life. Estimates vary of what the cost might have been: between 250,000 and 500,000 men, Truman said; 1,000,000 Americans alone, according to Secretary of War Henry L. Stimson. Japanese casualties would have been even higher. The argument is not entirely convincing, however, when we learn that a number of American military leaders, including Admiral William D. Leahy, Army Air Force Commander General Henry H. ("Hap") Arnold and General Dwight D. Eisenhower, the Allies' Supreme Commander in Europe, thought otherwise. Eisenhower, especially, was vehemently opposed to using the bomb, declaring it "completely unnecessary" because, he said, Japan was already beaten and ready to surrender. He added that by dropping the bomb, the United States risked condemnation by the entire world.

The civilian advisers appointed by Truman to an interim committee to report on whether the bomb should be used could not agree. Several were opposed, or vainly proposed restrictive conditions. Three groups of scientists, including several Nobel Prize winners, appealed urgently against using the weapon; one of the appeals carried seventy-five very well known signatures. The appeals were intercepted by General Leslie Groves, head of the Manhattan Project, and withheld from Truman. After the war, two great atomic physicists, Robert Oppenheimer and Edward Teller (known as the "father" of the A-bomb) admitted that in their opinion the use of the bomb had been mistaken or blameworthy.

Another argument in favor of the bomb is that Japan, even if it knew it was beaten—and it did know, as the preceding pages have clearly shown—would have been dragged by the extremists into the holocaust of a futile final battle and that only the bomb silenced these fanatics. Before Hiroshima and Nagasaki, surrender could not have been accepted because the war party was too strong, the people too blind to the disaster, the Emperor too weak. The bomb's value, according to this reasoning, was politi-

cal rather than military; it gave the sovereign a decisive argument
for stopping the massacre.

Despite all this, the case against the bomb is strong and not
well enough known. I will sum it up here in presenting what I
would call the "seven arguments against the atomic bomb."

1.   The bomb's power could have been demonstrated by
dropping it, say, on a desert island or a lightly populated one
close to the Japanese coast. This was proposed, notably by a
number of scientists, but the idea was rejected by American military leaders.

2.   Even without a demonstration, the Japanese nation could
have been informed of the bomb's existence and its incredible
power and warned of what Japan could expect if it continued the
war. This was also turned down in the United States.

3.   The bomb could have been used against a purely military
target, thus at least sparing the civilian population. But U.S.
strategists deliberately chose a mixed objective; that is, a city
where a single strike could hit both a military installation and a
large, surrounding civilian population, for its terror effect.

4.   The population of Hiroshima could have been told by
radio, in leaflets, etc., to evacuate it within a specified period and
advised to watch the destruction of their empty city from a distance.

5.   Even after Hiroshima, Nagasaki might have been spared.
The first bomb might have been excusable. The second was useless slaughter. Nagasaki added nothing to the wholly convincing
lesson of Hiroshima.

6.   Peace could have been pursued through the Japanese approach to the Soviet Union. U.S. intelligence agencies had informed Truman of the feeler before Stalin mentioned it, and the
President knew Japan was on its last legs. He could at least have
opened negotiations through Moscow.

7.   The phrase "unconditional surrender" could have been
eliminated in the first place from the ultimatum to Japan, as was
proposed by former American Ambassador to Tokyo Joseph
Grew, among others. To the military extremists in Japan, uncon-

ditional surrender meant the certain or probable abolition of Imperial rule and they used this as a convincing argument for continued resistance.

All this merely fuels debate on the bombs' strategic and political significance. This is the terrain on which the argument, infinitely repeated and already old, is usually fought out. But the debate should be pressed further, carried to a higher level; the real question is one of morality and humanism. From this point of view, are we not obliged to declare the Hiroshima bomb a crime, a crime against humanity? A crime with attenuating circumstances, no doubt, perhaps not exclusively an American crime but one in which all nations share, since the bomb was simply an extension of more established methods of warfare accepted and practiced everywhere. But criminal, too, because since Hiroshima, all kinds of countries have been coldly planning future nuclear massacres in tomorrow's wars.

A crime, then, that should be denounced and indignantly prohibited by humanism, morality and religion. With the Hiroshima bomb, atrocity in warfare crossed a threshold; it constituted a mutation in the collective criminality of war. It ushered humanity into an era of mass murder. Military plans are now calculated in terms of millions of dead. The aim of combat is no longer to kill soldiers or battalions, but a whole people, whole peoples. No more fronts in war, or rear; everyone, on both sides, is subject to destruction. By the thousands, the millions, children will die, women, old people. And, finally—look at the intolerable pictures of Hiroshima—nuclear fire promises its countless victims unimaginable suffering, the hell of Hiroshima multiplied, I repeat, a hundred times, a diabolical death for those who perish quickly, a still more abominable one for the survivors condemned to slow extinction. And a fatal sickness for generations to come, for the human race would be polluted in its very heredity by nuclear radiation.

And there is this, too: the white race dropped its Hiroshima bomb on people of another race, on a so-called "colored" people. Would the whites have dared use their bomb against their own race? There was an underlying racist idea that facilitated the use of this accursed weapon when a decisive argument against it should have been that it was one race's weapon against another race.

19

The Emperor
and the Bomb

In Tokyo on August 6, long hours were spent in vain attempts to communicate with Hiroshima before information from neighboring localities began to pile up, all of it about an extraordinary catastrophe. Some people already guessed at a new and unusually powerful weapon. But it was not until the night of August 6–7 that the mystery was solved when the government heard President Truman's radio broadcast concerning Hiroshima.

"Sixteen hours ago an American plane dropped one bomb on Hiroshima," the President announced triumphantly. ". . . . It is a harnessing of the basic power of the universe. The force from which the sun draws its power has been loosed against those who brought war to the Far East."

On August 7, army and navy investigators dispatched to Hiroshima confirmed American radio announcements. U.S. networks continued to pour out details on the apocalyptic force now threatening the Land of the Rising Sun. As information spread through the narrow, closed world of Japan's government, it generated wild excitement and endless speculation. Data about the bomb were not coming from Japanese sources but by radio from San Francisco, and they produced strong and immediate political repercussions.

To the peace party, the bomb was clearly an opening. Any argument for a final battle was now untenable because with one or more bombs the invaders could empty before them the coasts on which they proposed to land. How could Japan even risk waiting until September, when the invasion would probably come? What remained of Tokyo could be vaporized at any moment. The nature of the war had changed. If the fight continued, this would be a war unlike any seen before, an atomic war that could claim millions of victims in a few weeks, a few days. The partisans of peace, then, saw the bomb as a means of saving face. Passionate protest was already rising against the "atrocities" caused by nuclear bombardment, but these provided a valid excuse for surrender. It could be said that the Japanese Army was still in condition to win in case of a landing, but that an inhuman weapon forced it to lay down its arms to spare millions of civilians an atrocious death.

While these arguments rallied many undecided people to the cause of peace, they failed to dent the resolve of those calling for all-out resistance. The extremists were still powerful, first because they represented all the nation's armed forces and, second, because the country at large still did not know how desperate the situation was. Instead of frightening it into a dishonorable surrender, why not hide from it or minimize the new weapon's effectiveness? A fierce row blew up among the leadership over whether to tell the people the truth. The army opposed it, but was finally brought around to recognizing that this was not the kind of news that could be hushed up.

Military leaders finally agreed to publication of an ambiguous communiqué. This strange document, which appeared in the morning papers on August 8, was only a few lines long. It said that an enemy plane had dropped a new kind of bomb on Hiroshima and that the city had suffered considerable damage. But the Japanese language can be tremendously fuzzy and the communiqué took full advantage of this. It left readers unsure whether, as the text nevertheless implied, there had really only been one plane and one bomb. On the other hand, the way this brief morsel was headlined in all the papers suggested that the bomb or bombs constituted a very important event and that the adjective "considerable" authorized the gravest speculation.

In fact, the truth soon spread beyond the ruling circle and reached the people directly. The "bamboo telegraph," as foreign residents called the Japanese grapevine, for once functioned efficiently. Information and rumors circulating on August 8 furnished the first details on the catastrophe and the new weapon's real nature far better than the communiqué did. The explanation is probably that the small radios on which Japanese families heard the news in standard-wave broadcasts from Tokyo were also picking up the broadcasts the Americans were beaming to Japan from a powerful new transmitter on Okinawa; they may even have heard signals from U.S. ships cruising the Japanese coasts. In English and Japanese, the Americans were providing an endless flow of information about the origins, wonders and destructive capacity of atomic bombs. It left the people stunned, uncertain and frightened. No Japanese equivalent had even been found so far for the words "atomic bomb" and people invented makeshift expressions for the devilish new device. Speculation was rampant: all Japan might be razed; the whole earth could perish in a single explosion. These nightmare visions probably bred a secret wish that the war would end, but the people nevertheless passively continued to leave all decisions to their masters.

As though the bomb were not calamity enough, a second disaster shook the Japanese: the Soviet Union's declaration of war. The news broke on the night of August 8–9 in a Moscow Radio broadcast monitored by the Domei agency. At 5 P.M. on August 8, Moscow time, Ambassador Sato was called in by Molotov and, instead of the expected reply about the Konoye mission, was handed the declaration of war. Russia had not waited for the expiration of the neutrality treaty, which legally ran until April 5, 1946. In a note handed to Sato, Molotov argued that Japan's solicitation of Russia's good offices had been invalidated by Tokyo's rejection of the Potsdam Declaration. He added that the Soviet Union had therefore decided to subscribe to the declaration, which it had not yet signed, and that it would consider itself at war with Japan beginning at dawn on August 9.

Let's stop here a moment to weigh the event's implications. Russia's Far East war would last only a little over a week (the Soviet Union suspended operations at noon on August 17, not on August 15, as everyone else did). Was the Soviet move on August 9 a "stab in the back," like Mussolini's 1940 declaration of war against a France already beaten by Germany? Not at all.

Moscow was not trying to barge in when the fighting was over; it thought it would still have a major role to play in ending the war. It was at the Yalta Conference in the Crimea eight months earlier that Stalin had finally abandoned the hesitant policy of neutrality he had long maintained toward Japan, to his Allies' secret surprise and disgust. He had promised then to enter the Far East war within three months of the fall of Germany. American plans, of which Stalin and his generals must have had some inkling, were predicated on the possibility of the war lasting until the middle of 1946. This meant Russia had plenty of time; by entering the war in August 1945, it thought it could look forward to eight or ten months of campaigning. Attacking weakly guarded Manchuria and northern Japan across a land frontier would put Soviet forces in a better position than MacArthur's troops, who had to jump off from distant islands to make two landings, on Kyushu and then at Tokyo. Russia could carve out a large chunk of the Japanese Empire for itself, invade Japan from the north and the northwest and maybe even put its troops in Tokyo before the Americans. So, on August 9, exactly as promised—that is, three months after the German surrender—it kept its word and invaded Manchuria.

Too late! The colossal event that occurred two days earlier had canceled any effective Russian participation in Japan's defeat. Russia's entry into the war would be an important political element in the surrender, but its military effect would be virtually nil. The Americans dropped the first atomic bomb on Hiroshima on August 6 as though they had chosen that date to steal a march on the Russians and thereby avoid having to share their victory. All plans went askew. Now the facts were very different from Stalin's calculations. The war had only six days of life left. In a month, the United States, theoretically acting on behalf of all the Allies, would be the sole power occupying Japan. Russia would have to content itself with positions on the outer rim of the Japanese bastion. It was almost as if it were paying—and paying heavily—for its compliant neutrality toward Japan.

The bomb's potency, which was far more devastating than had been expected, had suddenly brought a tremendous and unlooked-for chance to end the war promptly. "We don't need the Russians any longer!" This was the discovery, the new policy that Churchill, at least, along with General Marshall, American Secretary of State James F. Byrnes and perhaps Truman himself, apparently formulated at Potsdam and confirmed after Hiroshima. The A-bomb, finally, was not merely anti-Japanese, but anti-Soviet as well. And MacArthur would profit from his advance over the Russians to make the occupation of Japan 100 per cent American. The cold war probably had not begun *before* Hiroshima, but it was certainly part of that first bomb's political fallout.

Without waiting for the official telegrams from Sato confirming the Soviet declaration, the Supreme War Council met in Tokyo on the morning of Thursday, August 9, in an atmosphere of catastrophe. By noon the Japanese command in Manchuria had sent the first phone and cable reports on the military situation there. The Red Army had attacked at dawn along the northern sector of the Siberian-Manchurian frontier, on the western edge of Outer Mongolia and in the southeast, on the Korean border. It had pushed the Japanese forces back everywhere. Tokyo's orders were to slow the Russian advance while the bulk of the Kwantung Army fell back as planned to Manchuria's southeastern corner. Japanese civilians were abandoned to their fate— particularly the big colonies of farmer-militiamen on the northern frontier that had been settled over the previous ten years by the forced emigration of poor Japanese peasants. Soviet planes bombed Hailar and Kirin in Manchuria and, in Korea, Yenzan and the Rashin naval base, a rival to the Soviet base at Vladivostok. At the same time, 1,700 carrier-based U.S. bombers struck at Akita and northeastern Japan.

In the council of war in Tokyo, Togo played his hand boldly. He had been received in audience that morning by the sovereign, whom he found more determined than ever to fight for peace, and he now felt bolstered by the support of the supreme head of the Empire. Didn't Togo, like the Emperor himself, have amends to make for Pearl Harbor? He had been Foreign Minister, we recall, under General Tojo. Nevertheless, the discussion dragged into a special cabinet meeting called for that afternoon. Appalling news had arrived to heighten the tension: a second city, Nagasaki, had been engulfed in an atomic holocaust—Nagasaki, of all cities, lovely Nagasaki, built in a crown around its blue bay at the foot of green mountains and terraced rice fields. For two and a half centuries before the Meiji restoration, it had been the only city opened to whites by hermit Japan. It had also been one of the places where Christianity in seventeenth-century Japan had lived its hours of triumph before its savage martyrdom. Now the men of the West had returned to its bay to take their turn as executioners, to inflict a fresh martyrdom on a city dominated by the Westerners' cross and Virgin. One of the few "valid" reasons, if there were any, for this second bomb was, as the Americans would later explain, that it was of a different type from the first: uranium at Hiroshima, plutonium at Nagasaki. The experts wanted to compare them. In fact, the comparison was unsatisfactory because the Nagasaki bomb, dropped in cloudy weather, missed its targets, the port and the city center. It wiped out most of an outlying sector of the city inhabited by the bulk of the working population and almost the entire Roman Catholic community, grouped around its now-obliterated Urakami Cathedral. The rest of the city had been devastated by a shock wave more violent than the one at Hiroshima, but had escaped burning.

In Tokyo, the cabinet session was feverish. Civilians and the military were split, although they did agree to conceal the Nagasaki catastrophe from the public for the time being. They discussed a proposal that the cabinet resign, but rejected it on the grounds that it would only further complicate the crisis. They talked of accepting Stalin's challenge by declaring war on the Soviet Union.

Then Togo stepped in. He pleaded strongly in favor of accepting the Potsdam Declaration—in other words, of surrendering. War Minister Anami protested vehemently and again spoke of Japan's chances of driving the enemy into the sea in a final battle.

The meeting hummed with controversy. Hadn't the atomic bomb swept away all these illusions? The ministers remained divided, incapable of decision. Confusion was compounded by a review of a proposal offered to the war council that morning for conditional acceptance of the Potsdam ultimatum. Japan would surrender, but on three conditions: (1) that the country not be occupied; (2) that the Japanese themselves, not the Americans, supervise the disarming of their own forces; (3) that war criminals be tried in Japanese courts.

The cabinet could not agree on the terms, which opponents said would be flatly rejected by the Americans. There was unanimous agreement, however, on a minimum condition for surrender: maintenance of the Emperor, or what had been called at the June 8 Imperial conference "safeguarding the national structure." General Anami, meanwhile, obdurately refused even to consider talk of surrender; he was backed by his chief of staff, General Umezu, and Admiral Toyoda, chief of naval operations, who as fleet commander had lost the final naval battle in the Philippines. Anami knew perfectly well that to continue the war in the face of atomic bombardment was tantamount to national suicide. His attitude suggested that he was mainly pushing the official line; its chances for approval were slim and he knew it, but he hung on, both to play his samurai role to the hilt and because he was losing control of the fanatics in the army and the military bureaus.

Prime Minister Suzuki took no position, merely directing the debate with unexpected energy. He finally ended the session at eight o'clock that evening without pressing for a decision. In fact, as he afterward confided to his intimates, he was going to put the decision up to the Emperor.

It was already dark when, less than two hours later, the ministers, in cutaway coats and dress uniforms, reached the palace, where they had been summoned for an Imperial conference; they would be joined by all the principal dignitaries of the state in Hirohito's presence. The theater of this historic scene was a semicircular hall in the Imperial shelter, fifty feet underground, with concrete walls more than twenty feet thick. The sovereign, in a khaki-colored general's uniform, entered quietly via a narrow staircase ten minutes before midnight and seated himself on the throne on a low dais before a golden screen. Bowing to him from their places at two long tables were the Prime Minister and his cabinet on the left and representatives of the armed services on the right. Baron Hiranuma, chairman of the Secret Council, was also present, as were a few highly placed representatives of the military and civilian bureaus and the secretary-general of the cabinet. The room was not air-conditioned and the heat on that summer night was exhausting; the wood paneling on the walls dripped with sweat, and so did the conferees' faces. In an assemblage made up for the most part of elderly men, the forty-four-year-old Emperor seemed amazingly young.

After distributing a Japanese translation of the Potsdam Declaration and a report on the Supreme Council's deliberations, the Prime Minister, still neutral, introduced Togo as the cabinet's spokesman. The Foreign Minister, who knew he had the Emperor's connivance, delivered a long report covering not only the international situation, which was his field, but a number of other pertinent factors as well: the exhaustion of the civilian population, the effective destruction of a hundred Japanese cities, public opinion, the desperate state of the nation's industry and transport, the probable consequences of an atomic war, the danger of a Soviet invasion of Japan itself, which was even more redoubtable than occupation by the Americans. It was an overwhelmingly pessimistic report and it concluded once again with a proposal to accept the Potsdam ultimatum. Togo did specify the usual condition: safeguard of the Imperial dynasty.

He was followed by the partisans of resistance, who disagreed strongly with his conclusions. With a violence barely restrained by the presence of his silent Emperor, Anami rejected any formula for peace that envisaged the occupation of Japan; he preferred a hopeless fight. In this he was supported by General Umezu and by Admiral Toyoda, in disagreement with his own minister, Admiral Yonai, who argued against him. This was the first time in modern Japanese history that the sovereign had presided over a discussion as passionate as that at an ordinary cabinet meeting. Until now, debates in his presence had been dryly academic, leading to his ratification of decisions already made. That night, for the first time, it was the Emperor who would make the decision.

At 2 A.M. on August 10, Suzuki finally rose and intervened in the discussion. After sweeping the room with a glance, he declared that the row had persisted for too long without agreement in sight. The situation, however, allowed for no delay. "In these circumstances," he said, "I shall humbly present myself at the foot of the throne and I will ask that the august Imperial opinion close the debate with such a decision as it may please His Majesty to take."

With this, in an unexpected and dramatic move, the octogenarian Prime Minister left his place, took a few wobbly steps and suddenly fell to his knees before the Imperial table, prostrating himself at the feet of his pale and motionless sovereign with his arms outstretched before the throne and his head touching the floor.

Violent sobbing broke out in the hall. In a faint voice, the young Emperor ordered the old man to rise and return to his place. When silence was restored, Hirohito straightened himself on his throne and began to speak. Admiral Suzuki, slightly deaf, leaned toward him with his hand cupping his ear.

The Emperor announced his position in a very few words. Citing Togo's proposition, he asked a simple question that broke with the usual solemnity of Imperial language: "Why not?"

That was it. Minds were made up. Sobbing broke out again, so loudly that the Emperor had to remain silent for a moment while tears flowed down lowered faces. When calm was restored, the sovereign said he would outline his reasons. The situation, he explained, had reached the point at which prolongation of the war would not only mean that Japan would be crushed forever, but would impose useless suffering and sacrifice on the rest of the world. He paid tribute to the soldiers and sailors who had died for glory in his name, to the civilians slain in the bombings, to all the wounded of this war. He recalled the wise decision of Emperor Meiji, who, after the Sino-Japanese War in 1895, bowed to the Triple Intervention (by Russia, Germany and France) that stripped a victorious Japan of part of its conquests. In thinly veiled reproach of the army and navy, he said that naval and military expectations, so often stained with overoptimism in the past, now were less likely than ever to be realized. No, the Emperor could not bear to see his people suffer any more; the limit had been reached. It was time to "accept the unacceptable, to bear the unbearable."

The Emperor had spoken. No one had the right to say another word.

Everyone in the hall was weeping quietly. The session ended at 2:30 A.M.

20

A Palace Revolt

On August 10, in execution of the Imperial decision, Foreign Minister Togo, through Japan's legations in Switzerland and Sweden, addressed an official note to the Allies announcing that Tokyo accepted the Potsdam Declaration. There was only one condition: Japan, the note said, accepted "with the understanding that the said declaration implies no demand that would impair the prerogatives of His Majesty as sovereign head [of state]." The language had been quickly approved at the cabinet meeting that followed the Imperial conference. Hirohito's decision had eased the minds of the people in the government. Tension, however, remained high among the people, who knew nothing of what was happening. On that day, the Tokyo area and central Japan were pounded by 1,600 carrier-based planes while, in the morning, over 200 B-29s bombed Chiba, the industrial area northeast of Tokyo, and the Yokosuka naval base.

America's reply, dated August 11 and signed by Secretary of State Byrnes, was picked up by radio on August 12 by Domei and officially received at the Swiss legation in Tokyo at 8 A.M. on August 13. It merely acknowledged Japan's acceptance and the condition posed, adding that "From the moment of capitulation, the authority of the Emperor and the Japanese government for direction of the state will be subject to the supreme command of the Allied powers, which will make the arrangements they deem necessary for applying the terms of surrender." This was not clear. It neither accepted the Japanese condition—maintenance of the Emperor—nor rejected it. Ambiguous was the word for it.

No more was needed to ignite furious quarrels in the government. Togo and the moderates wanted to give in and have done with it, since, after all, the American reply, while subordinating the Emperor to MacArthur, did maintain him on his throne and that was the important thing. Speaking for the extremists, General Anami declared such subordination intolerable. He remarked moreover that the United States had not committed itself for the future; after using the Emperor to carry out the Potsdam provisions, they could then discard him as a useless instrument.

Violent arguments raged at the cabinet meeting. Rumors raced through political circles that the colonels in the military bureaus were planning a coup d'état. The country, without news of the deliberations of the past four days, was alarmed. It was decided to issue an official communiqué informing them of what was going on. This led to fresh rows about what to say to the people. Anami formally opposed a flat revelation of the Imperial decision; spontaneous rebellion, he said, might break out among the civilian and military population throughout the country if the surrender were announced. The Information Bureau finally issued an obscure declaration in which the government proclaimed its resolve to "safeguard the Imperial structure."

To the few Japanese who could read between the lines, this was clear: all was lost except the Emperor. But for most of the Hundred Million, it was all still a mystery. And Anami added to the general confusion when, pushed by the superpatriots and the general-staff fanatics, he broadcast an unexpected proclamation appealing to the army to sacrifice itself in a final battle against the American invaders that would annihilate them just when they thought they had achieved their goals. On August 13, an apocryphal document, supposedly an Imperial Staff communiqué urging the army and the people to resist to the end, was caught and scrapped on the point of publication in the newspapers. Anami and his chief of staff denied they had written it.

While the political storm raged, the Allies resumed the air raids they had suspended for two days, Saturday, August 11 and

Sunday, August 12, as though in fear of disturbing the Japanese government's final deliberations on the eve of surrender. At dawn on Monday, August 13, bombers from some ten aircraft carriers struck at the industrial area of Keihin and the big factories at Kawasaki, between Tokyo and Yokohama, plowed up the airfields around Tokyo, attacked railway stations, strafed trains. It was rumored that the Americans had announced in a broadcast that Tokyo was to be obliterated by a third atomic bomb. Tokyo Radio, without ever mentioning the new bomb by name, contributed to the general anxiety by issuing some odd instructions with implications everyone understood. "Take shelter even from a single enemy plane!" the announcers warned. "Close your shelters hermetically! Wear white clothing that will protect you better from burns than dark clothes!"

From San Francisco, on the afternoon of August 13, broadcasts accused the Japanese government of delaying its reply too long. The executive secretary of the Japanese cabinet, Hitsatsune Sakomizu, without his superiors' knowledge, had the Domei agency radio a message, repeated five times, asking the American government not to lose patience and promising that the Japanese answer was about to be sent. But American service messages monitored by radio in Tokyo specified that MacArthur was in no way committed to permanent maintenance of the Emperor of Japan. This news reached the general staff that evening and refueled the quarrels. During the night of August 13–14, the army and navy chiefs of staff went to the Prime Minister's official residence and demanded that Suzuki alter his position. They wanted him to try to persuade the Emperor that he had made a mistake. Another note would be sent to the United States insisting on absolute guarantees for the sovereign; if Washington refused, the Emperor and his people would perish rather than surrender their honor. Togo, who was present, rejected the proposal. Nor was Suzuki shaken when old Admiral Onishi, the father of the kamikaze corps, who would commit suicide after August 15, made a tearful, violent scene. Having failed in their mission, the staff men left around 2 A.M., throwing full responsibility on the Prime Minister for the chaos in which, they said, the country would be plunged when it learned of the surrender.

A cabinet meeting was scheduled for ten o'clock on the morning of August 14 at Suzuki's residence. He appeared on the minute. He had been to the palace, had seen the Emperor, who had asked the members of the cabinet, the Prime Minister said, to postpone their session and appear before him for another Imperial conference. The meaning of the injunction was clear: the Emperor had again decided to settle the quarrels dividing the powerless government.

The session opened at 11 A.M., in the shelter. Present were the same men who had been at the conference on August 9; civilians who had not had time to dress formally for the occasion were given special permission to attend in business suits. This time, General Anami said only a few words and gave the floor to a very agitated General Umezu who, backed by Admiral Toyoda, once more affirmed his opposition to a surrender that did not include the necessary guarantees and did not clearly assure the security of the dynasty. The mute hostility of most of those present was patent during Umezu's speech. But this was not a decision to be taken by majority vote. Everyone recognized the basic problem: would the army refuse to capitulate? Would it rebel and drag the population with it into insurrection? Extremists were known to have been organizing for the past twenty-four hours to seize power, and a number of people, notably the kamikaze pilots, had gone over to them. Could the army be brought to heel?

Againt the Emperor intervened. This time he spoke more firmly than he had five days earlier, even though his nerves seemed ready to break. Weeping as he spoke, he repeated his unequivocal support for Togo's proposals; the Foreign Minister had played his hand skillfully and boldly. Then the sovereign expressed a formal desire that the government accept the American reply as it stood, without asking the United States for further clarification. Everyone understood that his desire was an order.

The Emperor stopped speaking for a moment to wipe tear-fogged glasses with his white-gloved hand. Then he resumed his improvised address. He sympathized profoundly, he said, with the feelings of the army and its leaders, who had shown throughout the war that surrender was a word banished from the Japanese code of honor. But more than one hundred of the nation's cities had been wiped out, the raids had left hundreds of thousands of people dead and millions of his subjects in misfortune. Even now, an atomic bomb might fall on the capital. "It is of the people that I am thinking," he said. Then he cried out, "I can no longer bear for them to continue their sacrifice." His audience listened with bowed heads, weeping openly. The sovereign himself constantly wiped away the tears flowing slowly down his cheeks; his voice was thick as he hammered home his words. Then, more calmly, he spoke of a "new Japan"—those are his exact words—that would be a member of the international community and would devote itself to peace. There was only one way to save the country from the most terrible of catastrophes and that was to accept the Potsdam Declaration. "Whatever may happen to me, I am determined to bear the unbearable. . . . I am ending this war on my own authority."

Decisive words that could redound to the Emperor's discredit, for the authority he now bared in all its power was the same authority he had failed to wield in 1941 to prevent the war. But those words can also absolve him, for they show that he alone amid the general chaos clearly saw the road to follow and courageously imposed his vision on the country, having understood the lesson of events and learned to put aside his former passivity.

The conference ended with a decision that, to make his will known to the nation, Hirohito would broadcast a proclamation to his subjects. Never before in history had a Son of Heaven addressed his people personally and directly or let them hear the sound of his voice. At the end of the day, the cabinet composed Japan's final reply to the Potsdam ultimatum, which this time was one of unconditional acceptance. The Emperor set his seal to it that evening and an English translation of the message was sent to the Allies via Bern and Stockholm.

The Imperial discourse was to be broadcast at noon on August 15, but it was recorded on the evening of August 14 to spare the sovereign's having to go to the studio. Under the direction of Information Bureau chief Kainan Shimomura, a group of Tokyo Radio technicians assembled at the palace shortly after 9:30 P.M.

The historic recordings were made in the Imperial apartments, which had been transferred to a Japanese-style pavilion still intact in the middle of the grounds. Hirohito read a message written by cabinet secretary Sakomizu based on the Emperor's speeches at the two Imperial conferences. Because of technical difficulties—the first recording had not been altogether satisfactory and a second one was made—and the demands of protocol, the session did not end until after midnight.

Shortly before that time, a group of officers from the War Ministry and the general staff entered the Imperial Guard's barracks and awakened the division's commander, General Takeshi Mori. With their revolvers trained on him, they told him to write out an order placing the guard at their disposal on the pretext of reinforcing palace security. Mori refused and was coldly chopped down by a hail of bullets in the chest. His killers then faked an order which they stamped with the general's seal, found lying on his desk. A few moments later, troops surrounded the palace. Shimomura and his radio team, leaving via the still-intact buildings of the Imperial Household Ministry, were suddenly surrounded by soldiers and officers and ordered at bayonet-point to hand over the recordings the Emperor had just made.

It was a crude enough plot: rebel officers were trying to block the next day's call by the Emperor to his people. Shimomura and his men refused to obey and insisted that they did not have the disks with them; their persons and equipment were searched and, when nothing was found, they were locked in a shed under armed guard. The furious troopers spread out through the surrounding buildings, searching everywhere and arresting everyone they found. They did not find the disks, which were safely locked away in a small safe concealed under a pile of papers in the Imperial apartments: Marquess Kido, Lord Keeper of the Privy Seal, and Household Minister Ishiwatari had foreseen the possibility of an incident and had taken precautions. The two men narrowly escaped arrest, they later related, by hiding in an alcove just before soldiers broke into the room.

Meanwhile, truckloads of armed civilians and soldiers surrounded the Prime Minister's residence on the Sanno Hill, near the Parliament building. After firing off a few machine-gun bursts, they broke through the gates, smashed in the doors and, brandishing naked swords, ransacked the house, obviously looking for Suzuki. But he was spending the night in his private residence. The rebels, informed by servants that Suzuki was not there, scattered gasoline over the floors, carpets and curtains, set them alight and left. They forgot to cut the phone wires, however; the Prime Minister was warned at his home in Koishikawa just in time to take refuge with one of his brothers, a general, who lived in another section of Tokyo. The rebels, furious at this second escape, sacked and burned that house as well.

The homes of other dignitaries were also attacked on that night of August 14–15, including those of Baron Hiranuma and Deputy Foreign Minister Matsumoto who, as Togo's Number Two man, had also worked for peace. All escaped; many, in fact, had opted to spend the night away from home: the 1936 rebellion was still fresh in their memories and everyone, feeling a coup d'état in the air, had taken his precautions. Besides, the conspiracy had obviously been bungled and poorly coordinated, perhaps because the archchampion of resistance, General Anami, was dead.

In the afternoon following the Imperial conference, Anami had visited the Prime Minister to offer his apologies in mysterious terms and express his remorse for having dared persist at that day's conference in an opinion the Emperor had discarded on August 9. Returning to his official residence, the Minister of War committed hara-kiri. It was later learned that fanatics from the military bureaus had hoped through their conspiracy to put pressure on the Emperor and force him to reverse his decision to surrender. Until the conference on August 14, Anami had let himself be persuaded that the plot was justifiable and had at least allowed them to mount it, becoming its passive accomplice if not its leader. The Imperial speech that day, however, was practically a personal reproach, and he decided to die. It was his way of breaking with the rebels; his death warned them that their uprising had failed. At the same time, he made honorable amends to the Emperor. And he remained true to his duty as a samurai, since his death also signified that he, at least, preferred to sacrifice his life rather than surrender.

In the early hours of August 15, information on the night's happenings began flowing into the headquarters of the police and the army high command in Tokyo. The palace was still under siege. A phone call from the studios warned that the Tokyo Radio building had been occupied by troops along with the Kawagoe transmitter outside Tokyo. Shortly before dawn, an officer at Tokyo Radio began preparing to broadcast what was purported to be an army appeal to the people. When air-raid sirens sounded an early warning, however, he was misled by one of the technicians with whom he had been working into thinking that radio silence had to be maintained until the alert ended. This gave a military police detachment time to reach the building. At dawn they surrounded it, disarmed the rebels and their leaders—who accepted their defeat fatalistically—and freed the radio staff.

It was also at dawn that General Shizuichi Tanaka, commander of the armies in eastern Japan and former chief of military police, stalked alone into rebel headquarters in the Imperial Guard barracks. After three hours of angry harangues, threats and outraged eloquence, he convinced the conspirators that they had failed: nothing would make the Emperor reverse his decision; those who opposed him would be treated not as patriots, but as rebels. Later that day, the rebels' four top leaders blew their brains out. The others were taken to military police headquarters, while the troops surrounding the palace were relieved.

A few other serious incidents were to occur on the night of August 15–16. A group of conspirators, members of a nationalistic terrorist society whose watchword was "Revere the Emperor and chase out the foreigners," staged an armed attack on Marquess Kido's home in Akasaka, but the marquess was not there. They had no better luck the next day when they attacked a nearby house in the hope of finding Kido hiding with a relative. Holing up in the Shiba district, on the hill where the famous Atago temple stood, the rebels—ten men and three women—committed suicide with grenades a few days later as police moved in to arrest them.

Some thirty persons killed themselves on the Imperial palace esplanade in the days following the surrender. Arriving singly or in groups, stationing themselves a little apart from the tearful crowds there to prostrate themselves before the double bridge leading to the home of the Son of Heaven, they committed ritual suicide facing a screen of pines that had resisted the fire. No one tried to stop them.

The Emperor's broadcast, made a little later than scheduled on the afternoon of August 15, had restored calm to the capital, but excitement spread through the provinces. A rumor obviously emanating from extremist military sources circulated that evening alleging that the proclamation was a fake fabricated by the defeatist Suzuki government. Young kamikaze pilots, especially those at the Atsugi base near Tokyo, and navy pilots from the Oppama airfield near the Yokosuka naval base, took off and scattered leaflets over the provinces of central Japan. "Do not obey the false orders to surrender," the leaflets exhorted. "Resist to the end!" They were signed, "The commander of Imperial naval air forces at Yokosuka." A number of these rebels were arrested. The most fanatical committed suicide by diving their planes into the ocean. Others at the Atsugi field were finally brought around through "negotiation," as the Japanese say. Their peasant fathers and mothers and relations were brought to the base from their distant villages in army trucks: ranking officers explained the situation to the elders, informed them of the Emperor's orders and begged them to persuade their children to obey. A dramatic scene then took place in a true *kabuki* atmosphere in which the young pilots, most of them not yet twenty years old, finally accorded their families the obedience they had refused their superiors.

At the air base at Oita, on the island of Kyushu, Admiral Matome Ugaki, hero of a number of Pacific naval battles, set the example of suicide. In the war's last kamikaze expedition, launched after the war ended, eleven planes piloted by suicide volunteers under the admiral's command took off to attack Okinawa. Four had to turn back with engine trouble and the other seven would be listed as missing. Shortly before their takeoff, Admiral Onishi committed hara-kiri in Tokyo, dying in slow agony. To the famous superpatriot Yoshio Kodama, whose saber he had borrowed for the ceremony and who was with him at the end, he said simply, "Doesn't cut, your blade!"

The wave of suicides still was not over. In one infantry regiment stationed near Tokyo, a battalion lost all its officers, including a major, three captains, ten first lieutenants and a dozen second lieutenants, as well as a number of noncommissioned officers. The major, setting the example, committed classical hara-kiri, opening his stomach with a dagger while kneeling on a rug in his office; he finally had himself beheaded, as the rules dictated, by a blow from an aide's saber. The other officers followed, some killing themselves as he had, others shooting themselves. Similar scenes, it was later reported, occurred even in distant garrisons in China, Korea, Formosa and the southern territories. The final count would reveal that hundreds of officers had swelled the suicide total in Japan.

But the great mass of the army obeyed its Emperor's orders. Hundreds of thousands of enlisted men and officers cheated of their final battle, especially those in Japan who had never seen action, gave in because the Emperor had ordered them to.

21

The Japanese Smile

Word of what had happened at Hiroshima reached the foreigners interned in Karuizawa on August 7. At first, the bomb seemed an incredible miracle that opened the doors to freedom to us. But our enthusiasm was short-lived. We soon found that what the bomb had brought us was anxious suspense because it made our fate terribly uncertain. Through what seemed to us interminable days, Japan hesitated between surrender and the supreme battle and, as we well knew, our lives hung in the balance. If the decision was to fight, we would be caught up in the bloody whirlwind that would finally crush Japan and our chances of coming out of it alive were slim. American radio broadcasts to which we listened clandestinely between August 7 and 14 kept us abreast of diplomatic and political developments in that crucial week. The former French Consul, Edme Gallois, a veteran of fifty years in the Far East, had been daring enough to bring a shortwave radio with him from Tokyo in the teeth of stern prohibitions against possession of such sets in wartime. Despite the danger of discovery by the Kempetai, some of us stayed secretly glued to the set to hear the reports from San Francisco on the backing and filling in the negotiations between Tokyo and Washington. The attitude of our guards and the local population also helped us measure the tension in the air. Reports I was to confirm after the surrender told us that police officials in Karuizawa had discussed what to do with us if the war continued. Executing us all was suggested and rejected, but the more likely alternative was not much more reassuring: to march us in a column to the northern mountains. In case of a general collapse, we could imagine where that would lead us.

August 14, in the morning: the rumble of a furious bombardment of the Tokyo plain came to us on the wind. So the war was still on! August 14, in the evening: from San Francisco came word of our deliverance. The war was over!

Secrecy was so strict that the Japanese still knew nothing of what was happening. As we have seen, they had been given only the vaguest information about the bomb. Of the peace negotiations it had provoked they were kept in the strictest ignorance. Finally, on August 15, the military police announced that the people would be briefed on the situation. The Emperor himself, in an unprecedented move, would be heard on the radio in a proclamation to his people.

As the time for the proclamation—4 P.M.—approached, I saw people in my corner of the village gather around radio sets, not in each house, but in groups in their tonarigumi leaders' houses. No one in these troupes of pantalooned housewives and runty elders clustered around the blue-and-white pennants of their civil-defense sections knew what the sovereign was going to say. A rumor had even circulated the previous day that he was going to sound a fiery call to resistance and many people believed this, here as everywhere in Japan.

People clustered in the doorways because the houses were too small to hold them all. Four o'clock: an announcer gravely introduced the Emperor. On an order from their leaders, the members of each group stiffened and bowed their heads in the respectful attitude prescribed in the Emperor's presence; in this case, the object of their anxious respect was a radio ceremonially enthroned on a straw-seated chair before the door.

Silence. And then that voice never heard before. A little hoarse, slow, too controlled, the voice of someone reading a speech. Surprise: for all practical purposes, no one understood a word of it! The sovereign was speaking the learned and solemn language reserved to the Son of Heaven alone: an antique, almost Chinese, language that had little in common with the language the people spoke and was made even more unintelligible by the fact that while the people may sometimes have read Imperial proclamations, they had never before heard one spoken by the Emperor himself. As soon as he finished speaking, an official commentator had to come on with a vernacular translation of what the Emperor had said. Only then was the speech really understood.

Yet even while the sovereign spoke, the common people (I watched as they listened in a kind of stupor) probably understood the general meaning of those august words. Their faces went white. Everyone stood rooted in place, but tears were furtively brushed away, stiff little gestures in pure classical-theater style in which actors use a minimum of movement to show that fierce emotions are boiling behind their rigidly passive expressions. And that monotonous voice was shot through with distress. My irreverent gaijin's ear caught a resemblance to a Nō player reciting a lamentation. The Imperial voice talked and talked and then abruptly broke, as though it could produce no more sound, as though the effort of maintaining that doleful note had suddenly become unbearable.

When the announcer came on to explain the Emperor's speech, the people remained stiff and silent for a few moments more in the intensity of concentration. Then it was over. They had understood, and the sobbing broke out. The knots of people dissolved in disorder. Something huge had just cracked: the proud dream of Greater Japan. All that was left of it to millions of Japanese was a true sorrow, simple and pitiable—the bleeding wound of their vanquished patriotism. They scattered and hid to weep in the seclusion of their wooden houses. Absolute silence prevailed in the village. As you walked down the street, all you saw through the doors left open in the August heat was an occasional tear-stained face that turned quickly away as you passed.

The next day, the Japanese snapped up their single-sheet newspapers to puzzle out the Imperial proclamation in all its details. How odd that proclamation was, and how Japanese in spirit! How prudently it dealt with the future, how careful it was not to tarnish the book of Japanese history with the forbidden word "surrender"! And how solid it was in having the courage, in the depths of its despair, to hope!

After pondering deeply the general trends of the world and the actual conditions obtaining in Our Empire today, We have decided to effect a settlement of the present situation by resorting to an extraordinary measure. We have ordered (*an unusual expression*) Our Government to communicate to the governments of the United States, Great Britain, China and the Soviet Union that Our Empire accepts the provisions of their Joint Declaration.

To strive for the common prosperity and happiness of all nations as well as the security and well-being of Our subjects is the solemn obligation which has been handed down by Our Imperial Ancestors, and which We lay close to heart [sic]. Indeed, We declared war on America and Britain out of our sincere desire to ensure Japan's self-preservation and the stabilization of East Asia, it being far from Our thought either to infringe upon the sovereignty of other nations or to embark upon territorial aggrandizement. . . . But now the war situation has developed not necessarily to Japan's advantage. . . .

Very cautious, all this, but wait:

Moreover, the enemy has begun to employ a new and most cruel bomb, the power of which to do damage is indeed incalculable, mercilessly spreading injury and massacre through an innocent population. Should we continue to fight, it would not only result in an ultimate collapse and obliteration of the Japanese nation, but it would lead to the total extinction of human civilization. Such being the case, how could We then protect Our countless subjects, who are to Us as new-born children? How could We atone for ourselves before the hallowed spirits of Our Imperial Ancestors? . . . When Our thoughts revert to those officers and men as well as others who have fallen in the fields of battle, or died at their posts of duty, or those who met with untimely death, and all their bereaved families, We feel Our five viscera break. . . .

Not once was the word "defeat" mentioned in all this, much less surrender. Should the military, in the future, have occasion to rewrite history to their liking, they will be able to cite the proclamation as witness that Japan had ended the war only because of the inhumanity of her enemies and that, even though his armies were intact, her Emperor had agreed to end the carnage because he wished to be not only the savior of Japan, but the defender of human civilization.

Here is what the Emperor said about the future:

It is Our wish to open an era of grand peace for all the generations to come, by suffering the insufferable, by bearing the unbearable. Having been able to safeguard and maintain the structure of the Imperial State, and relying upon your sincerity and integrity, we will always be with you, Our loyal and good subjects. . . . Let the entire nation continue as one family from generation to generation, ever firm in its faith in the imperishableness of the Land of the Gods, mindful of its heavy responsibility and of the length of the road it must travel. Unite your total strength for the construction of the future. Cultivate the ways of rectitude. Foster nobility of spirit, and swear to enhance the innate glory of the Imperial State, resolved to keep pace with the progress of the world. May you, Our subjects, be the incarnation of Our will.*

So it was all over. Japan had surrendered. The drama was acted out and at that terminal moment we thought the players had given all their secrets up to us. We believed that we at last understood them completely, that this surprising people had forever lost its power to surprise us. We thought we had learned to read clearly the blurred portrait of its vices and virtues: its mad ambition and its splendid capacity for work, its violence and its brave endurance, its disorder and docility, its admirable patriotism and its intolerable vaingloriousness.

Well, no—it wasn't over. That final tragedy reserved one more surprise for us. Seventy-five million people were supposed to have died to the last man. Even the poorest of them swore, and doubtless believed, that they would commit hara-kiri rather than surrender. And when, after averting its face to weep, Japan looked up again—it entered tranquilly into its defeat. There seemed a disconcerting facility in that acceptance; the page was turned with seeming effortlessness. And on Japan's new face was

* These extracts from the statement are from an official Japanese translation.

a glimmer of something that had not been seen in a very long time: the special Japanese smile.

The smile bloomed first on the faces of the police, those masters of our fate. Not three days had gone by before these black-uniformed men, who had so long made us feel the weight of their hate and their petty persecution, visited each foreigner, one by one, bowing endlessly and, flashing broad, gold-toothed smiles, offered their amiable services. "What can we do for you, sir? . . ."

The tonarigumis smiled too, the masters of rationing and forced dieting: two days after the surrender, they issued to the French—along with the Koreans and the Chinese—a special ration of sake, almost a kind of ceremonial libation, in addition to cans of salmon, a pair of cotton shorts for each person, a short-sleeved rayon shirt, a pair of shoes and bath towels.

Then there were the official smiles: an amiable diplomat from the Foreign Ministry, which, in concert with the army, had persistently refused to authorize Red Cross inspection of Allied prisoner-of-war camps, now phoned Swiss Minister Camille Gorgé to protest, "Minister, why didn't you ever visit the camp where American fliers were held? It was right near Tokyo, after all, near the Ofuna station." Neutral diplomats knew of this secret camp and they had guessed at the suffering of the men in it, but its location had been carefully hidden from them and they had never discovered where it was. Now, suddenly, *eighty* POW camps came to light as though by magic—eighty camps no one had known about, or visited before.

Smiles for strangers from the man in the street. When I took the chance of leaving Karuizawa by train for Tokyo, the only white man in a throng of Asians, I did not feel the slightest hostility around me—anything but. The trip was an adventure—passengers packed even on the cars' roofs, the trains themselves in a shambles, interminable stops—but a completely safe one despite the pessimistic predictions of my fellow internees, who envisioned my being lynched by the crowd. Indeed, as though the courtesy and hospitality of a long-vanished Japan had been reborn, amiable volunteers kindly offered their assistance: "Can I help you carry your baggage? Can you find your way? Everything has changed so, hasn't it?" And my unpaid guide gestured toward the ruined station, toward the ravaged plain that was once Tokyo, and he laughed that Japanese laugh. . . .

Japanese smiling to each other, for they were still in possession of their Japan—the Americans hadn't yet arrived. The conquerors may have feared that despite the nation's promises and the Emperor's orders, the first units to set foot on Japanese soil would be treacherously attacked; they had been surprised by the speed of events, which had outstripped their preparations. In any case, the Americans waited two weeks before landing an airborne division at Atsugi and armored units at Yokohama. This gave the Japanese two weeks in which to compose their collective face. Two precious weeks, too, for the former leaders the new Japan would sweep aside: they had time to burn their records, hastily and everywhere, even in the street, indifferent to the public and to foreign eyes; to whisk away compromising papers and probably people too; to cache arms and money, only part of which would ever be found by the Americans. And demobilization was rushed through before the invaders arrived. Feverishly, disbanded military and naval units and abandoned factories distributed their supplies to soldiers, sailors, workers to keep them out of the victors' hands.

The train that took me back to Tokyo through ruined stations passed interminable convoys heading north, toward the regions that would be invaded last, carrying thousands of khaki-clad men: demobilized soldiers, discharged crews, workers sent home to their villages. In the stations, unarmed groups standing stiffly at attention meekly obeyed officers who had already stripped off their braid but had not yet given up their long samurai sabers. The Ueno station in Tokyo was a disintegrating antheap. Countless men in new clothes milled around, their backs burdened with everything they could carry to escape American requisitioning. Excited, lively, this rabble of troopers was almost merry, as happy as old campaigners on leave. And to the satisfaction of returning home was added the bonus of all that frantically distributed equipment.

Even the press smiled. With a single twist, all the newspapers turned their coats at once. In only a week, the famous *Nippon*

Times, fascistic and militaristic before, became a champion of democracy, parliamentary government and people's rights; having shouted itself hoarse about "American bestiality" and done its best to imitate the Goebbels style, here it was informing its readers of the impatiently awaited invaders' generosity of soul and protesting that only rude and stupid Japanese provincials could imagine that an American soldier was a gangster in uniform. Then, at last, it happened: American planes landed at Atsugi and discharged onto Japanese soil a vanguard of blond giants armed to the teeth. "Frank Cordiality Marks American Landing," blithered the *Nippon Times* headline. Japanese reporters, praising the new arrivals' perfect courtesy, told of trading their caps for chocolate and Lucky Strikes.

Smiles, finally, from the common people. Touchy at first, under strict discipline, proceeding by degrees to a cautious occupation of the country, the Americans gradually came to understand that they were not going to be double-crossed. The Japanese could see them relax, put aside their machine guns, spread out wherever the trains would take them, grin at the trafficking in cigarettes and chewing gum, begin to cast interested glances at the still timid bar-girls. These amazing, incredibly large creatures whose pockets were always full and who let you feel the wonderful cloth of their uniforms, who casually displayed the marvels of their equipment, their leather, their polished boots, their rubber raincoats, their jeeps, their enormous trucks with their colossal tires, their terrifying bulldozers—why, these were good lads, rich and laughing.

Tension vanished; hardly a shot was fired at the invaders anywhere in Japan. Invaders? Not at all. They were already guests for whom one took enormous pains and who revived around them the merriment so long forbidden. Was this the forced laughter of the defeated? No indeed. It was merely the sudden reemergence, after the war and the country's long nightmare, of everything Japan's military adventure had repressed in a people simply and naïvely given to joyfulness and now, at last, allowed to confess its frivolity.

For here we may have the final key to the whole tragedy; here, at least, was the trait in the Japanese character that we who lived through it all had not yet properly gauged. It takes a great crisis to judge a great people. For the handful of foreigners who had been miserably trapped in Japan, the surrender reserved the privilege—one they would gladly have passed up—of appreciating this national frivolity at its full strength. You had to have seen the sudden airiness with which the Japanese adapted themselves to defeat; you had to have watched them turn the page, collaborate unresistingly with the American occupation in a spirit of real goodwill, and you must have witnessed the surprising birth of the "New Japan," to understand a final paradox: that the Japanese adventure that weighed so heavily in the catastrophe of world war was launched, prolonged and finally canceled by the lightness of a whole nation.

A kind of obstinate, unreflecting absurdity, we recall, had marked Japanese policy in the 1930s and 1940s. Now we had the explanation. Remember Japan's mad involvement in the Axis, the way it shamelessly abandoned Germany in its war with Russia, the blindness that propelled it into a war with America it could not win. Later there were the occasions missed, after Singapore and Saipan, to ask for or offer peace, and the way a whole people let itself be dragged toward mass suicide in a final battle, until the atomic bomb quenched its warlike enthusiasm and it about-faced with a rapidity the world had never seen before. Trickery or blindness? Frivolity, rather, lack of seriousness. Nothing in all its recent past could be fully explained without this essential factor: that 75 million Japanese were frivolous. And we will avoid a great many errors now and in the future if we remember to give due weight to their lightness—to their smile.

The Japanese smile! The most disconcerting of Japan's "secrets," the most resistant, the one most fraught with meaning for anyone who tries patiently to decipher it. While no Westerner can put himself inside the Japanese mind, much less speak for this complex people, here is the autocriticism *this* Westerner thought he caught behind that smile—a self-examination that would mold the future of the new Japan then being born.

"We smile first of all because a smile effaces trouble, makes us forget it," the smile says in its silent language. *"We have powers of forgetfulness in us, of inconsistency and fatalism that no other people can equal. We suffered frightful air raids and the abominable bomb, but there is no hatred in our welcome to the big, appealing fellows who rained those horrors on our heads only a few months ago. 'Shikatta ga nai!' we say, our version of nitchevo—so what! We couldn't change anything and neither could they; they were just instruments of fate. We have absolutely no scruples against treating them decently.*

"When it comes to ideas, we are the most changeable of peoples. For fifteen years we tolerated a hateful militarist regime, we gave it our enthusiasm and our blood, yet our loyalty was no deeper than a passing passion. Our soldiers waged war in frenzy, our civilians obstinately, and yet our warlike enthusiasm was never anything but enthusiasm on order. And now we are enthusiastic about peace.

"We are unalterably polite. We exalted the Axis, praised Mussolini, showered Hitler with flattery, but this was pure courtesy; we did not like such arrogant people, in fact, we detested them. We cursed America because insults are part of our combat arsenal and are prescribed in military regulations. But even during the war our hatred for the Americans was never more than transient. Perhaps we are too frivolous to sustain real hatred. In any case, we find our prewar admiration for wise and powerful America has survived almost intact.

"Of all the world's nations, ours is the most attentive and the most permeable to the seasons. Our ideas and our fancies also have their changing, colorful seasons. The wind carries them off as it brought them. Our feelings are more volatile than a spring day. There are fewer flights of migrating birds in autumn than there are flights of our fads and fashions. We loved the West madly and wound up Orientals in spite of ourselves. We have fallen suddenly and successively in love with baseball, horsemeat, zeppelins, birth control, French painting and camping. Our heroes were Washington and then General Araki. We adored Britain, then the Reich, and in between we read Karl Marx. Now we

shall love socialism, democracy and disarmament; we shall have labor unions and a free press and our women will vote.

"Our smile is the mark of our flexibility. For we are awesomely flexible. For ten centuries we have been limbering up by bowing to those who direct us. Have we new masters now who want to teach us the use of freedom? We are so used to having masters, to indulging their whims and applauding them. You can be sure this has never prevented us from laughing up our sleeves in their presence, and in such situations it is in fact very convenient to have your forehead pressed to a mat and your nose in the dust.

"We have emerged from the war with quiet consciences. There is one thing we know, and that is that we've been beaten, but what we will never believe is that we are guilty of anything. We don't take anything too tragically because we have no sense of sin. How tormented you are, you people! And how burdened you are with your anxiety and your depth, all you who have known Christ. Alone among the great peoples of today's world, we have shielded ourselves from the Evangels and because of that the war did not singe our souls as it did yours. As one of your people said, 'Where no law is, there is no transgression.' We know nothing of sins of the flesh, nor any more of the sin of war. We are to be put on trial with the Germans to be condemned together. What a mistake! Germany betrayed your civilization after centuries in its bosom. We haven't turned our backs on civilization, but we believe that it was by trying to fit ourselves to it that we went wrong. And if, to borrow your vocabulary, there is sin in us, we think it is partly yours. We copied you all too well.

"We smile because we suffer. With us, smiles do not always mean pleasure; an injury, a failure also solicit our smile. We smile, sometimes we guffaw, when we're embarrassed, when we lose a match or lose face. This is our courtesy toward destiny; bad luck and pain are masters and we must be amenable to their pleasure. This is also our revenge, for we in turn make adversity lose face. There are millions of smiles on Japanese faces today because there are millions of aching hearts in Japan.

"We smile, too, because we joyfully welcome a new world we hope will be a better one. For in Japan we also smile to express

satisfaction. The war unburdened us of a myriad things, begin-
ning with our possessions, our money, the roofs over our heads.
Peace will complete the job: it will lift from us the weight of mili-
tary oppression, of the war, the bombings. It will free us from
fifteen years of servitude. For the great mass of our people, the
bitterness of defeat is offset by a feeling of true liberation; we feel
light without our chains.

"Our mind is as happily unencumbered with logic as our
rooms are with furniture. Can any situation be more illogical
than ours? We are supposed to hate the Americans as invaders
but acclaim them as liberators. We choose to consider ourselves
liberated rather than defeated, liberated of the military clique we
sincerely learned to detest, free of the nationalistic swindle that
so long abused our faith and which, as we now know, led us into
catastrophe. Liberty agrees with our lightness and we try not to
think too much about the fact that we had to lose a war to win
that liberty.

"We have come out of the war without remorse, because our
people, those at home in Japan, knew absolutely nothing about
the cruelty and the atrocities of which the Japanese showed
themselves capable when they're away from home. It will do you
no good now to offer them proof; they'll never believe you. A
Japanese, remember, is not a personality; he is a possibility. Cir-
cumstances alone decide without his having to choose, between
the violence and the gentleness that cohabit in him. Our educa-
tion isn't like yours: it has never attempted to quell the natural,
original man. On the contrary, it carefully cultivated him in
every citizen. From childhood, the schools have nurtured forces
of explosiveness and violence in every Japanese as you would put
together a bomb, but they have carefully screwed down over
them the lid of discipline and self-mastery. As circumstances dic-
tated, almost by virtue of where they were geographically, the
Japanese during the war were either tigers or sheep—tigers at the
distant fronts, sheep at home. But how can you make the sheep
understand that they too might have been tigers and that some of
their brothers and friends who left home as sheep became fero-
cious animals when far away? The war brought out our dark
side; wait for the pleasant surprises we are saving for you in

peacetime. Ordinary Japanese have always been bursting with goodwill and perhaps this was the cause of all our troubles, for it serves the bad as well as the good; in us, our leaders found the most docile and tractable of human flocks. Many of us gave the worst of wars all that was best and nicest in us.

"We smile because Japan is accustomed to catastrophes and always survives them. In our destitution we still had at least three gifts you could not take away from us. The first was our number; there were 75 million of us after the war who wanted to live. The second was our will to work. We did not wait a year—not even six months—to get going again, clearing our ruined cities, rebuilding our shacks, reopening our shops. And the third Japanese gift? The country's powerful agricultural economy, the foundation of the New Japan.

"The time is coming when you will wonder if you really beat us, if it was really you who won the war. We never took seriously those of you who talked of wiping us off the face of the earth. Governors, businessmen, the common people, everyone here was sure that Japan would always have its place among the nations of the world. What conspired with us after our defeat was primarily our place on the map. An earthen dike between the American tide and the Russian flood, a pontoon bridge over which to accede to or retreat from the adjoining Asian continent, Japan is one of the places in the world where the welfare of the planet forbids too long a depression. The first to help us rise again were the Americans who defeated us. They fed us to keep us from making trouble. They once more transformed us into the factory of Asia to prevent us from becoming its barracks. They were nice to us to keep us from being nice to the Russians.

"Our smile is like the mysterious smile of the Kamakura Buddha meditating on reincarnation. We know we are changeable, elusive, many-faceted and yet what we are pursuing in our own way through all these changes is really stability. We are thought of as flighty and mobile, yet the very principle of our national life is immobility. People talk of the 'New Japan,' but can so old a country ever be new? Two thousand years of immobility—that's the meaning of our whole history, the mark of our dynasty, the explanation of our people's tragedy in its sudden telescoping by

*the mobile West. The New Japan will not succeed unless it
makes an effort to bring back to the surface part of its old, solid
base, the good side, the best side of a very ancient Japan.*

*"Like our Buddhist sages, we know that in plunging deep
down inside of us we will find something essential that will never
change even if the world changes. This something absolute, un-
determinable and interminable, is what survives our fashions; it
is stronger than our defeat. It is the bedrock over which our fluid
appearances flow, enduring through our metamorphoses, the immobile object of our contemplation. We do not know what it is,
but we know that it is. We call it Japan."*

Autumn 1945. The surrender was signed aboard the battleship
Missouri on September 2 in the roads of Tokyo Bay. American
troops occupied the archipelago from north to south. MacArthur, a new emperor in a general's cap, reigned from the heights
of his massive, ultramodern palace, the Dai-Ichi, once the headquarters of an insurance company, and the shadow of the Stars
and Stripes fell across the moat before the Imperial palace. The
American occupation spread unimpeded across a horizontal land
of razed cities and one-story shacks and flattened pride. Tokyo,
metropolis of horizontality, offered no resistance to the general's
debonair dictatorship, for the supreme command's orders rained
on millions of bowed backs.

Prince Higashikuni headed the capitulation cabinet. The first
batch of war criminals, the members of the Pearl Harbor cabinet,
were in the Sugamo prison awaiting the Yokohama trials, doubtful duplicates of the Nuremberg trials. Prominent people continued to commit suicide. Among them were the unfortunate Prince
Konoye, unjustly accused of war crimes, who preferred death to
humiliation by the conquerors; Marshal Sugiyama, and General
Tojo, who bungled his suicide as he had bungled his war and
who ended on the gibbet. A reconstituted Communist party
dared to criticize the dynasty. Emperor Hirohito moved around
unescorted. He and MacArthur met, but it was not the general
who went to the palace, it was the Emperor who was granted an
audience at the American embassy, where MacArthur received

him—this was malice on a historic scale—in his shirtsleeves, tieless and with his collar open.

What did the Japanese crowds care? They were still wrapped up in two basic problems: getting enough to eat to stay alive and rebuilding a roof over their heads. Tokyo was a sinister image of the Year One of the atomic age, fire-swept, empty, where everything had to be rebuilt, the ground level of a world in reconstruction. To this the Japanese people brought uncommon zeal and courage. It was as though their solid virtues had finally taken over, cleansed of the hard and violent character traits the war had placed in command. Now they applied their extraordinary patience and their incredible frugality to the terrible problem of getting enough to eat. They went to work at once, ardent and undiscouraged, on the enormous enterprise of rebuilding an entire city.

Tokyo would sprout like grass, like a forest. On the field of ash and twisted steel into which that capital of unpainted wood had dissolved, three million people were already busy. At first, the eye took in nothing but a sort of mass of shifting human particles. Slowly, sense appeared in the confusion; there were patterns, nuclei. Razed zones—poles of repulsion—remained persistently empty, deserts of rusty steel and charred debris shunned by life. Magnetic poles—the blocks of buildings that survived the disaster—attracted the multitudes toward the only district remaining almost intact in the city's center. People trotted along the sidewalks, peering at the immense flea market spread out on the ground. And, now, the crowds drifting by the Imperial palace moat turned their faces not to the palace, but to MacArthur's headquarters, hoping to catch a glimpse of their new master.

But Tokyo had to be inspected under a magnifying glass to bring out the details of its activity. The obstinate work of renascence was already under way. Back came the crowds that had fled from the terrible Superfortresses, reinforcing a segment of the population that had never deserted the wreckage. At first, these uncertain survivors simply wandered among the ruins. Then little men in khaki caps and women in silk pants began fluttering about like agitated birds building their nests. From this incoherent caroming there gradually emerged a sort of reclassification of the ruins, an organization of the debris. The twisted metal was gathered in piles, so were the blackened beams and the charred iron plates, the piles rising as high as a man's head. Then, suddenly, they vanished, doubtless to half-ruined work sites or to the riddled factories rearing their smokeless chimneys against the horizon. In the cleared areas, a few bright beams of new wood appeared, then coalesced into frames, and were clothed in corrugated iron. A shack was born, then another nearby and another; a shantytown sprang up along the old streets' courses among washlines and yowling babies and the songs of busy mothers who had a new infant on their backs and another already in their wombs.

The winter of 1945–46. Tokyo in defeat was not only a razed city, it was also three million obligingly flattened people. Then slowly, timidly, the heads came up. Institutions were rebuilt. Japan's bureaucracy flourished anew after the purges. A new police force rewove its net. The Diet, with a fresh coat of white paint, was reanimated by the debates of a resuscitated Parliament. A new, democratic Constitution ignored Amaterasu, the Sun Goddess, but the Imperial dynasty miraculously survived the violent shocks of the war and the atomic bomb. It was indeed the same dynasty the old Constitution had proclaimed as "unbroken through ages eternal": Hirohito, whom the Chinese were eager to hang and the Russians wanted to dethrone, is still there.

Revenge? Secret preparation for revenge? We wondered, we few foreigners who were witnesses of this surprising before-and-after. We did not think so—not for the moment, at any rate. But it did not take us long to realize that Japan's real revenge for losing the war was to win the peace and that its sole and astounding ambition was to equal its conquerors in trade and in the arts, not in war.

There was a conspiracy just the same, one the newly arrived and naïve occupants did not notice, but that we old-timers observed with amusement. That was this country's eternal conspiracy to japanize everything brought in from outside. American order was absorbed in the protective coating of Japan's occult manners, its secret psychology, the complexities of its language, its code of hieroglyphics. MacArthur sent Washington glowing reports on the success of the democratic reforms he had ordered;

the Japanese bowed respectfully and set busily about deforming the reforms. Parliament was purged and the outs installed other members of their clans in their places while waiting to return in person. The trusts dissolved their holdings, were broken up and, within a few years, reglued the pieces together. The Foreign Ministry was closed? Its diplomats in their cutaways reappeared on the huge "liaison committee" that formed the link between the Japanese government and the Allies.

The best model offered by the occupiers to the Japanese people were the GIs, whose noisy niceness was totally successful at all hours of the day or night. When passersby formed circles around them, the Yanks laughed, ate, turned up the volume of their radios, drank, played jazz, hugged the bar-girls and discovered the remarkable purchasing power of chocolate. Around them, the little people stood openmouthed, not so much in admiration of this free show as in their eagerness to absorb the lessons to be learned as though they were a kind of food. They learned to say "Hello!" instead of *"Anoné!,"* to add a handshake to the inevitable bow, to chew gum; boys and girls learned to kiss each other on the mouth. Japanese cabinet ministers learned English and got used to shaking hands instead of bowing when they went to SCAP—the supreme Allied command in the Pacific—to receive their orders.

But neither the people nor the politicians lingered too long where Americans habitually gathered. Carrying their lessons and their orders like loot, they scurried back to where they had come from, threaded their way through the humming hive and vanished in its depths. There, everything brought in from outside was examined by delicate antennae, worked by countless mandibles. Everything was reformed and transformed: translations revised their originals, plans were changed in the copying, figures were altered by conversion, schedules stretched in the calculating. Everything stored up was first bathed in a solution that dyed it all in Japanese colors. Indigenous acids began to eat away everything that was not japanizable, while gastric juices went slowly to work assimilating everything absorbable. Strengthening itself for its coming recovery, the New Japan was secretly digesting the American occupation.

Index